HOW CHANGE HAPPENS

HOW CHANGE HAPPENS

Why Some Social Movements Succeed While Others Don't

LESLIE R. CRUTCHFIELD

A project of the Global
Social Enterprise Initiative
at Georgetown University's
McDonough School of Business

WILEY

Cover design: Wiley

Published by John Wiley & Sons, Inc., Hoboken, New Jersey.

Published simultaneously in Canada.

For general information on our other products and services or for technical support, please contact our Customer Care Department within the United States at (800) 762–2974, outside the United States at (317) 572–3993 or fax (317) 572–4002.

Wiley publishes in a variety of print and electronic formats and by print-on-demand. Some material included with standard print versions of this book may not be included in e-books or in print-on-demand. If this book refers to media such as a CD or DVD that is not included in the version you purchased, you may download this material at http://booksupport.wiley.com. For more information about Wiley products, visit www.wiley.com.

Library of Congress Cataloging-in-Publication Data

Names: Crutchfield, Leslie R., author.
Title: How change happens : why some social movements succeed while others don't / Leslie R. Crutchfield.
Description: Hoboken : Wiley, 2018. | Includes index. |
Identifiers: LCCN 2017057782 (print) | LCCN 2018006548 (ebook) | ISBN 9781119413707 (pdf) | ISBN 9781119413783 (epub) | ISBN 9781119413813 (hardback)
Subjects: LCSH: Social change. | Social movements. | Environmentalism.
Classification: LCC HM831 (ebook) | LCC HM831 .C78 2018 (print) | DDC 303.4–dc23
LC record available at https://lccn.loc.gov/2017057782

Printed in the United States of America

10 9 8 7 6 5 4 3 2 1

For Caleigh, Quinn, and Finn

Contents

Foreword

THIS IS AN important book, and it comes at an important time. Leslie Crutchfield has given us a well-researched, highly readable examination of how the messy, complicated world of social change works, and does not.

There's no real recipe for social change, no "movement in a box" that we can put in place to create a more equitable, just society. This shouldn't be a surprise. But Leslie has studied a number of organizations and changemakers and given us conclusions that we can apply—if we have the courage and the ability to take up a cause worth fighting for. In other words, we *can* make change happen.

Most big, important social and environmental issues are daunting and scary, and seem beyond solutions. But this book tells us otherwise. It also shows us that champions and leaders come in all sizes and shapes. And that *we* can do it, too. In fact, that's the only way positive, sustainable change will happen.

I've been involved in many social change endeavors, including high blood pressure control through my social marketing work at Porter Novelli; striving for women's empowerment and education at CARE; fighting the tobacco wars at the Campaign for Tobacco-Free Kids; advancing age-related causes at AARP; and reforming advanced illness and end-of-life care at the Coalition to Transform Advanced

Care (C-TAC). I've got the scars to prove it, and Leslie's insights and conclusions strike me as being right on target.

She gives us a big-picture perspective so that we can look back on what's happened as a way to inform how we can look forward and plan for future challenges.

More specifically, she shows us how networks and coalitions are critical to success. No single organization is big enough or wealthy enough to tackle huge social and environmental problems alone. Strategic partnerships and alliances across sectors are necessary for change. This requires patience, skill, and ego adjustment. I recall a frustrated participant at an unruly public health meeting saying, "I know how to defeat the tobacco industry; let's make *them* work in coalitions!"

Sometimes—or, rather, oftentimes—it takes incredible optimism to fight these battles. Today the gun lobby seems undefeatable. But we can all remember when the tobacco industry was so big and bad (it still is, especially internationally) that it lied to Congress, hired a hoard of law firms, PR and advertising agencies—and had an addictive product to boot. Tobacco's story seemed unassailable: cigarettes are sexy and alluring; tobacco use is a right (after all, it *is* a legal product), disease is the smoker's responsibility, government intrusion is bad, the scientific evidence is in doubt, kids will be kids, and on and on. Take heart; nobody is too big to fall.

Leslie tells us we have to change both hearts *and* policy, that is, achieve policy reform as well as shift social norms and individual behaviors. So true. Her examination of changing norms and expectations in drunk driving and marriage equality are important examples of how it can work. Media, technology, and policy are important levers for change. Then–vice president Joe Biden helped tip the issue of same-sex marriage when he surprised the nation, and his boss, Barack Obama, by saying he was "absolutely comfortable with . . . men marrying men and women marrying women." Biden credited his change of heart to the TV show *Will & Grace*. And for good measure he officiated at the wedding of two gay White House officials at his home a few years later.

But it's also important to know what stories *not* to tell . . . what won't work in shifting norms and expectations. At the Campaign for Tobacco-Free Kids, I wanted to attack tobacco company executives. So we came up with a communications concept we called "Does your mother know what you're doing?" It was about shaming their senior executives. Consumer testing showed us that the concept didn't work. People hated the industry, but attacking specific individuals seemed to make them too uncomfortable.

Persuasive stories that change minds have to be fact-based, as well as emotional. For example, in our Global Social Enterprise Initiative here at Georgetown, we're working with the Viscardi Center and the U.S. Department of Labor's Office of Disability Employment Policy to encourage companies to hire and retain more people with disabilities. We want to persuade human resource professionals that this is the right thing to do and that there is a logical business case, as well. But our research among small- and medium-sized businesses operating at local and regional levels in different parts of the country showed that many HR directors don't even think of disability as part of diversity and inclusion. So we need to start there, not down the road.

Leslie also shows how the private sector plays an important role in social movements, today, more than ever. Decades ago, in the National High Blood Pressure Education Program (led by the National Heart, Lung, and Blood Institute at NIH), companies became involved in a quiet way because they realized that we were creating a market for their medications.

But today, as Leslie points out, companies are much more up-front and engaged. They increasingly see that speaking out on public issues, involving their employees, and appealing to their customers can make a positive difference for them and for society. This will probably increase, because the opportunity to create business value through creating social and economic value—with company shareholders and societal stakeholders both benefiting—is one of the most powerful forces driving growth in the global economy. So whether companies are completely or only partially on board with our issues, we need and want them at the table. (Exclude the tobacco companies, please.)

Many of the movements Leslie studied are decades old, and despite their successes, there's no end in sight. That's because social change is seldom permanent, and it can be reversed. New generations grow up, lessons are forgotten, program funds are diverted, and technologies emerge.

Again, consider tobacco. While smoking among kids and adults has declined dramatically in the United States, the industry is still an evil global empire. As this is written, Big Tobacco has enough signatures for a ballot initiative to reverse San Francisco's ban on menthol in cigarettes. Menthol is an alluring flavor that is the choice among half of all kids who begin smoking—and has even greater appeal among African American beginning smokers. At the same time, the industry is working on a new technology that they "promise" will reduce harm while providing the nicotine and flavor smokers crave. Internationally, it's the wild, wild west; the industry is using many of the same tactics—from advertising to women and children, to product sampling and sponsoring music festivals—that they used to get away with in the United States. No, you can never drop your guard.

Finally, Leslie's emphasis on leadership cannot be overstated. Leaders make the difference in social movements, as in most human endeavors. But her finding—and our lesson—is that good leaders exist throughout a movement. You don't have to be the woman or man at the top to be a leader. You can lead from the front, the middle, or the back of the parade. Colin Powell understood that. He said that real leadership is the capacity to influence and inspire. Powell asked this question: "Have you ever noticed that people will personally commit to certain individuals who, on paper or on the organization chart, possess little authority, but instead possess pizzazz, drive, expertise, and genuine caring for teammates?"

Leaders set the direction and take us there. It's not so much yelling "Charge up that hill," but more like "Come with me." And that's why we *can* create social change, despite all the obstacles. That's what makes Leslie's book so hopeful. She calls it being "leaderfull." Not "leaderless" or "leader-led." We can all be engaged, and we can all make a difference.

A few years ago a newspaper article reported that a newly discovered bacterium was apparently eating much of the oil spill in the Gulf of Mexico and could potentially take care of this enormous problem. Wouldn't it be great to have a bacterium to attack other big problems, like obesity, socio-economic inequality, or Alzheimer's?

But no such luck. It turns out the article was inaccurate. There's no virtuous bug to "eat" the oil spill or any of the other huge problems we face. So we have to tackle them ourselves. That's what this book is about, and that's why it's so important.

Bill Novelli

Introduction: How Change Happens

W<small>HY DO CERTAIN</small> social changes happen, while others don't? The answer is not simple. Take smoking. It's hard to imagine now, but just a few decades ago, walk into a restaurant or fly in an airplane, and every third person could have been holding a cigarette. Just watch an episode of *Mad Men* to recall how ubiquitous tobacco was. Smoking was synonymous with an American way of life—glamorized by celebrities, promoted in glossy advertisements, and even tacitly endorsed by doctors and nurses, many of whom smoked on the job despite U.S. Surgeon General warnings.

Today, the harmful habit has largely been eliminated. Youth smoking rates have dropped down to 6 percent.[1] For adults, from an all-time high when more than half of men in America smoked, rates have flat-lined to around 15 percent on average.[2] Tobacco is banned from most places in the United States—offices, airports, malls—and, in some states, even in casinos. Joe Camel has evaporated from youth media, and the Marlboro Man is dead, literally. One of the recognized actors who posed for the ads, Wayne McLaren, died in 1992 (of lung cancer). Smoking today is infrequent, unfashionable, and unwelcome almost everywhere.

The abandonment of smoking is one of the most remarkable societal shifts in modern U.S. history. It has resulted in huge health gains: No other single social change has saved more lives or prevented more disease in the last few decades. How did this landmark achievement

1

occur? How could one of the most prevailing trends and addictive habits dissipate so dramatically? It is unlikely smoking simply "went out of fashion," like big hair, Jordache jeans, or moonwalking, among other 1980s fads.

Consider another groundbreaking social change in the United States: marriage for same-sex couples. Just two decades ago, the proposition of legally recognized homosexual marriage was roiling the nation. President Bill Clinton had signed the Defense of Marriage Act, defining marriage as only between men and women, and thirteen states had ballot measures under way attempting to ban same-sex marriage, fueled by powerful anti-gay conservative and religious groups. But the U.S. Supreme Court settled the matter with its 2015 ruling that same-sex couples must be treated the same as heterosexual couples in every state. How did this flip occur in less than a generation?

Gun rights expansion is another remarkable phenomenon to gain momentum since the 1980s: Gun laws today are more lenient than at any point in modern U.S. history, and firearms are ubiquitous. Guns are ingrained in American culture—glorified on TV, movie, and video game screens, legally owned at home, openly carried in most U.S. states, and easily purchased. There are more gun shops in the United States than there are McDonald's and Starbucks *combined*.[3] Like cigarettes just a couple of decades ago, guns today are *everywhere*.

It's astounding, given that 95 percent of Americans—including Democrats and Republicans, gun owners as well as non-owners—support more "common sense" gun laws such as universal background checks, and 64 percent oppose assault weapon sales.[4] Yet when a tragic mass shooting occurs—Las Vegas, Orlando, Sandy Hook, Columbine—public outcry for gun control surges; vigils, protests, and "die-ins" are mounted; reform bills are proposed; but ultimately, little changes.

How We Got to Now

These are just a few of the many examples of the sweeping social changes to occur in recent U.S. history. This book is about how these changes happened. We wanted to understand how society got to a place that allows almost limitless access to guns, celebrates gay weddings, and, at the same time, bans smoking in public and has strict laws so that most drinkers don't dare drive drunk. This book explores how these seismic social and environmental shifts came about. In essence, we are trying to explain *how we got to now.*

In writing this book, we specifically wanted to understand what makes the movements and campaigns behind certain causes so successful. The range of issues covered here is purposely broad: How did members of the LGBT movement triumph in their quest to make marriage legal for same-sex couples in the United States? What did members of Mothers Against Drunk Driving (MADD) do to cut by half alcohol-related driving deaths since the 1980s? In the same timeframe, the National Rifle Association (NRA) has successfully advocated to expand gun access and Second Amendment rights, markedly easing restrictions on firearm purchases and sales. Teddy bear manufacturers are now subject to greater regulation than gun makers are.

This book is also about why certain changes *don't* happen. Gun safety advocates have fought the NRA on the national stage for decades, and have largely lost. Why is it that most American voters support tighter gun laws, and yet the NRA continues to win so resoundingly? Or consider other vexing modern issues, such as climate change. Environmentalists were able to eliminate acid rain in North America by the turn of the 21st century, but have since struggled to cut carbon emissions in the United States and globally. And despite public health officials' best efforts to promote healthier eating and exercise habits, rates of obesity and diabetes have climbed to epidemic proportions.

Why do some changes occur, but others don't? What are the factors that drive successful social and environmental change campaigns, while others falter? This book examines the leadership approaches, campaign strategies, and ground-level tactics employed by a range of modern social change efforts peaking since the 1980s. Some changes were achieved through full-fledged social movements, like tobacco control and gun rights expansion—causes that entailed contentious battles with fiercely divided opponents. Other changes involved sustained campaigns, like the worldwide polio eradication effort. (See Table I.1 for a listing of the causes we explored and Appendix A: Research Parameters for more details.) But whether a movement or a campaign, these major societal shifts have a few factors in common that separate successful efforts from the rest. This book is our attempt to parse what sets apart today's winning movements from others and to find what lessons can be gleaned for change makers in the 21st century.

Table I.1.   Select Societal Changes (1980–2016)

Changes That Happened	Changes "in Progress"
Acid rain reduced	Carbon emissions reduction
Drunk-driving reduced	Criminal sentencing reform
LGBT marriage equality established	Gun violence prevention
Gun rights expanded	Living wage increase
Polio eliminated (globally)	Obesity and diabetes control
Mass incarceration increased	Racial tolerance and justice
Smoking reduced	Public education equity

Changes in this study had:

- Tipped (or not) during recent decades
- Occurred in the United States or were largely U.S.-led
- Focused on specific social or environmental outcomes (that is, were not primarily political movements)

Approach

During three years of intensive inquiry into some of the most significant social changes to occur in the last few decades, we investigated what worked, mistakes made, and lessons learned. We wanted to understand why successful movements triumphed over others, attempting to extract insights and advice to help advance today's causes. (The "we" in this book refers to the author, Leslie Crutchfield, and her twenty-one colleagues and graduate student assistants who made up the *How Change Happens* book research team housed at the Global Social Enterprise Initiative at Georgetown University's McDonough School of Business.)

Working together in rolling shifts over the course of several years, we set out to study each movement's unique history and spoke with many of its leaders, members, and supporters, as well as opponents. We reviewed materials created by, for, or about the movements, available online and off. When there were visible opponents, we tried to examine all of these same factors from opposing or alternate viewpoints.

We also tried to take under consideration the unique contexts that underpin each cause. Advancements made in these various areas weren't attributable to the actions of one particular leader or approach. Luck, misfortune, timing, and changing cultural attitudes also influenced outcomes in any given social change effort. So we've tried to take all relevant factors into consideration.

But we also recognized that significant societal shifts do not occur at random. Americans didn't suddenly stop smoking because it simply "went out of fashion." Gun enthusiasts weren't able to stock up on semi-automatic assault weapons without legislative and regulatory allowances. Heterosexuals didn't embrace marriage for same-sex couples because it seemed like "the right thing to do." These changes occurred because of the relentless advocacy of vast networks of individuals and organizations, campaigning in the face of seemingly insurmountable obstacles and often against entrenched, powerful opponents. In spite of it all, they prevailed.

Context

This book is about changes that happened as society careened into the 21st century. It's set during a time when social movement organizations had one leg in the past century, planted squarely in the successes of earlier movements such as civil rights, environmental, worker, and feminist pushes that had peaked in the 1960s and 1970s. The other leg stretches into the 2000s, as new social sector organizations have come online in response to fresh threats and opportunities, just as many movements have spread globally. Meanwhile, new ways of organizing metastasized with the dawn of the Digital Revolution; through the newly ubiquitous Internet, suddenly millions of activists could immediately connect to each other through social media platforms. Campaign messages could go viral in a nanosecond, and anyone could shape the course of an entire movement because now anybody could communicate directly with everybody—without filters, for better or for worse. As *Here Comes Everybody* author Clay Shirky writes, "When we change the way we communicate, we change society."[5]

Just as civil society and social movement organizing were shifting with the advent of social media, the private sector was evolving—at exponential rates. Technological innovation ushered Western society into a post-industrial Digital Age and catalyzed the supply chain revolution. With innovations in sourcing and logistics, suddenly businesses were freed up to purchase inputs from and create their products in almost any nation on earth. As supply chains opened up, the world turned flat once again, and globalization brought a new world trade order. This unleashed boundless new frontiers for fortune-makers— and also new responsibilities. Companies that had been profiting off environmentally unsustainable sourcing practices, or perpetuating cruel and unsafe worker conditions, were exposed to global glare. In the United States, the environmental impact of more than a century of coal-fired industrial progress had laid waste to the air, water, and ground that supported life. Citizen groups and advocates rose up in protest, and the corporate responsibility movement was spawned, as companies scrambled to clean up their acts under new government regulations and, more importantly, consumer and citizen scrutiny.

By the 2010s, some forward-thinking businesses were getting ahead of the environmental and human rights problems that vexed them by adding social and environmental impact to their financial bottom lines. Strategy gurus Michael Porter and Mark Kramer proposed in *Harvard Business Review* that companies generating shared social, environmental, and financial returns promised to "reinvent capitalism." Today big businesses don't just compete to make the "Fortune 500" list of most profitable companies by sales; now they jockey for slots on the more elite "Fortune 50 Companies Changing the World" list of billion-dollar-plus businesses creating *shared value*.

Policy Matters

The political sphere during the past several decades was rife with foment as well. In response to the progressive movements of the 1960s and 1970s, conservative forces geared up in the 1980s to resist and dismantle progressive-era programs and policies. President Reagan attempted to disassemble the Environmental Protection Agency and built on President Nixon's attempt to spawn "law-and-order" federal policies with a cascading affect that rippled through the following decades and down into state and local jurisdictions. The result: The United States today is the world's leader in incarceration, with more than two million people in prisons and jails—mostly men of color. What explains the 500 percent increase in imprisonment over the last four decades? Not increased crime rates, says Michelle Alexander, author of *The New Jim Crow*. Rather, changes in sentencing laws and other government policies resulted in minor drug offenders being punished and branded on par with murderers and other felons.[6]

Paradoxically, while conservative officials started the United States on this path decades ago, new ultra-conservative forces are pushing back today: The Koch brothers are fighting on the same side as Black Lives Matter activists against the "overcriminalization of America"— although it's principally Koch's Tea Party–infused quest for deregulation and sequestering government spending that puts them in the company of such unlikely bedfellows.[7]

Other vexing paradoxes permeate this period. During a time in the 2000s when more black men became incarcerated than had been enslaved in the 1800s,[8] the United States also elected its first black president. President Barack Obama symbolized for many the dawn of a new era of racial tolerance, a harbinger of hope for a "post-racial" society. One challenging reality of his presidency was that, when Obama took office, the United States—and by extension the world—had cratered into the deepest financial crisis since the Great Depression. A fierce conservative backlash quickly formed, with the populist Tea Party insurgents rising up with anti-immigrant, libertarian, nationalist bents. They railed against President Obama's proposed bailouts for homeowners hurt by the Wall Street mortgage debacle, and later against Obamacare.

Tea Partyers captured a sizeable number of Congressional seats, but their impact was felt far beyond the political sphere: They provided fertile ground for the offensive "Birther" movement (of which Obama's successor, President Donald Trump, was a prominent and vocal chieftain) and fomented a new caste of global warming skeptics. According to a Pew Research Center poll, by 2013, Tea Party Republicans were the only group of Americans who still believed the earth was not warming.[9] By sowing seeds of scientific doubt and emboldening climate skeptics, as well as fostering nationalist and, by extension, racist views, the Tea Party contributed to an unprecedented polarization in U.S. politics and society.

By the time of this writing, the Tea Party–infused conservative movement had reached its apex by winning the presidency. In Republican candidate Donald J. Trump, they found the bona fides they were looking for, given his "Birther" background and his anti-immigrant, nationalist stances. But it's important to note that Trump didn't *create* the populist movement that ultimately ushered him into office; rather, he shrewdly *tapped* the anger and disaffection of white working-class voters in coal country and other parts of the United States who felt left behind by a vanishing industrial economy and increasing cultural diversity.

And it's precisely because of the some of the successful social and environmental movements profiled in this book that big blocks of white Americans had become increasingly disenchanted: They were incensed by environmentalists who prioritized clean air over coal workers' livelihoods. They resented heavily pedigreed elites from either coast telling them what they should not eat, drink, smoke, or shoot. Trump's victory may be interpreted as the apogee of a nation's hillbilly elegy as told by Kentuckian J.D. Vance or a crippling case of "whitelash" as tagged by civil rights environmentalist Van Jones.[10,11] It depended on which side of the Rust Belt you were on.

Deconstructing the Dissonance

Whether or not whitelash explains the 2016 presidential election results, by the mid-2010s, American society was undeniably experiencing a severe case of whiplash. We had allowed almost unlimited gun stockpiles and freed up gay and lesbian couples to wed, and at the same time banned almost everyone from smoking in public, and no friend would dare let a friend drive drunk—all during the same timeframe. The movements that drove these changes are both catalysts and harbingers of our time. Like canaries in a coal mine, movements are manifestations of the polarizing, contradictory, ever-changing values and beliefs that constitute a democratic society. And they are the engines of change.

Think about it. In the past few decades, "nanny state" tobacco controllers have managed to snuff out smokers' abilities to light up in most places—including bars, restaurants, and most casinos. They've jacked up prices by slapping on sin taxes to the point that a pack of Marlboros today costs a New Yorker $13. (This is, incidentally, nearly double the hourly minimum wage most smokers earn, since unemployed or low-income workers are among the few people still smoking these days). Anti-tobacco groups also stamped out cigarette companies' license to advertise to young people in the United States, effectively curtailing the industry's chances of hooking its next generation of consumers—although some teens are now using "smokeless" e-cig-arettes, enticed by the sweet flavors these liquid nicotine-delivery devices are designed to emit through vapor clouds.[12]

But during this same timeframe, gun rights advocates have swung the country to the opposite extreme. Pro-gun activists have managed to loosen gun laws to such lenient levels that almost anyone twen-ty-one or over can legally purchase a handgun at one of the thousands of gun shops, trade shows, and online venues. People can openly carry firearms into almost any place in more than thirty U.S. states. And gun collectors and mass murderers alike can stockpile as many weapons as they wish: In the worst mass shooting in modern U.S. history, the Las Vegas shooter who in October of 2017 murdered fifty-eight con-cert-goers and injured hundreds more had stockpiled more than forty firearms, many with semi-automatic capability, no questions asked. He was allowed full access to these weapons after passing background checks because he exhibited no prior criminal record or mental health history at the time of purchase. Besides, if it had taken more than three days for gun vendors to complete his background checks, they would have been allowed to sell him the guns anyway.

Or consider this other curious quandary: Same-sex couples in every U.S. state won the right to marry in 2015 when the U.S. Supreme Court decided *Oberfell v. Hodges*. The ruling followed on the heels of hundreds of local and state court cases and dozens of U.S. states passing measures in support of LGBT rights to marry, establish civil unions, and receive other protections from discrimination. That same year, then-governor Mike Pence (R-Indiana) signed a Religious Free-dom Bill that would allow businesses to discriminate against custom-ers based on their sexual orientation; Memories Pizza, a family-owned business in Walkerton, Indiana, became the first company to publicly refuse to cater a same-sex wedding as a result of the law.[13] The follow-ing year, Pence's conservative credentials bolstered Donald Trump's presidential ticket, helping clinch the election.

Darkness and Light

"It was the best of times, it was the worst of times . . . it was the season of Light, it was the season of Darkness." So wrote Charles Dickens of the French Revolution. ". . . it was the spring of hope, it was the winter of despair, we had everything before us, we had nothing before us." So sits society as it edges up to the 2020s. It's a time of disturbing societal incongruities—while some people are filled with great hope for a better future, others are slouching in depressive regress. We've needed help making sense of it all. In one poignant *Saturday Night Live* skit that aired a few weeks before the 2016 election, actor Tom Hanks donned a comfy knit cardigan and spoke as "America's Dad."

"You may have noticed that your complexion is changing—you're getting a little darker, and you're freaking out about it. Well, that's natural for a nation of immigrants like yourself," quipped Hanks. "Also, you're a lot gayer than you used to be. . . . And you have a lot more guns. Do you really need all of those?" But he assured everyone, "It's gonna' be fine."

Embracing the Dissonance: Why Some Movements Succeed and Others Don't

As we examined some of the most successful modern movements of our time, we marveled at the dizzying juxtaposition of outcomes that had occurred. How could society simultaneously grow "more gay," stockpile unprecedented caches of guns, quit smoking, stop driving drunk, and remove the toxins from the air that created acid rain and destroyed the ozone, only to later fail to cap carbon emissions in any meaningful way? Taking comfort in Hanks's soliloquy, we needed a way to make sense of it all.

First, as disjointed as circumstances are today, we did find one thread of continuity: Among all of these jarringly juxtaposed outcomes, it was clear no single political ideology or set of religious values was emerging as "right" during the 1980–2016 period. Republicans, Libertarians, and Tea Partyers gained ground on certain issues, while Democrats, progressives, and liberals won others. God didn't appear to be favoring any one side. And if multiple Gods were involved, there clearly wasn't consensus.

In the absence of a predominant ideology or values set that might explain why certain sides prevailed, we knew that the answer to why some movements catapulted forth to victory while others faltered had to do with how they were *organized*. We looked at how each movement and campaign was structured and led and at what strategies and tactics each employed. We wanted to understand whether certain elements were common among the winning sides that the others lacked.

This didn't tell us much at first. All sides of each cause we studied had impressive leaders, strategies, and many of the same campaign tactics. They organized, mobilized, and canvassed door-to-door; they educated, persuaded, and lobbied—and when that didn't work, they sued, protested, marched, and demonstrated; they held vigils and town halls and prayer breakfasts; they gathered signatures, got out the vote, and some backed political candidates and influenced elections. They raised money (some more than others) and pitched the press. They did most if not all of the myriad things required to move public opinion, shift behaviors, and reform laws, policies, and regulations to favor their side. And when the Internet became ubiquitous, they used social media— friending, texting, and tweeting up storms. So what differentiated the best from the rest?

We started to look more closely at these movements, observing not just what they did or the number of supporters they had, but how the various pieces fit together. That's when we started to see patterns emerge. We saw distinctive approaches and different emphases among the winners. It's not that they had something the others completely lacked, such as charismatic leaders with deep-seated passion for the cause—all causes had plenty of those. Also neither luck nor financial fortune explained why some prevailed over others: The tobacco industry *dwarfs* the gun industry in revenues, yet anti-tobacco activists prevailed against their powerful corporate opponents. And it's not simply that certain causes have public opinion in their favor—more Americans want "common sense" gun laws than not. Yet today's policy outcomes reflect the opposite.

Basically, winning movements and also-rans alike started out with mixed bags of advantages, disadvantages, and neutral factors. It's what they *did with it* that matters. The success of winning movements— we found—had to do with their approach and the *degrees* to which they emphasized certain aspects of their campaigns. It had a lot to do with the strategic choices winning movement leaders made, and how they got their movement's myriad parts aligned to advance a common cause, despite odds set heavily against them most of the time. In short, *winning movements made their destinies come true, rather than being destined to succeed.*

As Jim Collins writes in *Good to Great*, "Greatness is not a function of circumstance. Greatness, it turns out, is largely a matter of conscious choice, and discipline." Collins was writing about companies that had massively outperformed their industry peers, but his insights are just as applicable to movements. Winning causes didn't simply get lucky, and they don't just coalesce out of thin air. The best movement leaders had well-thought-out plans, made tough strategic choices, and led from the grassroots up. They realized they needed to amass armies to advance their causes, and that victory would be secured by unleashing that grassroots energy and channeling it—somewhat like catching lightning in a bottle.

Findings

After several years of intense scrutiny and careful thought about a range of movements, six patterns emerged that seemed to distinguish the effective movements from the others. These patterns are:

1. *Turn Grassroots Gold:* Winning movements are fueled by energy that materializes from the bottom up. The most successful organizational leaders understand they must turn their approach to power upside-down and let local activists lead. They recognize seeding and growing vast networks of millions of passionate individuals organized around a common cause is infinitely more powerful than any single organization or association—no matter how well-resourced or branded. They invest their assets—money, time, know-how, and political clout—into ensuring the grassroots not only survive but thrive. They do this by fostering bonds *between* individual members as well as by empowering them to collectively fight for the cause. It can be tedious, expensive, and time-consuming, but when done right, the investment pays off.
2. *Sharpen Your 10/10/10/20 = 50 Vision:* Successful U.S. movements plow through all fifty states with their change campaigns, rather than focusing only on sweeping federal reforms. They do the yeoman's work of pushing for improvements at the state and local level, advocating town by town, racking up small wins and building momentum incrementally, rather than going for national change at the start. The movements that successfully drive change across

all fifty states win big when their grass-tops are organized in *net-worked* leadership structures—coalitions of leaders who recognize they need to forge pathways so all of the players *around them* can collaborate rather than compete and achieve collective impact.

3. *Change Hearts* and *Policy:* Great social change leaders refuse to choose between either pushing for policy reform *or* shifting social norms and individual behaviors. They realize that to achieve last-ing systems change, they must change public attitudes so people believe the changes they seek are fair and right. They strive to make the change they seek the *new normal*. Whether emotional, visceral, heartbreaking, or inspiring, winning movements lead with messages that connect with people at their human core. They put the individuals with the *lived experience* of the problem out in front of the cause—whether they are victims, survivors, or in some other way inured to the issue. And they use all the tools—social and traditional media, sophisticated Madison Avenue–style adver-tising, and old-fashioned boots-on-the-ground organizing—to get their messages out.

4. *Reckon with Adversarial Allies:* If your movement is crippled by pol-icy disagreements, personality conflicts, territory fights, or scraps over which organization gets the credit, or the donor list, or the prime-time media slot, you are not alone. Every movement—whether winning or struggling—faces intra-field challenges. In all fields, multiple organizations that are ostensibly allies co-exist across a spectrum that spans from extreme left to right. All players jockey to have *their* vision for change dominate the agenda. The dif-ference in winning movements is that leaders manage to put their egos and organizational identities to the side (if only temporarily) so disparate factions can come together around a common agenda—although the path to victory can be arduous and never linear.

5. *Break from Business as Usual:* Traditionally, social and environ-mental activists were seen as largely pitted *against* business. But it turns out that corporations have influenced the outcomes of many modern movements in more positive and nuanced ways than conventional wisdom would suggest. Businesses can affect major change by altering their employee policies; raising their influential voices in public debates; and leveraging their innovation capa-bilities, as well as their brands and customer loyalty, for causes.

It doesn't work for every company. Those businesses that continue to employ negative practices harmful to the environment or society suffer even harsher consequences under today's heightened consumer and social media scrutiny. But companies willing to risk proactively pushing for positive social and environmental changes demonstrate that capitalist market forces can contribute to advancing many important causes.

6. *Be Leaderfull:* The conventional mental model of social change evokes images of mass protests, with waves of activists spontaneously rising up and agitating for change. In crowds that big, no single leader is in charge and the collective appears to move of its own accord, "leaderless." It's the opposite of the structured, hierarchical, top-down management approach embodied by traditional corporations and nonprofits, where a CEO is clearly in charge and calls the shots. But the notion that modern movements are "leaderless" isn't quite right. Rather, we observed winning movements to be "leaderfull." Instead of small handfuls of elites dictating to troops from the top down or an amorphous mob of activists genuflecting for change from the bottom up, the most effective movements find balance between the "leaderless" and "leader-led" extremes. We observed movement leaders who both empowered and encouraged their grassroots counterparts to take action at the state and local level, while helping guide the movement toward collective goals at the national and federal levels through *networked* leadership approaches. Effective movement leaders share power, authority, and limelight and lead from behind, embracing a long-term view. This is very hard to do—it involves letting go of ego, as well as putting cause and mission ahead of personal or organizational power. It's the main reason why some movements fail—and why the best movements win.

Research Frames

We came to these insights through an iterative, inductive process. We started with bottom-up research, interviewing leaders past and present from the movements; reviewing organizational documents and public records; and studying the extensive literature about many past and present movements. We started our analysis by borrowing frameworks from social movement theorists. We thought these frames would help us separate the best movement approaches from the rest.

Having studied politics and sociology and the extensive writings on movements from the 1960s, we consulted books on our shelves like *Poor People's Movements* by Piven and Cloward and Saul Alinsky's *Rules for Radicals* and Taylor Branch's *Parting the Waters: America in the King Years*. In the works of historian and sociologist Charles Tilly, we found one definition of social movements that crystallized the thinking of that time around the idea of *contentious collective action*: "The irreducible act that lies at the base of all social movements and revolutions is *contentious collective action* . . . not because movements are always violent or extreme, but because it is the main, and often the only, recourse that most people possess against better equipped opponents."[14]

The problem was, while many of the changes that have occurred in recent times have involved "contentious collective action," others did not. While protests, demonstrations, and anguished vigils were part and parcel of mothers fighting drunk driving, gun-toting Second Amendment rights supporters, and non-smokers' rights groups, they weren't as much a part of other changes. The push to eradicate polio from the face of the earth has been arduous, but it hasn't involved protest marches. And while the fight to pass the original U.S. Clean Air Act in 1970 was a contentious battle between green groups and their opponents, passage of the Clean Air Act Amendments in 1990 that led to the reduction of acid rain was achieved entirely differently. The cap and trade policy solution that ultimately cleared the air of acidity in the United States and Canada was crafted by environmentalists teaming up with economists to jury rig a market-based solution allowing companies to compete to lower toxic emissions—and to make money when successful. Instead of protesting or suing businesses, environmentalists were essentially advocating to allow some businesses to *pay to pollute*. While repugnant to many, it *worked*. Acid rain was dramatically reduced—more resoundingly and quickly than anyone had anticipated.

New Lenses

It seemed what was needed in studying societal changes since the 1980s was a fresh framework, an updated way of thinking about movements and campaigns that built on, but was different from, the previous received wisdom. Since all of the movements and campaigns we studied were trying to achieve change on a systems level, we decided to look to systems design and complexity theory for alternate lenses to help us make sense of them. This turned out to be quite fruitful. Systems lenses enabled us to move out of the black versus white, friend versus foe dualistic orientation social movement theorists had historically used to understand earlier conflicts. It enabled us to see how modern movements connected with the other political, economic, and cultural currents moving during this same time and to think more about the interplay among these sectors.

What do we mean by "systems"? Environmental scientist Donella Meadows offers this lens: "A system is an interconnected set of elements that is coherently organized in a way that achieves something."[15] It isn't merely a collection of things. A system has a function (if a machine) or a purpose (if a social grouping), and it consists of elements that are interconnected. Examples of systems, according to Meadows, include the human digestive track, a football team, global trading markets, and the solar system. A defining feature of systems is that they are made of interrelating, interdependent parts, rather than isolated components. "Systems need to be understood not by focusing on what each part is doing, but on how each part is interacting with the rest," says social innovation scholar Frances Westley.[16]

Applying a systems lens allowed us to see social change movements, for instance, not simply as extensions of charismatic gifted men and women fighting for societal change, but as systems in and of themselves. Instead of focusing mainly on movement leaders, we focused on the relationships *between* leaders—*how* they related to each other, as well as much as *what* they did and *who* they were as people. The systems lens enabled us to see how the various parts of a social change movement added up to a whole greater than the sum of its parts. It also freed us from only focusing on bilateral dynamics that traditionally defined social change campaigns in terms of contentious battles between deeply entrenched opponents. Most importantly, thinking in terms of systems helped us see more clearly what made the successful movements work and what made others seem to falter. So readers will see we've framed insights throughout this book in these terms, using metaphors and analogies from networks, complexity, and systems dynamics.

We also refer at times to insights from *Forces for Good: The Six Practices of High-Impact Nonprofits* (Leslie Crutchfield's earlier book co-authored with Heather McLeod Grant). Not surprising, the organizations in *How Change Happens* that are driving the successful movements of our time—whether for LGBT marriage equality, gun rights, tobacco control, or other causes—share similar traits with the high-impact nonprofits featured in *Forces for Good*. For instance, in *Forces for Good*, it was observed that the most effective nonprofits adopt a "network mindset," working with and through other groups in coalitions and alliances instead of simply shoring up their own organizations. This theme and others are threaded—and amplified—in the pages of *How Change Happens*.

Believing in Systems

Systems and network thinking also provides a larger, macro lens to view the way the world has evolved around the turn of the 21st century. The rise of the Digital Era has ushered in profound shifts in the way society thinks, works, socializes, and organizes. If the 20th century was the age of *organizations*, marked by industrial companies and traditional nonprofits structured under command-and-control hierarchies, the 21st century emerges as the age of *networks*. The Industrial Age was a time of "machine age thinking." With the invention of clocks, production assembly line workers could be "managed." There was the appearance of order, the ability to control, as people at work cooperated in linear, hierarchical relationships, and chains of command extended from the CEO and board down to the front-line factory worker. The "machine age" was perhaps best symbolized by the atom. "The atom whirls alone. It is the metaphor for individuality," write Cleveland, Plastrik, and Taylor. "But the atom is the past. The symbol for the next century is the net. The net has no center, no orbits, no certainty. It is an indefinite web of causes . . . whereas the atom represents clean simplicity, the net channels messy complexity.[17] (See Table I.2.)

Table I.2.   Transformational Societal Shifts

Organization Era (19th and 20th Centuries)	Network Era (21st Century)
Organizations	Networks
Linear	Relational
Centralized	Centerless
Top-down	Bottom-up
Closed, controlled	Open, transparent
Newtonian (physics)	Networks (complexity)
Illusion of control	Reality of chaos
Nonprofits	Causes
Profits or purpose	Shared value

In the following chapters, we explore how networks and systems theory inform the messy, nonlinear, emergent world of social change movements. We use these lenses to help make sense of it all and to answer the driving question behind our research: Why do some movements succeed and others do not? While we haven't unearthed every answer to this question, we found what we believe to be some of the most important ones.

One of our foremost revelations was this: Change happens not by chance. It is determined by individuals and the organizations and networks that bind them together in common cause. Many of the protagonists in the stories you are about to read had no background in nonprofits or politics, and no prior interest in social activism. While some were lawyers or lobbyists, most were not. The leaders of the winning movements we studied brought a truly mixed bag of experience and expertise—they were real estate agents, homemakers, PR professionals, veterans, teachers, nurses, and small business owners, among others. One thing that unites the eclectic groups of people who made the changes featured in this book is: Each was compelled in its own unique way to stand up, speak out, and take the lead on behalf of a cause the group cared about. Just like each of them, you have the power to change things, too.

To find out how, dive into this book and learn more about *how change happens*.

Notes

1. "Youth Smoking Rate Falls to 6 Percent." Truth Initiative official Web site, https://truthinitiative.org/news/youth-smoking-rate-falls-6-percent.
2. Adult smoking rates have been reduced to 15.1 percent on average nationally. However, smoking rates are considerably higher in some U.S. regions such as in the South, where in a state like West Virginia, adult smoking rates are closer to 25 percent. Campaign for Tobacco-Free Kids. https://www.tobaccofreekids.org/problem/toll-us/west_virginia. Accessed November 12, 2017. Also, in 1955, 52.6 percent of males smoked on average across all age categories (21 to 65+). "Smoking and Health: A Report of the Surgeon General," Appendix A: Cigarette Smoking in the United States, 1950–1978, Table A2. Official Web site of NIH. https://profiles.nlm.nih.gov/ps/access/nnbcph.pdf.
3. *Under the Gun*, directed by Stephanie Soechtig. Epix 2016.
4. Quinnipiac University National Poll. "Latest Massacre Drives Gun Control Support to New High, Quinnipiac University National Poll Finds; Voters Reject GOP Tax Plan 2-1." November 15, 2017. https://poll.qu.edu/national/release-detail?ReleaseID=2501.
5. Shirky, C. *Here Comes Everybody: The Power of Organizing Without Organization.* New York: Penguin Books, 2008.
6. Alexander, Michelle. *The New Jim Crow: Mass Incarceration in the Age of Colorblindness* (rev. ed., 2010, 2012). New York: The New Press, 2011.
7. Ball, Molly. "Do The Koch Brothers Really Care About Criminal-Justice Reform?" *The Atlantic.* March 3, 2015. Available at https://www.theatlantic.com/politics/archive/2015/03/do-the-koch-brothers-really-care-about-criminal-justice-reform/386615/.
8. Alexander, Michelle. *The New Jim Crow.*
9. Funk, Cary, and Rainie, Lee. "Americans, Politics and Science." Pew Research Center, http://www.pewinternet.org/2015/07/01/americans-politics-and-science-issues/.
10. Vance, J.D. *Hillbilly Elegy.* New York: HarperCollins Publishers, 2016.
11. Ryan, Josiah. CNN Politics.com. November 9, 2016. http://www.cnn.com/2016/11/09/politics/van-jones-results-disappointment-cnntv/index.html.
12. While smoking rates are down in the United States, the tobacco industry is taking its products global and ramping up sales in other countries where tobacco control is weak or non-existent.
13. Wikipedia contributors. "Religious Freedom Restoration Act (Indiana)." *Wikipedia, The Free Encyclopedia,* https://en.wikipedia.org/w/index.php?title=Religious_Freedom_Restoration_Act_(Indiana)&oldid=807613408. Accessed November 9, 2017.

14. Tarrow, Sidney G. *Power in Movement: Social Movements and Contentious Politics*. Cambridge University Press, 1994, page 2.
15. Meadows, Donella H. *Thinking in Systems: A Primer*. London: Earthscan, 2008, page 12.
16. Westley, F. "Social Innovation and FSG: The Challenges of Re-Imagining Social Change." Presentation at FSG company retreat in Boston, MA, February 2015.
17. Cleveland, John, Plastrik, Peter, and Taylor, Madeleine. *Connecting to Change the World: Harnessing the Power of Networks for Social Impact*. Washington, DC: Island Press, 2014.

1

Turn Grassroots Gold

Grassroots *[grass-roots] noun: The common or ordinary people, especially as contrasted with the leadership or elite of a political party, social organization, etc.; the rank and file.*[1]

IN ONE OF the worst mass shootings in modern U.S. history, Omar Mateen killed or injured more than one hundred people in a popular gay night club in Orlando, Florida, in a hateful terrorist act on June 12, 2016. Furor ignited when Donald Trump, then the presumptive Republican presidential nominee, tweeted hours after the tragedy, "Appreciate the congrats for being right on radical Islamic terrorism. . . ." Democrats reacted on Capitol Hill, shouting "Pass the Bill" over a stalled vote for a proposed "no-fly, no-buy" law to prevent suspected terrorists from purchasing guns. Some Democratic leaders walked off the floor as Republican Speaker of the House Paul Ryan called for a moment of silence in memory of the victims and then launched an unprecedented fourteen-hour Senate floor filibuster to force a vote on tighter gun laws for suspected terrorists. The NRA countered that radical Islamic terrorists would not be deterred by gun control laws, and its supporters protested any infringement on Second Amendment freedoms. Meanwhile, thousands of the surviving victims and family members and friends joined with LGBT rights activists and gun control advocates to hold candlelight vigils, mount protests, and stage "die-ins"—one outside NRA headquarters in Virginia. The

21

entire spectacle was covered 24/7 by cable news and other media, with many reporters reminding viewers the vast majority of Americans favor "common sense" gun measures.

And then, not much changed.

Drive about a hundred miles south of Washington, D.C., to Charlottesville, Virginia, to understand why. There, a more muted scene unfolded during that same summer month of June 2016: A few days after the mass shooting in Orlando, the Charlottesville City Council met and discussed a resolution asking state and federal law-makers for stricter gun laws. The resolution passed 4 to 0. Despite the unanimous vote, the majority of local residents attending the meeting objected. "My hope for tonight is that the Charlottesville City Council, in all it's [sic] wisdom, decides to forget about this whole thing," said Albert Shank, an Army veteran and Charlottesville resident. "And they let us go on to continue to observe our rights, and obey the Second Amendment."[2] The council members didn't actually have any legal power over gun rights, and their vote was merely a "call to action" due to the Virginia state preemption laws, which prevented local jurisdictions from enacting gun laws that were stricter than what the state had already ruled.[3] The Charlottesville City Council—and every other local council in the state of Virginia—was rendered impotent on imposing any kind of further firearm restriction.

The situation in Charlottesville mirrors that of the vast majority of communities across the country. At the local level, even when the most seemingly innocuous resolution is up for consideration by city councils, NRA members and gun rights supporters mobilize to express their views and defend Second Amendment rights. They show up, they speak up, they vote—and dutifully persuade family members, neighbors, and friends to do the same. The NRA projects a visible, palpable presence at statehouses, council chambers, and courtrooms across the country whenever a piece of legislation or law related to guns is up for consideration. It's the dutiful activism of citizens like Albert Shank—and hundreds of thousands of others like him across the country—that shore up the phenomenal legislative and electoral victories of the NRA.

The NRA's grassroots organizing strategy is the *single most important reason* why the movement has been so successful in defending and expanding the rights of gun owners in the United States. Its grassroots membership is far more important than the financial support the NRA receives from gun manufacturers, which historically have provided only a minor percentage of the budget.[4] And it's the fundamental reason why even the most unorthodox NRA policy proposals are enacted. The gun rights movement's grassroots army is the reason why, despite the waves of angry anti-gun protests, heartbreaking vigils, and pleading calls for reform that erupt after each tragic mass shooting—from Columbine to Sandy Hook, Orlando to Las Vegas—gun violence prevention groups still largely lose ground. On the surface, it's baffling, because the vast majority of Americans support "common sense" gun policies such as universal background checks, including Democrats and Republicans, gun owners as well as non-owners.[5] Given the widespread public support of measures like these, it would seem gun safety advocates should be winning handily. But except in a handful of progressive states, they don't. The main reason for their defeat nationally is that gun control advocates historically failed to match the scale and intensity of the NRA's grassroots-fueled movement.

Leading from the Grassroots

As we examined a range of social and environmental movements surging since the 1980s, it became irrefutably clear that those with strong and robust grassroots—measured by both size and intensity of the base—win. It is the single most important factor in the NRA's success since the group first politicized in the mid-1970s and then intensified its grassroots organizing efforts starting in the 1990s. And in almost every other winning modern societal change we studied, grassroots activism played the key role.

The war to secure marriage rights for same-sex couples was waged at local and state ballot boxes, coordinated in large part by Freedom to Marry campaign leaders who successfully galvanized memberships of major national LGBT groups like Lambda Legal, GLAD, and NCLR, and hundreds of state and local groups, forging coalitions to galvanize grassroots action. Likewise, the anti–drunk driving movement was almost entirely predicated on chapter-based strategies of Mothers Against Drunk Driving (MADD), RID, and others to mobilize survivors and victims' families and friends. The modern tobacco control movement was sparked by grassroots activists who rallied in the 1970s to pass the first community bans in Arizona and Minnesota.[6]

California soon followed suit, and with the 1976 launch of Americans for Nonsmokers' Rights (ANR) by a group of Berkeley-based advocates, ANR (formerly Californians for Nonsmokers' Rights) expanded the grassroots charge against the tobacco industry to protect non-smokers from secondhand smoke. The tobacco control movement accelerated again with the 1995 launch of the Campaign for Tobacco-Free Kids (the Campaign). A national organization created to provide technical support and critically needed resources to state-based grassroots coalitions, the Campaign also mounted national media and public norm change campaigns and provided a powerful counterweight to the influential tobacco industry lobby at the federal level.

Even the global polio eradication movement credits its success in large part to Rotary International's grassroots membership, which puts more than a million boots on the ground through its thirty thousand chapters as Rotarians marshal the social and political will to fight polio in each country where the disease remains—eliminating it in 99.9 percent of the world to date.

Conversely, the causes that are faltering in the early 21st century can attribute their struggles in some part to weak or uneven grassroots efforts. One example is gun violence prevention. Prior to when Everytown for Gun Safety formed in 2014, for nearly forty years, two main groups had dominated the gun control agenda: the Brady Campaign to Prevent Gun Violence and the Coalition to Stop Gun Violence. The Brady Campaign was founded in 1974 (named National Council to Control Handguns, and later re-named Handgun Control, Inc., from 1980 to 2000). The Brady Campaign quickly became the wealthiest and most politically important gun control group in America—"the de facto chief."[7] The Coalition to Stop Gun Violence represented a consortium of women's, civic, labor, and religious associations; both organizations advocated for national legislation to prohibit gun use and ownership among the general public. What was missing, however, was a robust sustained movement of individual activists and local groups pushing for gun control from the grassroots up. As Kristin Goss noted in *Disarmed: The Missing Movement for Gun Control in America*, ". . . the gun control 'movement' was [oriented] toward elite politics at the national level, rather than mass political or social change at the grassroots. Their goal: push a comprehensive gun control bill through Congress."[8]

There were points, however, in modern gun control movement history when grassroots activists led the charge. These include, for instance, the years immediately following the Million Mom March Across America, when on Mother's Day in 2000, more than one million gun control supporters demonstrated on the National Mall and in city satellite marches across the country. They ushered in a wave of some of the strongest state gun violence prevention legislation to pass in recent decades. But when the Million Mom March folded into the Brady Campaign, and most chapters were re-branded as Brady/MMM chapters, momentum stalled nationally.

Locally, MOM activists and their supporters continued to work in local communities, campaigning for gun safety candidates and successfully fighting gun lobby initiatives in Congress such as Concealed Carry Reciprocity. Brady/MMM chapter members also promoted the ASK Campaign, a nationwide effort to educate parents about the risks associated with having guns in the home; the ASK Campaign has been federally recognized as the most effective national safe storage awareness program.[9]

The dichotomist trajectories of the gun rights versus the gun control movements were not inevitable. As we'll see in this chapter, among the successful movements we studied, deliberate choices were made by leaders to grow and embolden their grassroots base. And in the struggling movements, we observed choices being made to the contrary, whether deliberate or by default—sometimes prompted by excruciatingly challenging external circumstances. But the end result was the same: weakened or nonexistent grassroots. While many factors fall beyond the control of a movement, there is one thing every movement has within its purview: the care and feeding of its most ardent base of supporters. Perhaps the single most important decision movement leaders must make is whether to let their grassroots fade to brown or to turn their grassroots gold.

Turning Grassroots Gold

To understand the power of grassroots in driving winning movements, it's first important to understand what we mean by "grassroots." A movement's grassroots are its everyday people, the "rank and file," in contrast to the leaders or "elite." Most movements start out as grassroots phenomena, with small groups of concerned individuals banding together to solve a problem and collectively advocating for change. A successful movement wins when its members are nurtured locally, and simultaneously encouraged and supported to channel their energy—whether fueled by anger, anguish, hope, or idealism—into targeted campaigns at local, state, and federal levels. When properly organized and mobilized, grassroots members make a whole movement greater than the sum of its parts.

"Grassroots" also evokes meanings that go beyond basic definitions. Grassroots activism conjures up images of extreme, even radical change tactics, whether in the civil rights vein of progressive organizing techniques governed by Saul Alinsky's *Rules for Radicals* or in the more recent ultra-conservative Tea Party Patriots mix of anti-government, libertarian, and populist activism. In this extremist light, disempowered and angry grassroots groups are pitted against powerful elected officials, corporate executives, and cultural elite. It's an "us versus them," "black versus white" mentality. But as noted in the Introduction to this book, we considered not only the classic social movement organizing frameworks to inform our study of modern movements, but also frames from other disciplines such as systems, complexity, and networks. From these vantage points, we looked at grassroots not just as armies of activists fighting against a common enemy, but as collectives of individuals who were part of *networks* and who gained as much from being deeply connected to each other *within* the movement as they did from outwardly attacking foes.

As networks, grassroots constituencies can be seen as important in their own right. They are not just a means to a movement's end goal, they *are* an end goal. As noted in *Forces for Good*, referencing Joel Podolny, ". . . the solution is to treat the network not as a tool for information or resources but as a community defined by a common set of values. . . . Ultimately, the community should be treated as an end in itself."[10] This comes into view when looking at grassroots elements of movements as part of larger *systems*. When we employ a systems lens, we can understand more clearly what differentiates the best movements from the rest.

Thinking in Systems

Consider a social or environmental movement as a type of "system." What do we mean by system? "A system is an interconnected set of elements that is coherently organized in a way that achieves something," writes environmental scientist Donella Meadows.[11] Systems have a function (if a machine) or a purpose (if a social grouping), and they consist of multiple elements that are interconnected. Examples of systems, according to Meadows, include the human digestive track, a football team, global trading markets, and the solar system.

Systems have a number of unique properties. As social innovation scholar Frances Westley observes, they:

- Are made of interrelating, interdependent parts,
- Cannot be understood as a function of isolated components,
- Need to be understood not by focusing on what each part is doing, but on how each part is interacting with the rest, and
- Are subjective: What we call the parts and their relationship is fundamentally a matter of perspective and purpose, not intrinsic to the real thing.[12]

Based on these factors, what doesn't qualify as a system would be a group of things that don't add up to a whole greater than the sum of their parts, a pile of sand grains, for instance. Take away some of the parts, and it doesn't change purpose or function. But take away a piece of a human's digestive system, such as the kidneys, and the system would cease to function properly.

What's important to note about every well-functioning system is that it's the relationship *between* the parts that make it work. The parts themselves, of course, need to be in good working order, but alone, they are powerless to achieve the greater goal or purpose. But when properly linked together, they can create a whole that's greater than the sum of its parts.

Great movements have at their core strongly connected grassroots members. Leaders of movement organizations understand they need to invest in building member relationships—not just between the members and the organization or movement, but *among* the members *themselves*. They nurture intense, personal bonds that engender trust and mutual obligation. Building on those bonds, they then encourage activists to collectively take charge in their communities to advance the cause at the local level. The network also becomes an end in and of itself. This approach comes more naturally for some causes than others.

Take the NRA. Founded in 1871 as a nonprofit charitable organization, for the first one hundred years of its history the NRA was essentially a membership organization dedicated to marksmanship training and education. Its founders were two Union veterans concerned by the lack of shooting skills among their troops, so they set out to "promote and encourage rifle shooting on a scientific basis."[13]

It wasn't until relatively late in NRA history, in the 1970s, when the group politicized and pivoted to focus on aggressively defending what it saw as constitutional protections in the Second Amendment for gun ownership.

Today, the NRA continues to nurture its membership even as it lobbies to influence legislation and elections. Members enjoy attending NRA-sponsored gun safety and marksmanship trainings; they visit gun shows and join hunting clubs. Members join to receive the NRA magazine and watch pro-gun content on NRA TV and social media. NRA outings are family affairs, featuring clam bakes and potlucks replete with music, children's games, and more. For instance, attendees of the Virginia-based Tidewater Friends of NRA annual event in 2017 were beckoned on the group's Facebook page to "come to this year's banquet and fight for freedom, family, and the future of the second ammendment [sic] while enjoying a night of auctions, raffles, games, and FUN! We average 1 firearm for every 10 people as prizes!"[14]

Members of the NRA are a *community*. They live near one another and hunt together; they often socialize, worship, and work together. So when it is time to show up at a town hall meeting—as Al Shank and his fellow gun rights supporters did in Charlottesville, Virginia, in the wake of the Orlando massacre—it's a no-brainer. NRA grassroots members are *all in*.

Forging Bonds Under Fire

For other movements, fostering a grassroots community of members is harder. Take MADD: as founder Candy Lightner bleakly admits, losing a child to a drunk driving crash "instantly makes you a member of a club you never wanted to join."[15] While MADD is most renowned for its fiery fights to change social norms around drinking and driving and for aggressively advocating for stronger laws to reduce and prevent drunk driving, from the beginning, the group was doing something that would prove vital to its long-term impact: supporting the victims of drunk driving crashes, including survivors and victim's friends and loved ones.

Support circles sponsored by local MADD chapters forge bonds of trust and mutual obligation among people at the most personal level. They provide bereaved and injured victims and their family members and friends what they need most in the immediate aftermath of a drunk driving–caused crash: one-on-one emotional support from counselors and connections with local support groups comprised of other victims and survivors facing similar experiences. MADD also provides advocacy support, information, and referrals to victims and survivors through its more than three thousand trained victim advocates located across the country, which MADD promotes on its Web site and via social media.[16] (See Figure 1.1.) Programs and services like these have ensured that MADD would have a formidable grassroots army of ready-made soldiers fired up to do battle for the cause. Founder Candy Lightner was smart to focus what resources she could muster on chapter support groups from the outset. For instance, when MADD received its tax-exempt status in 1981, the organization soon had raised $100,000 in private donations, and $60,000 from the National Highway and Traffic Safety Administration specifically to support chapter development.[17]

MADD Victim Support Services

We help survivors survive by . . .

- Providing you and your loved ones with emotional support
- Guidance through the criminal and civil justice systems
- Accompanying victims and survivors to court
- Helping you prepare a victim impact statement
- Referring victims and survivors to appropriate resources for additional help
- Offering support groups in some areas
- Connecting you with other victims and survivors who've had similar experiences
- Providing you supportive materials on victimization topics
- We also have a private Facebook group exclusively for victims and survivors of drunk and drugged driving. This group offers the opportunity for victims and survivors to connect, share, and seek support

If you, or someone you love, has been the victim of a violent crime, you can contact a MADD Victim Advocate, 24 hours a day, at 1-877-MADD-HELP.

Figure 1.1   MADD Victim Support Services

Source: Excerpts from MADD Official Web Site[18]

We also saw examples in other winning movements of how well they treated and nurtured their grassroots—from LGBT proponents advocating for same-sex marriage equality to the tobacco control movement's grassroots base that blanketed the country through groups like Americans for Nonsmokers' Rights and the myriad state-based coalitions that the Campaign for Tobacco-Free Kids supported with technical assistance and advocacy tools. The state coalition work had been catalyzed by several big health charities, including the American Cancer Society, American Heart Association, and American Lung Association, whose members recognized that the diseases that killed or hurt them and their loved ones were preventable through not smoking.

Building networks among grassroots members is vitally important; movements that skip this step are not as well-equipped to achieve their policy and social change goals in the long run. Most movements require their members to take big risks—advocates are called to stand up to powerful people and institutions and often face criticism in their own communities, sometimes confronting their peers. What fortifies advocates in stressful situations like these are the bonds they have with each other—what Malcolm Gladwell refers to as "strong ties."

As Gladwell writes in *The New Yorker* "Small Change: Why the Revolution Will Not Be Tweeted," there is a big difference between "strong-tie" and "weak-tie" networks.[19] He examines the networks of activists who advanced the civil rights movement, specifically students who participated in non-violent civil disobedience campaigns such as sit-ins at Woolworths. He concludes it was because of their strong friendships and mutually felt obligations to one another that they held fast in the face of physical violence and emotional adversity. Gladwell could just as easily been writing about mothers angry about a child killed in a drunk driving crash or gun owners afraid their Second Amendment freedoms were threatened. The collective strength of grassroots members comes in part from the support they feel and receive from each other, as well as from their connection to a larger cause. It's important to disaggregate these two different, but equally vital, points of connection.

Organizing in Systems

Viewing movements through a systems lens allowed us to see how grassroots members of movements relate to *each other*, as well as to the larger cause. It also helped us understand how the various constituent parts of a movement work collectively to achieve the larger purpose. It's not enough to connect members to each other and foster bonds of trust; grassroots advocates also need help coordinating their local actions to advance a larger common agenda. So we looked very closely at how the *grass-tops* leaders of social movement organizations inter-acted with the grassroots and at how they managed to channel all of that collective energy in productive ways. By studying the approaches of the Campaign for Tobacco-Free Kids, Freedom to Marry, the NRA, and other influential organizations employing *networked* leadership strategies, we learned how they *turned their grassroots gold*.

Going for Gold: The NRA-ILA Grassroots Division

"If you want to understand why the National Rifle Association is suc-cessful, look at the structure of the association as being an inverted pyramid. At the top of the pyramid, the largest constituency and base of support is our membership. And the reason they're at the top is because they are the most important."

This is how Glen Caroline, director of the NRA-ILA Grassroots Programs and Campaign Field Operations Division, starts out a typi-cal lecture to policy students.[20] "The reason we succeed is that we try to divest control from our headquarters and really empower our vol-unteers in their communities to be grassroots activists and grassroots leaders," said Caroline in an interview conducted at NRA headquarters in Fairfax, Virginia. The NRA doesn't just *talk* about the importance of grassroots. They *act* on it, giving grassroots activists the resources they need to succeed—from tangible assets like political connections, educational and training materials, to moral support and camaraderie.

The NRA's focus on the grassroots coalesced in the early 1990s, after Caroline started working in NRA-ILA in 1991. Caroline says that at that time, NRA-ILA had a "very loosely defined grassroots office" consisting of one staff member.[21] Part of his first job as an employee of the NRA-ILA's Research Division was to answer incoming calls and letters from people who had either complaints or suggestions. It struck Caroline and his colleagues that "somebody who is taking the time to contact NRA to complain, give suggestions, and ask questions is demonstrating the virtues of good volunteer." They were clearly willing to take initiative and speak out. So responsibility for answering the incoming inquiries was shifted from the research division into a newly emerging grassroots division. Around 1993, the Grassroots Office transformed into a Grassroots Division, and the NRA began to formalize and build programs designed to "harness that energy and passion into a more focused goal."[22]

This shift proved to be the modest beginnings of what eventually would emerge as the most powerful drivers of the NRA's future legislative and electoral success. Through its grassroots, the NRA figured out how to transform the passion and enthusiasm of its supporters into direct influence on the outcomes of elections and legislation proposals.

The newly formed Grassroots Division was deliberately structured to respond to individual member concerns. For instance, the NRA installed a 1–800 toll-free hotline, which any member could call to lodge complaints or concerns. They designed it specifically in this way because, as Caroline explains, "We know we cannot monitor every single activity in every corner of every state. It would be presumptuous for me to think that, sitting out in that gigantic blue building we have off Route 66 in Fairfax, Virginia. We can't know everything."[23] Volunteers and supporters alert the NRA to situations that would go unnoticed and receive training and field support from the NRA. Through this training and support, the NRA-ILA puts its emphasis on grassroots and grassroots members out front. Instead of elite leaders dictating from on high down to the grassroots which actions to take, Headquarters envisions its role as largely *listening* and *responding* to constituent concerns, and then forging the network so local grassroots individuals can coalesce and take action.

It's a key lesson every consumer-facing business must learn—the customer comes first and the customer is always right. Most businesses have elaborate mechanisms for gathering customer feedback and data and for transparently responding to their suggestions and concerns. By staying "close to the customer," organizations like the NRA sharpen their ability to respond and adapt. At the extreme level, it's the way open-source, consumer-driven platforms like Wikipedia, Linux, and Mozilla are successful—their consumers are in charge. It's the difference between a traditional company like Encyclopedia Britannica with its handful of elite experts deciding on which content belongs on its limited pages, and Wikipedia, which allows virtually anyone to contribute to building the knowledge base. It's not that Wikipedia allows just any content—there are paid editors involved who are empowered to monitor and control the forum to some degree—but it's mainly a bottom-up rather than a top-down enterprise.

Getting Out Grassroots Votes

Just as the Grassroots Division at NRA-ILA was supporting NRA members in the field around advocacy campaigns, in 1994 they were launching an Election Volunteer Coordinator Program, now known as Frontline Activist Leaders (FAL). The original goal was to identify NRA members in as many of the 435 U.S. Congressional Districts as possible to act in a liaison role between NRA members and gun owners and the campaigns of candidates the NRA supported. The effort was focused on building pockets of grassroots activists that could help with door knocking, phone calling, material distributions, and other get-out-to-vote efforts, explains Caroline. For the first few election cycles, they only ran the program during election years; by 1998 they converted to a year-round program, with more than two hundred volunteers and NRA coordinators working continuously to build and sustain grassroots activism through networks in their local communities, supporting other political and legislative actions.[24]

Putting It All Together

NRA Grassroots Division volunteers and field staff are the glue that binds the NRA membership together and harnesses their energy to impact legislation and elections. They are successful because they don't just give the grassroots attention when there's a bill up for consideration or a tight race for elected office; they maintain a visible and constant presence throughout the broader gun-enthusiast community. They visit gun shops, attend gun shows, and show up at gun hunting clubs. They appear at Friends of the NRA fundraisers—and not just the staff: NRA Executive VP Wayne LaPierre is a fixture at NRA events large and small. The NRA-ILA staff make a point of being present at many different community forums because "having a presence allows us to have a continuous dialogue with potential supporters and remind them that their activism is important," said Caroline. And all of this lavish attention is undergirded by the range of products and services offered or sponsored by the NRA membership organization—the magazine, gun shows, shooting competitions, BBQs, and more. NRA staff and Front-line Activist Leaders are an integral part of a much broader community.

The NRA could have gone a very different way. With policy experts and well-connected lobbyists working from its headquarters located just outside the Washington, D.C., beltway, they could have chosen to focus on federal legislative priorities and primarily advancing a national agenda. But they didn't. They put their members at the "top of pyramid," because they realize their lobbyists are just the tip of the spear. Without the outspoken, vigorous activism of its core volunteers organizing across its nearly five million members, the NRA wouldn't be able to pass the legislative changes it wants.

Many Pathways to Gold

Each of the successful movements we studied had at its center a vigorous base of passionate, energetic, and well-organized grassroots support. However, the ways in which the grassroots movement evolved for each issue varied. Many factors impacted the scope and formation of grassroots efforts. These factors include the competitive landscape of the field—whether crowded or relatively unpopulated—as well as the structure of the organizations—whether they arose as associations, charitable nonprofits, advocacy or membership-based groups; whether they had c4 and PACs; and more. As noted before, the NRA had a natural grassroots base built into its membership when it politicized in the late 1970s, and while there were other gun rights groups, it was the clear national frontrunner. But in other fields and causes, the competitive landscape was quite different.

Consider the competitive fields and inter-organizational challenges facing these three very different, but equally successful, movements: drunk driving reduction, tobacco control, and same-sex marriage equality. Like the NRA for gun rights, MADD emerged as the clear national leader for the anti–drunk driving cause. There were, of course, other players in these causes: the NRA co-existed with other gun rights groups, which were often more conservative than the NRA and held extremist policy stances that made the NRA's positions appear relatively moderate by comparison at times. But the NRA has always been the largest and most influential player in gun rights. Likewise, MADD was the dominant national anti–drunk driving group. MADD had at

One Major Leader	Very Crowded Fields
Gun Rights NRA	*Marriage Equality* ACLU Anti-Defamation League Freedom to Marry GLAD and GLAAD Human Rights Campaign Lambda Legal NCLR
Anti–Drunk Driving MADD	*Tobacco Control* Americans for Nonsmokers' Rights American Cancer Society American Heart Association American Lung Association American Medical Association Campaign for Tobacco-Free Kids Robert Wood Johnson Foundation Truth Initiative

Figure 1.2   Select National Movement Landscapes

least one antecedent: RID, a regional group based in New York that had not gone fully national. And although other groups like SADD cropped up, none matched MADD in size or scope of influence. As a result, front-running organizations like NRA and MADD did not face significant direct national competition within their own fields.

By contrast, the landscape for same-sex marriage and tobacco control looked quite different. Multiple powerful national organizations co-existed, many with far-flung state and local affiliates, making the challenge of mobilizing and emboldening the grassroots a more complicated feat, as it was difficult to rally disparate activists who joined or supported different organizations, and therefore channeled their energy into sometimes competing agendas. In Chapter Four, "Reckon with Adversarial Allies," we explore intra-field dynamics in depth. But for the purposes of this chapter, Figure 1.2 is a depiction of how the national competitive landscapes appeared for each major movement we studied.

Going for Gold Via the Grassroots

Keeping these competitive landscapes in mind, let's now delve into how other movements employed winning grassroots approaches to drive their causes to victory. In the realm of public health, Mothers

Against Drunk Driving (MADD) provides an excellent example of how concentrated grassroots activism can turn the tide for any movement. It also offers a compelling story of how one social entrepreneur and activist, Candy Lightner, sparked a formidable movement by building from the grassroots up.

Lightner founded MADD in 1980 after her thirteen-year-old daughter, Cari, was killed by an intoxicated driver. The driver had been involved in multiple other driving arrests, and Lightner quickly learned from investigating officers that her daughter's killer was unlikely to serve any jail time.[25] Distraught about her daughter's tragic death, angry her killer would likely go unpunished, and frustrated he had not been prevented from driving in the first place, Lightner and a group of her friends decided to create an organization, Mothers Against Drunk Drivers ["Drivers" was later switched to "Driving"].

Within the year, Lightner had chartered dozens of chapters in California. By 1981 MADD had been incorporated as a 501(c)3 organization with chapters in more than six states, then grew to more than ninety chapters by the next year. By the time Lightner left the organization in 1985, MADD had more than 450 local chapters and two million members and donors.[26] The chapters spread like wildfire in part because of Lightner's passionate charismatic leadership and her broadened definition of drunk driving crash "victims" to include not only those people directly killed or injured, but their family, friends, colleagues, and larger social networks. MADD connected with the victims and their families, tapping into their most primal emotions— grief and anger and revenge and bitterness—and supported them and provided them with outlets to advocate for solutions.[27] (We explore in greater depth in Chapter Three, "Change Hearts *and* Policy" how successful movement leaders use emotional, visceral messages to change social norms around their issues, rather than just focus on advocating for policy solutions.)

MADD chapters also flourished because of the loosely federated structure of the organization. It had a central office in Texas (moved from California) and semi-autonomous local chapters, which were free to appoint their own leaders, raise their own money, and promote their own programs.[28] When a victim of a drunk driving crash or a family member of a victim called MADD and asked, "What can I do?" the answer was, "Start a MADD chapter." Lightner didn't open field offices; she simply sent packets of information to victims and their families with guidelines on how to understand the motor vehicle code, monitor court cases, and interact with officials in law enforcement, the courts, and the legislature.

Lightner left the organization five years after founding it.[29] But MADD overcame the potentially debilitating loss of its visionary, charismatic founder, precisely because *the power of the organization was vested outside of headquarters and away from its founder.* MADD pushed power out to the chapters, which were free to act locally and advance the drunk driving cause in ways that worked in each community's unique political, legal, and social context. It turns out that MADD's decentralized structure was perfectly suited to encourage and enable the local leaders to assume leadership and maintain autonomy. Like the NRA-ILA, MADD had turned its grassroots gold.

Untangling Tobacco Control's Twisted Grassroots

The modern tobacco control movement faced a very different competitive landscape than the one MADD operated in: The tobacco wars were fought in fields that were crowded, cantankerous, and at times rife with conflict.

Tobacco control's grassroots were planted back in the 1970s, when the first local activist campaigns were firing up across the country. Influential leaders such as University of California professor Stanton Glantz and community organizer Julia Carol were "true believers" in the anti-smoking cause. Incensed by the tobacco companies' unapologetic lies about the harmful and addictive qualities of cigarettes, these activists helped drum up a vigorous non-smokers' rights movement, advocating in towns and counties for non-smoking ordinances. Their organization morphed into Americans for Nonsmokers' Rights (ANR) as they took their California-based local ordinance strategy national.[30] They also worked in alliance with other public health groups to create smoking bans in the airline industry in the 1980s.

The fact that the movement launched locally—from small communities outward—turned out to be an extremely effective inoculation against the powerful tobacco industry. Tobacco companies had elite relationships with state and national political leaders, cemented with generous campaign contributions and lobbying prowess. But companies did not have a depth of reach at the local level. As Stanton Glantz recalls, "Tobacco companies realized that they were dominating in the state legislatures, but getting their lunches eaten at local level . . . they gave money, hired lobbyists, and could dominate [at the state level]. But at the community level, in smaller places, politicians care a lot more what their voting constituents think."

By rallying local activists to show up at even the smallest town council meeting and stand up for their health and rights as non-smokers, ANR was doing for tobacco control what the NRA was doing for gun rights with its rank-and-file members like Al Shank in Virginia advocating after the Orlando mass shooting—showing up, speaking out, and making elected officials aware they cared about the issue— and they would vote on it.

In 1995, when the Robert Wood Johnson Foundation (RWJF) jumped full force into the tobacco wars and provided seed funding for the Campaign for Tobacco-Free Kids (the Campaign), it sought to fuel federal policy and regulatory change by creating a group that could directly counter the powerful tobacco lobby, represented by the Tobacco Institute. While working nationally, the Campaign also expanded the breadth and diversity of state-based advocacy campaigns, providing technical assistance to state-level coalitions and helping them push for reforms, such as passing state excise taxes, which were proven to reduce smoking. RWJF also had funded the *Smoke-Less States*® initiative, which provided financial support to coalitions of state and local groups advocating for the state excise tax policies, among other changes. These resources provided much-needed fuel for local grassroots groups to succeed. Tobacco control movement leaders at the Campaign and RWJF understood the importance of caring for and feeding the grassroots.

This did not mean the path to victory was smooth or straight. Tensions flared between grassroots advocates like Glantz, based far outside of Washington, D.C., and national leaders like those leading the Campaign inside the beltway. Their clashing visions for the movement came to a head in 1997, when lawsuits were brought by several state attorneys general against major tobacco companies, and the Campaign's executive vice president and legal counsel, Matt Myers, was asked by the attorneys generals and White House officials to join in negotiations with the heads of major tobacco companies about a potential settlement, the Global Settlement Agreement (GSA). Even though the Campaign had backing from formidable proponents like the American Cancer Society, American Heart Association, and American Medical Association, a perfect storm of political and intra-field events conspired to prevent the agreement from going forward. Grassroots advocates like Glantz and Carol were outraged. They torpe-doed the GSA, concerned that loopholes and other concessions to the tobacco industry were fraught with danger. Some advocates publicly excoriated leaders of the Campaign for "dealing with the devil." (This fissure is further explored in Chapter Four, "Reckon with Adversarial Allies.") The following year, a revised Master Settlement Agreement was made, producing key wins for tobacco control. But it would be another decade before a federal law regulating tobacco under the FDA would pass and the balance of the tobacco control movement's agenda could be realized.

Smoking was curbed in the United States because of the vast, unruly network of individual activists, charitable nonprofits, lobbying groups, business and policy leaders fighting to advance the cause—and sometimes despite it. But it never would have advanced as far as it did without the grassroots efforts that first popped up in the 1970s and later were nurtured with technical assistance from the Campaign for Tobacco-Free Kids and ANR, and bankrolled with RWJF's more than $500 million in financial support through *SmokeLess States*. It was a classic David versus Goliath matchup. Only in this case, it took thousands of grassroots "Davids" banding together to undercut the giant tobacco industry.

Building Grassroots Momentum for Same-Sex Marriage

In the fight for same-sex marriage rights, LGBT advocates faced a sim-ilarly competitive and crowded field. And although the success of the movement is credited in large part to Freedom to Marry, a national organization founded in 2003 by activist Evan Wolfson, the roots of the marriage equality movement ran much deeper—underlying a grassroots membership both broad and complex.

The ninety-four-year-old American Civil Liberties Union (ACLU) brought the first marriage lawsuit on behalf of a same-sex couple in 1971. Legal defense groups like Lambda Legal Defense and Education

Fund, GLBTQ Legal Advocates & Defenders (GLAD), ACLU, and others had been working for decades to advance LGBT issues in the courts. The largest LGBT membership organization, Human Rights Campaign (HRC), has connected more than 1.5 million members and notable celebrities with LGBT causes since 1980. Meanwhile, the National LGBTQ Task Force (the "Task Force" also formerly known as the "National Gay Task Force"), had been advocating since 1973 when it was founded in the wake of the Stonewall Riots—the first major grassroots protests supporting equal rights for gay people. This panoply of legal, policy advocacy, and membership groups was working vociferously to advance a range of causes that affected LGBT community members when Freedom to Marry entered the scene.

As the marriage equality cause started to gain traction, all of these disparate groups clamored for money, media attention, and power to advance their various agendas. In this crowded field, the proposal of pushing for full marriage rights was not popular—a relatively new concept, it was embraced only by some LGBT advocates. Meanwhile, the dominant groups were founded or had become engaged in LGBT causes at an earlier period of U.S. history, when homosexuality was still considered a mental illness; many states had anti-sodomy laws; and children were often sent away to mental institutions when their parents discovered they were gay.[31] As a result, organizations were working on a range of issues, from employment and housing discrimination to adoption and custody rights, and more. (By contrast, when MADD launched, the drunk driving issue was not yet widely perceived by the public as a dominant cause for concern.)

Because of the crowded field and the many disparate agendas, leaders in the fight for marriage equality were forced to find ways to join together in coalition and embrace a common strategy to promote marriage equality. They did this primarily by engaging and focusing on grassroots engagement at the state and local level (which we explore in more detail in Chapter Two, "Sharpen Your 10/10/10/20 = 50 Vision"). In order to be successful, they had to energize the memberships and grassroots supporters of various groups like HRC and ACLU, while widening the base to include new supporters who had never been active in LGBT issues before.

LGBT efforts in Massachusetts make an excellent case study: There, to drive a campaign for a constitutional amendment allowing same-sex marriage, Freedom to Marry and other national and regional groups forged a coalition, MassEquality, in the late 1990s. Their first objective: Galvanize a grassroots base of support and organize it to advance legislative and electoral wins. The groups pooled resources to hire a campaign coordinator and brought in Marty Rouse, a seasoned political organizer who'd worked on Democratic election campaigns. HRC opened up its membership list, enabling the coalition to raise initial funds and start to expand the base. Rouse used some of the funds to recruit a team of field organizers and jumpstart the grassroots movement. By 2004, email was available as an organizing tool, which enabled many more people to easily contact their legislators, and one hundred people quickly metastasized into a network of 400,000.[32]

Rouse operated shrewdly offline, too. He organized postcard campaigns and targeted certain senators' neighborhoods to give greatest visibility. Rouse recalls, "People would say 'MassEquality is EVERYWHERE!' No, we weren't everywhere. But we were very strategic, we knew where [the senator] went for coffee every morning, so we would postcard there and get people talking so they would bump into him in the supermarket and say 'Hey, we heard about the marriage ballot initiative and we're for it.'"[33] By galvanizing a savvy and relentless grassroots campaign, which involved issue-organizing as well as electoral influence, MassEquality was eventually able to win over enough legislators to amend the Massachusetts Constitution to recognize same-sex marriage.

Marriage equality advocates parlayed their successful Massachusetts strategy to win next in several other states, including New York (which we explore in detail in the following chapter). They won in large part because they *turned their grassroots gold*.

Fading Grassroots

Just as we explored the important role grassroots activists played in *winning* movements, we also looked at movements that seemed stuck or were "in-progress" as of the 2010s. It became immediately clear that movements that failed to nurture their grassroots, either because they didn't recognize their importance or couldn't muster the resources to do so, were often on the losing side of battles.

Take the gun control movement. Its leaders had, until very recently, followed a different approach with regard to grassroots than the NRA had. Until Everytown for Gun Safety coalesced in 2014 with the merger of Mayors Against Illegal Guns and Moms Demand Action and quickly grew within a few years to four million support-ers,[34] no other major gun group came close to matching the breadth of the NRA's grassroots. At almost every turn, it appears gun control leaders historically made choices that had left local grassroots activists relatively under-resourced and on the fringe—at the very same period in history when the NRA was doing exactly the opposite.

The history of modern gun violence prevention is not entirely devoid of grassroots activism, however. A few notable exceptions in the movement do exist when grassroots activism appeared to match the level of intensity and volume of the NRA. These were the points at which modern gun control activists had won ground. One remark-able national grassroots effort was ignited by Donna Dees-Thomases, a working mother living in a New Jersey suburb who organized the Million Mom March Across America in 2000. The idea hatched after a tragic incident on August 10, 1999, when a white supremacist had opened fire with a semi-automatic weapon at the North Valley Jewish Community Center in Granada Hills, California. A horrified Dees-Thomases wanted to take action and looked for ways to join the gun violence prevention movement (then commonly known as gun control). Finding no place to plug in, she decided to do something on her own. Drawing on her professional career in media and communi-cations—she'd been working for Late Night with David Letterman as a publicist—she envisioned staging a "million mom march" on Wash-ington. As she started searching for partners to help mount it, initially she was rebuffed by the established gun control groups of the time. One male representative of Handgun Control, Inc. (later re-named Brady) told Dees-Thomases there was no "movement" and doubted anyone would actually show up at a march on Mother's Day.[35] Coa-lition to Stop Gun Violence (CSGV) leaders Michael Beard and the Reverend Jim Atwood expressed support and provided help, despite limited resources.

Dees-Thomases eventually clinched a partnership with Bell Cam-paign, a nascent grassroots gun violence victims and survivors sup-port network founded in California by burn trauma expert Andrew McGuire, executive director of the Trauma Foundation. Launched under the fiscal umbrella of the Trauma Foundation, what became known as the Bell Campaign was modeled after MADD, and McGuire early on formed an advisory board comprised of nine gun violence advocates, including Tom Vanden Berk (whose teenaged son had been fatally shot), and Mary Leigh Blek, who had also co-founded another gun control group, Orange County Citizens Against Gun Violence. McGuire received an initial $4 million over three years from the Goldman Family Fund, and by the time Dees-Thomases contacted the Bell Campaign, McGuire's group had established more than eighty chapters across the United States.[36]

The Million Mom March and the Bell Campaign together mounted what became the Million Mom March Across America, ultimately galvanizing more than 750,000 protestors to march on the National Mall, recalls Dees-Thomases, along with tens of thousands of satellite marchers in other cities on Mother's Day in 2000. One of the largest marches on Washington, D.C., the Million Mom March to this day is the largest single day of protest against gun violence in U.S. history.[37] It ultimately succeeded with help from established gun violence prevention groups at both the state and national level.

In the wake of the Million Mom March (MMM) and with the influx of new activists, stricter gun laws were either enacted or strengthened at local and state levels as a result of the vigorous activism of MMM chapters and other like-minded organizations across the country. But momentum soon fizzled. After the big event on Mother's Day, the Bell Campaign changed its name to Million Mom March (MMM) after the Trauma Foundation helped establish MMM as a separate 501(c)4 organization.[38]

Plus, clashes among various leaders at the previously established gun control groups arose—all of whom were male, notes Dees-Thomases, who bristled when she recalled many of them dismissing her and the growing army of MMM activists as "just moms."[39] Soon, squabbles ensued among the established gun control group leaders over everything from who got "credit" for the enormous success of the march (which MMM founder Dees-Thomases and the Bell Campaign's McGuire had bootstrapped and independently funded) to who owned the donor list; financial control and leadership succession issues erupted into a perfect storm.[40] By early 2001, MMM was merged into the Brady Campaign.

On the surface, this appeared to be a win-win: Brady could offer fiscal sponsorship and policy expertise, and the MMM chapters would drive grassroots activism. But a key funder pulled support when the merger with Brady was announced, and Brady soon suffered a cratering financial setback in the wake of the 9/11 terrorist attacks, as the organization lost a significant chunk of funding as the nation's attention turned to terrorism.[41] Under then-president Michael Barnes's leadership, the Brady Campaign managed to keep most of the remaining 236 MMM/Brady chapters afloat (some chapters opposed the merger, as did McGuire). But Brady did not deeply invest in them—or support the original MMM chapter model, which had been based on Mothers Against Drunk Driving's decentralized, locally driven chapter approach—at the level originally intended. "The MADD chapter model had at its foundation state council leadership," notes Dees-Thomases. "When the MADD chapter model was abandoned, the chapters began to diminish in size."[42]

Study in Contrasts

The difference between how the NRA handles its grassroots versus how Brady did couldn't be starker. While the NRA has put grassroots "at the top of the pyramid" since the 1990s, whereas Brady historically put them near the bottom. Brady had historically worked only with the "grass-tops" organizations and state-based groups until its merger with Million Mom March (MMM) in 2001 and the Brady/MMM Chapters were formed.

This was in part due to the fact that Brady was originally not conceived as a chapter-based organization. As former Brady Campaign grassroots division leader Brian Malte explains, when Brady merged with MMM, "the mentality was not 'everything we're going to do now is wrapped around [the chapters], [they] are an important piece of the organization.' But I guarantee that's not what the chapters thought. They thought, 'We *are* the organization.' So I had the difficult task of trying to get the chapters what they needed, yet knowing we're not solely a chapter-based organization."[43] (Malte served in various leadership roles at Brady for more than twenty years before leaving the organization in 2017.)

Today, more than ninety Brady/MMM chapters continue to operate nationwide. The California chapters in particular have successfully advanced policies restricting gun use and ownership, and the state is among a handful in the United States with relatively robust gun safety laws. At its peak, the Brady Campaign counted approximately half a million members. But it's proven no antidote to the five-million-strong membership the NRA claims forms its grassroots base.

Meanwhile, it took fifteen years after the Million Mom March and multiple mass shootings—including the tragic Sandy Hook School massacre—for a new, grassroots-driven gun safety organization to emerge. Everytown for Gun Safety formed in 2014, created with the merger of activist Shannon Watts's organization, Moms Demand Action for Gun Sense in America, and Mayors Against Illegal Guns (MAIG), and was co-founded and funded by former New York City Mayor Michael Bloomberg. Bloomberg pledged $50 million in the new organization's first year, and with its number of supporters surging to four million by 2017, the newly formed Everytown for Gun Safety presents a considerable counterweight to the NRA.[44]

Ironically, when Shannon Watts launched with a Facebook page what became Moms Demand Action in the wake of the Sandy Hook School shooting, she did so because she couldn't find an obvious way to become involved. "I wanted to join the gun safety movement and looked for something like MADD. I went online, [but] there really wasn't a grassroots effort, at least not one that spoke to me."[45] So in a painful illustration of what's past is prologue, like Dees-Thomases more than a decade before, Watts set out to build a grassroots movement once again.

While it remains to be seen whether Everytown will be able to translate its growing ranks of moms, mayors, and other grassroots supporters of "common sense" gun control measures into national legislative and social norm change, there are promising early signs. Since the 2012 Sandy Hook School shooting, twenty-five states and the District of Columbia have enacted laws to keep guns from domestic abusers, and eight states have extended gun-sale background checks. Everytown also clearly prioritizes the involvement of survivors in the movement through its national Survivor Network, as well as its broader network of Moms Demand Action for Gun Sense in America volunteers, who are motivated and equipped to turn up in town hall meetings and on Capitol Hill and raise their voices alongside their equally vigorous gun rights opponents. So now, every time dozens of guys like Al Shank show up at a town council meeting in their neon orange hunting garb, an equal number of passionate women sporting bright red Moms Demand Action T-shirts show up on the opposite side. Everytown appears to understand the vital importance of its grassroots base of energy and of not letting it fade.

"It's like catching lightning in a bottle," explains Shannon Watts. The trick is not to snuff it, but channel it into social change.

Golden Grassroots Systems

According to a teaching by the Sufi mystic Rumi: "You think because you understand 'one' you must also understand 'two,' because one and one make two. But you must also understand 'and.'"[46]

This chapter is all about the "*and*"—the stuff that connects people at the grassroots of a movement to each other and also tethers them to a common cause. Winning movements foster the "*and*." That's what turns grassroots gold. Conversely, less successful movements fail to focus on the "*and*"—their leaders skip the step of creating deep, visceral connections among the individuals who make up their movements, or they don't recognize the critical importance of building on momentum from the grassroots up. It's a pattern we observed time and again as we looked at some of the struggling movements of modern times. These include gun control and other causes, such as climate action and public education reform.

In the environmental arena, one key explanation for why recent attempts failed to curb U.S. carbon emissions through federal measures can be found in how environmental groups handled the grassroots. In her unsparing analysis, "Naming the Problem: What It Will Take to Counter Extremism and Engage Americans in the Fight Against Global Warming," Harvard University Professor Theda Skocpol examines why environmentalists ultimately did not convince the U.S. Senate to pass "cap and trade" legislation during the 2009–2010 fight for the Waxman-Markey American Clean Energy and Security Act.[47] She analyzed how leaders of the U.S. Climate Action Partnership (USCAP), a coalition of business chieftains and heads of major environmental groups, attempted to place a cap on carbon emissions and create an open market for energy producers to trade allowances under a cap. Since a cap and trade mechanism worked to cut the toxic emissions causing acid rain in the 1990s, it could work for carbon, too. Or so the thinking went.

It turns out it wasn't the policy solution that was faulty. What was wrong, concludes Skocpol, was the largely top-down leadership approach deployed by environmental reformers at that time, and their failure to engage effectively with and to embolden the grassroots. Whereas the opposition—driven by Tea Party–backed climate skeptics and a growing mass of angry, disenchanted, conservative grassroots activists—were actively and vigorously mobilizing to the contrary. Conservatives had taken the fight out to U.S. states and local jurisdictions, whereas environmentalists were mainly trying to persuade elites inside the Capitol beltway of their cause. This was a mistake.

"To counter fierce political opposition," advises Skocpol, "[environmental] reformers will have to build organizational networks across the country, and they will need to orchestrate sustained political efforts that stretch far beyond friendly Congressional offices, comfy board rooms, and posh retreats . . . insider politics cannot carry the day on its own, apart from a broader movement pressing politicians for change."[48]

For the causes struggling to gain ground in the 2010s, such as gun violence prevention and carbon reduction, movement setbacks can be attributed in large part to relatively weak or under-organized grassroots. In other cases, sometimes it's not that the grassroots were downplayed or disorganized; it's that the grassroots seem to be altogether *missing*. Case in point: recent efforts by reformers to close the U.S. educational equality gap. While Teach for America has set about galvanizing a new vanguard of education reform to realize founder Wendy Kopp's vision that "one day, all children will have access to an excellent education," today it seems more dream than reality. Teach for America has successfully inspired tens of thousands of young people to teach in under-resourced public schools and go on to start schools or to leave teaching and go on to advocate for education reform from positions of influence in government or the private sector. Meanwhile, the bottom-up, state-based charter school movement has unleashed a new cadre of publicly funded, independently run schools flowering largely in lower- and middle-income communities. But what's been missing, says TFA alum and community organizer Mark Fraley, is a true *grassroots* educational equity movement.

Fraley argues in "History Matters," an analysis of the key success factors across a range of historical movements including LGBT, civil rights, and women's rights, that there is currently no social change "movement" for educational equity, only fragmented pieces of one. As a whole, the educational equity movement is "principally driven not by people whose families are directly affected by our education system's failures, but rather by a loose network of allies and advocates."[49]

Galvanizing a movement from the grassroots up requires mobilizing people who live at the grassroots—the rank and file, the everyday individuals with the *lived experience* of the problem at hand. These people are the most inseparable from the cause. They are the most viscerally connected to it. They have the most to lose if a movement fails, and the most to gain if it succeeds.

Whatever the cause, there is one fundamental strategy to win that supersedes all others: Figure out how to turn grassroots gold.

Notes

1. Dictionary.com definition, accessed February 2, 2017. http://www.dictionary
   .com/browse/grassroots.
2. Cairns, Taylor. "Charlottesville City Council Passes Stricter Gun Legislation."
   http://www.newsplex.com/content/news/City-Council-passes-resolution-
   for-stricter-gun-legislation-383725281.html. Posted: June 20, 2016, updated
   June 21, 2016. Retrieved January 26, 2017.
3. *Ibid.*
4. According to one summary, "Who Funds the NRA?" the NRA's finances
   became more entwined with the gun industry starting around 2005. By 2013,
   membership dues totaling $175,577,863 contributed the largest percentage
   (50.5 percent) of the NRA's total revenue of $347,968,789. The next biggest
   sources were $96.4 million from private contributions and grants (27.7 percent),
   $27.61 million from unrelated business income (7.9 percent), and $24.5 million
   from advertising income (7 percent). Since 2004, fundraising revenue from contributions had grown twice as fast as income from membership dues. The $96.4
   million in contributions in 2013 represented a 108.2 percent increase over the
   $46.3 million in contributions in 2004. This difference can be attributed to a
   shift in fundraising strategy starting in 2005, when the NRA put more focus on
   soliciting donations from individuals and corporations, including twenty-two
   gun manufacturers. http://www.amarkfoundation.org/nra-who-funds-the-
   nra-11-13-15.pdf. Retrieved October 25, 2017.
5. Quinnipiac University National Poll. "Latest Massacre Drives Gun Control Support to New High, Quinnipiac University National Poll Finds;
   Voters Reject GOP Tax Plan 2-1." November 15, 2017. https://poll.qu.edu/
   national/release-detail?ReleaseID = 2501.

6. Reports on State Tobacco Policy Making by the Center for Tobacco Control Research and Education at the University of California San Francisco. Official Web site of University of California San Francisco. https://tobacco.ucsf.edu/states. Retrieved December 19, 2017.

7. Goss, Kristin. *Disarmed: The Missing Movement for Gun Control in America.* Princeton, NJ: Princeton University Press, 2006, page 150.

8. *Ibid.,* page 40.

9. "Personal Firearms: Programs That Promote Safe Storage and Research on Their Effectiveness," September 2017. United States Government Accountability Office Report to Congressional Requesters. http://www.gao.gov/assets/690/687239.pdf. Retrieved December 15, 2017.

10. Crutchfield, Leslie R., and McLeod Grant, Heather. *Forces for Good: The Six Practices of High-Impact Nonprofits* (2nd ed.). Hoboken, NJ: John Wiley & Sons, 2012, pages 106 and 121.

11. Meadows, Donella H., and Wright, Diana. *Thinking in Systems: A Primer.* Charleston, NC: Sustainability Institute, 2008, page 12.

12. Westley, F. "Social Innovation and FSG: The Challenges of Re-Imagining Social Change." Presentation at FSG company retreat in Boston, MA, February 2015.

13. National Rifle Association official Web site. https://home.nra.org/about-the-nra/.

14. Tidewater Friends of NRA Facebook Page. https://www.facebook.com/events/1243190809103648/. Accessed October 27, 2017.

15. Candace Lightner interview, August 8, 2016.

16. Mothers Against Drunk Driving, https://www.madd.org/get-help/victim-assistance/. Accessed October 27, 2017.

17. Fell, James C., and Voas, Robert B. "Mothers Against Drunk Driving (MADD): The First 25 Years." *Traffic Injury Prevention,* 2006, 7(3), 197.

18. Mothers Against Drunk Driving, https://www.madd.org/get-help/victim-assistance/. Accessed October 27, 2017.

19. Gladwell, Malcolm. "Small Change: Why the Revolution Will Not Be Tweeted." NewYorker.com. October 4, 2010. https://www.newyorker.com/magazine/2010/10/04/small-change-malcolm-gladwell.

20. Caroline, Glen. Grassroots Mobilization at the NRA American University Institute for Lobbying Lecture. Hosted by the American University's Center for Congressional and Presidential Studies. https://www.c-span.org/video/?154618–1/grassroots-mobilization-nra. January 10, 2000. Accessed October 12, 2016.

21. Interview with Glen Caroline conducted at NRA Headquarters in Fairfax, Virginia, November 16, 2016.

22. Caroline, Glen. Grassroots Mobilization lecture, 2000.
23. *Ibid.*
24. Caroline, Glen. Grassroots Mobilization lecture, 2000.
25. Weed, Frank J. "The MADD Queen: Charisma and the Founder of Mothers Against Drunk Driving." University of Texas at Arlington, *Leadership Quarterly*, 4(3/4), 329–346. JAI Press, Inc. 1993.
26. Candace Lightner interview, August 8, 2016, and email exchange December 19, 2017. See also Fell, J., and Voas, R., "Mothers Against Drunk Driving (MADD): The First 25 Years."
27. Weed, Frank J. "The MADD Queen," page 335.
28. *Ibid.*, page 337.
29. *Ibid.*
30. Julia Carol stayed on to become co-director of ANR; Glantz left the organization, but remained a strong, although unaffiliated, presence in the tobacco control movement.
31. National LGBTQ Task Force Official Web site. http://www.thetaskforce.org/about/mission-history.html. Accessed February 6, 2017.
32. Marty Rouse interview, April 20, 2016.
33. *Ibid.*
34. John Feinblatt interview, August 1, 2017.
35. Donna Dees-Thomases interview, June 3 and 7, 2016.
36. Andrew McGuire, email exchange December 26, 2017.
37. Dees-Thomases interview.
38. A Million Mom March Ed Fund was also created as a separate 501(c)3 so the Trauma Foundation could transfer funding to support it. The organization was overwhelmed by the bursting energy of thousands of new activists and the enormous effort and cost entailed in forming and maintaining chapters nationwide, which had expanded to more than 280 after the march. Andrew McGuire, email exchange December 26, 2017.
39. Dees-Thomases interview.
40. Andrew McGuire, email exchange December 26, 2017.
41. Interviews with Donna Dees-Thomases (*Ibid.*), Andrew McGuire (June 20 and 22, 2016), and Michael Barnes (July 11, 2016).
42. *Ibid.* Dees-Thomases.
43. Brian Malte interview, June 9, 2016.
44. Everytown for Gun Safety. "New Gun Violence Prevention Group 'Everytown for Gun Safety' Unites Mayors, Moms, and Millions of Americans. https://www.mikebloomberg.com/news/new-gun-violence-prevention-group-everytown-for-gun-safety-unites-mayors-moms-and-millions-of-americans/. April 16, 2014.

45. Shannon Watts interview, August 1, 2017.
46. Jalaluddin Rumi, a 13th-century Sufi mystic.
47. Skocpol, Theda. Symposium on the Politics of America's Fight Against Global Warming, co-sponsored by the Columbia School of Journalism and the Scholars Strategy Network, February 14, 2013, Tsai Auditorium, Harvard University.
48. *Ibid*, page 11.
49. Fraley, Mark. *History Matters: Building Towards an Educational Justice Movement*. Washington, DC: Leadership for Educational Equity, 2016.

2

Sharpen Your 10/10/10/20 = 50 Vision

"The powers delegated by the proposed Constitution to the federal government are few and defined. . . . Those which are to remain in the State governments are numerous and indefinite."

—James Madison

ON MAY 10, 2005, Freedom to Marry founder Evan Wolfson, GLAD attorney Mary Bonauto, and a handful of other LGBT movement leaders quietly gathered at the invitation of mega-donor Tim Gill for a closed meeting in Jersey City, New Jersey. The outlook for the same-sex marriage movement on that day looked dour: Seventeen U.S. states had proposed constitutional amendments that explicitly banned gay marriage—thirteen of them freshly adopted after President Clinton had signed into law the 1996 Defense of Marriage Act (DOMA), which denied federal recognition of any state-issued marriage licenses to same-sex couples. The California Supreme Court had voided same-sex marriages in 2004. And while the Massachusetts Supreme Court had just allowed the first state-sanctioned marriages of same-sex couples, a vigorous opposition ballot referendum was under way, spearheaded by conservative leaders like then-governor of Massachusetts Mitt Romney, Catholic Church officials, and other conservative and anti-gay groups. A few rays of hope remained in

Vermont and two other states, which had passed either civil unions or similar relationship-recognition laws.[1] But these developments were considered by some a dubious half-step toward full marriage, evoking the ignominious 1896 *Plessy v. Ferguson* U.S. Supreme Court case, which had allowed states to segregate public facilities by race under the notorious "separate but equal" doctrine.

It was a moment of reckoning for the marriage equality cause. Proponents of legal marriage for same-sex couples had ginned up an audacious and extremely contentious campaign. By the mid-2000s, LGBT advocates had achieved hard-won victories on issues they'd been trying to advance long before gay marriage was considered even a remote possibility. More non-discrimination bills were passed in 2005 than any year since 1992. The U.S. Supreme Court had struck down the nation's remaining sodomy laws. States like California, Connecticut, and Vermont had passed sweeping protections for same-sex relationships.[2] So although in 2005 it wasn't legal for gays to *marry* anywhere in the United States except Massachusetts, *being* gay was no longer effectively illegal, and bashing or discriminating against LGBT people at work, in homeownership and rental transactions, and in every other public setting was now unlawful.

At their Jersey City gathering, the small working group of concerned LGBT leaders faced a crossroads. The movement was splintered, as same-sex marriage advocates wanted to win the legal right to marry, but at what cost? They faced vehement opposition from conservative forces, and they didn't even have full support from *within* the LGBT community. Some members rejected traditional marriage as, well, too *traditional*—mainstream, conformist, untrue to their "queer" identity roots. Another big LGBT segment wanted to push for more civil union–type arrangements—"separate but equal" seemed far better than virtually no legal protections at all. Another camp advocated for changes that mattered to the entire LGBT community, not just to couples; they wanted to focus on eliminating existing discriminatory laws.[3] And then there was the "marriage equality" camp, which was hell-bent on winning full, legal marriage for same-sex couples nationwide, but flummoxed about how to move forward in the face of both fierce conservative backlash and deep discord among their own allies.

A student of civil rights history, Freedom to Marry founder Evan Wolfson understood the way to win over the country was to get one of the two national players, either Congress or the U.S. Supreme Court, to act. But history also showed that a critical mass of states and a majority of public support were necessary before either entity would do so.[4] As one of the Jersey City meeting participants, ACLU deputy legal director Matt Coles, notes: "The women's vote wasn't won because advocates mounted a constitutional amendment campaign. It was won because a majority of states already had suffrage by the time it reached the national courts. By the time the 1964 Civil Rights Act was passed, half the U.S. states had already enacted employment laws banning discrimination based on race."[5] To win at the federal level, a movement cause must first create the right climate in the states.

With this knowledge in hand, and faced with a fractious group in Jersey City, Wolfson and his colleagues tackled the challenge of trying to align each of these various LGBT constituencies around some kind of unified, workable strategy. Stymied, someone at the meeting suggested a simple thought experiment: "What if we have a conversation about what we thought we could accomplish in particular states over the next ten to fifteen years?"[6]

And that's when their 10/10/10/20 = 50 vision came into focus. Members of the group asked each other, "What if we could get ten states with full marriage, ten with full civil unions, ten with some . . . form of relationship recognition laws (like domestic partnerships), and the remaining twenty with either non-discrimination laws or significant cultural climate change?"[7]

It was a breakthrough moment. First, because it allowed each "camp" of the LGBT community to work on what *it* thought was most important. Instead of forcing consensus among deeply divided groups, each segment could move forward in ways that were individually distinctive, but collectively nudged the entire country toward greater LGBT equality. Second, the state-by-state strategy was uniquely tailored to fit the very different political, legislative, and cultural landscapes in each of the fifty U.S. states. Those states in which advocates believed there would be the strongest appetite for (or at least tolerance of) same-sex marriage would become the first battlegrounds for full marriage. In other states, advocates could push for stronger relationship recognition laws. And progress could also be made in even the most conservative states, which might be nudged to at least drop existing discriminatory LGBT laws and policies.

By the next day, the group had coalesced around a working plan. They committed to a strategy dubbed "10/10/10/20," and ACLU Deputy Legal Director Matt Coles wrote it up in a paper, "Winning Marriage: What We Need to Do," which was endorsed by major groups working for LGBT rights.[8] The next step was to execute against the plan. Their first objective: Win and hold the right for same-sex couples to marry in one state—*any* state. They homed in on Massachusetts as their best shot. In 2003 the Massachusetts Supreme Judicial Court ruled in *Goodridge v. Department of Public Health* in favor of same-sex marriage, and just as the first couples celebrated legal marriages, opponents snapped into activist mode and proposed a constitutional amendment to withdraw the right. Marriage equality activists recognized they would need to fight the amendment in both legislative halls and at the ballot box. They mounted a formidable campaign that mobilized grassroots volunteers to lobby lawmakers and turned out voters to support election bids of candidates who would support the right to marry. By 2007, they'd won. Meanwhile, they pushed ahead in New York, California, and other states, as LGBT leaders waged dozens of other state-based electoral and legislative campaigns.

Meanwhile, attorneys from GLAD, ACLU, Lambda Legal, and NCLR mounted lawsuits against the federal government to challenge DOMA, resulting in the 2013 Supreme Court ruling that nullified this federal law, which since 1996 had effectively denied married gay couples the more than eleven hundred federal protections and responsibilities triggered by marriage.[9] LGBT activists organized efforts in various states to advance their causes, whether securing relationship rights or simply more tolerant laws toward their constituencies.

Ultimately, by the time the Supreme Court decided *Obergefell v. Hodges* in 2015, the marriage equality movement had achieved what civil rights and women's suffrage activists had achieved in prior eras—a groundswell of momentum across a majority of states that tilted the balance toward accepting, or at least recognizing, same-sex marriage. They'd demonstrated, just as in centuries past, that the winning path to national change in the 21st century was to first plow through all fifty states, rather than go directly to Congress or the Supreme Court. As history has shown time and again, "Change doesn't come *from* Washington. It comes *to* Washington."[10]

Go National *and* Federal

Although it may seem like 20/20 hindsight, it's difficult today to imagine marriage equality would have been affirmed nationwide for same-sex couples had that small group of LGBT activists not coalesced around a "10/10/10/20" plan to win all fifty states that day in Jersey City. "We realized we needed a national strategy, not just a federal one," says Freedom to Marry National Campaign Director Marc Solomon.[11]

This incremental, state-by-state approach that ultimately tipped the nation in support of the LGBT cause was not unique. Other winning movements followed the same recipe for success, even if they didn't follow precisely the same "10/10/10/20" divisional rubric. The key insight movement leaders embraced is this: Don't push directly for any sweeping federal change until a solid majority of support has already been cemented in most of the U.S. states. The winning movements that have peaked since the 1980s have all adopted this states-first approach—including gun rights, tobacco control, and drunk-driving reduction. Conversely, those causes that did the opposite—when leaders focused first or almost exclusively on federal legislation or Supreme Court rulings and placed a lower priority on state and local efforts—largely lost ground.

It's a strategy that makes sense—in theory. The United States is organized as a federalist system, with limited powers accorded to the federal government and the bulk resting with states. So why doesn't every movement adopt a state-by-state approach? There are many reasons, with lack of resources to effectively compete in all fifty states and divergent levels of interest and support for the issue across states being two frequent ones. But the most important reason, we believe, lies within movement leaders themselves. The protagonists of winning causes *recognize* that they must first win at local and state levels, before going for any big federal changes. With that knowledge in hand, they then *act*—either by empowering and emboldening grassroots efforts already in place, or by *seeding and supporting* state-based grassroots campaigns where none previously existed. It requires enormous resources, incredible discipline, and relentless commitment to orchestrating a differentiated yet coordinated strategy across all fifty states. But the fundamental distinguishing factor between triumphant movements and the rest is they pursue some variation on the "10/10/10/20 = 50" theme.

The next important factor is for successful movements to have in place the right kind of leadership structure to work across all fifty states. By structure, we don't mean a traditional hierarchy, with a CEO issuing commands from on high and hogging all power. While this top-down approach has been repeatedly tried, it almost always fails. Instead, in winning movements, we observed what might be called a *networked* leadership structure. In each of the successful movements we studied, the organizations and leaders most central to the change conceived of themselves not as *commander* at the helm of an army, but rather *a coordinator* at the center of a *network*. It's a concept explored in *Forces for Good,* where it was revealed that high-impact nonprofits adopt a *network mindset.* They work *with and through their nonprofit peers* to drive greater impact, rather than directly competing with other nonprofits or trying to go it alone.[12] The *networked* structure is expressed slightly differently in each movement, but the spirit is the same: A group of key organizational leaders conceives of their role as coordinating and supporting the efforts of a wider spectrum of organizations and individuals rallying for the cause, helping them engage in differentiated but coordinated work at local, state, and national levels.

Achieving Impact Collectively

A useful analogy to understand how *networked* leadership structures work is the systems leadership approach central to "collective impact." In their *Stanford Social Innovation Review* article of the same name, John Kania and Mark Kramer describe how effective local change efforts emerge in local communities when groups of actors from different sectors align around a common vision for impact. Successful collective impact efforts involve a centralized infrastructure, a dedicated staff, and a structured process that leads to the desired societal outcome; they also encompass continuous communications and mutually reinforcing activities among the actors.[13] At their core, successful collective impact efforts have a "backbone" organization, which is where dedicated staff and centralized infrastructure reside. *Networked* leadership structures can be thought of in some ways as movement "backbones," in that they allow leaders to work behind the scenes coordinating and supporting the work of others around them. Successful "backbone" leaders don't give specific orders; they provide high-level strategic direction. They don't dictate what each actor should specifically do; rather, they ask how they can help others around them do things better. It's a complex feat, because movements are complex, messy affairs—and although select individuals and organizations undoubtedly amass more power and resources than others, no single movement leader is ultimately "in charge."

Taking a *systems* view is helpful here in seeing the difference between organization-centric leaders who try to lead movements from the top down and *networked* leadership structures. As we discussed in the previous chapter, "Turn Grassroots Gold," movements can be thought of as systems—phenomena made up of many different but interdependent parts that collectively achieve a certain function or purpose. Each part individually is powerless to achieve the end goal; but collectively, the parts add up to a whole greater than the sum of the parts. In successful social change campaigns, movement leaders act as part of a larger *network*, positioning themselves to enable the parts of the system around them to succeed, rather than trying to shore up resources and do all the work themselves—and soak up the credit, media limelight, or other valuable assets.

For the same-sex marriage cause, this networked leadership role was played by Freedom to Marry. The founding *raison d'etre* behind Freedom to Marry was to be a *campaign*, not an organization, one specifically designed to propel the marriage equality cause forward. So even though Wolfson launched it as a singular 501(c)3 charitable organization, Freedom to Marry didn't act like a traditional nonprofit. Instead, Freedom to Marry and its emissaries went to local communities and joined or helped foster coalitions of LGBT groups, both driving and supporting joint advocacy, lobbying, and electioneering campaigns.

For the tobacco control movement, Campaign for Tobacco-Free Kids (the Campaign) has played the crucial *networked* leadership role. Seeded with funding from the Robert Wood Johnson Foundation, the brilliance of the Campaign's approach was twofold: First, while RWJF funded the Campaign and helped establish its headquarters in Washington, D.C., the power and authority to lead the movement was vested in founding staff members, executive vice president and legal counsel Matt Myers and president Bill Novelli, and wider networks of leaders with a vested interest in winning the tobacco wars, including CEOs of major health charities such as the American Cancer Society,

American Heart Association, and American Lung Association, among others. Second, a much larger chunk of RWJF's money went to its *SmokeLess States* initiative, pushing more than $200 million to seed state-based coalitions to advance tobacco control policy and social norm change campaigns—efforts which were led by coalition leaders at the state level and supported by national leaders at the Campaign and ANR, who provided technical assistance and other kinds of support.[14]

For other movements, the networked structure looked different: For anti–drunk driving, MADD played a central leading role and also had the largest membership of any organization in the field. But MADD founder Candy Lightner and her colleagues saw from the beginning that building up chapters, first in California and then in almost every state, while working nationally and locally through coalitions of diverse—and sometimes unlikely—allies was the key to advancing the cause. And as for the NRA, it's bottom-up, "upside down pyramid" view of its millions of members (as described in Chapter One, "Turn Grassroots Gold") illustrates how NRA leaders see their main job as figuring out how to support their many disparate members to work individually at the local level, and collectively at the national level, to advance a common gun rights agenda.

Regardless of whether there was one dominant membership organization or a coalition of groups at the center of these winning movements, the unifying thread was that their leaders saw their rightful place as *central though equal part of a network*, rather than at the top of a rigid hierarchy. And they recognized that their path to victory would be achieved by coordinating with and empowering people and groups around them to align around some sort of 10/10/10/20 = 50 vision.

Let's look now at how some other successful movements brought their 10/10/10/20 = 50 vision into focus and coalesced around differentiated but coordinated state-based efforts that both supported and freed up local organizations and coalitions to pursue separate but coordinated campaigns that made sense for *their* communities—and also added up to a collective national win.

Backing into a National Strategy

Like the LGBT campaign for marriage equality, the NRA-led gun rights movement in the United States owes its national victories in large part to incremental, state-by-state campaigns. Interestingly, the NRA didn't start out with an incremental approach; it originally chanced a head-first federal gambit, and lost.

The pivotal early gun rights case came about in 1981 with the Village Board of Morton Grove, a suburb of Chicago, which had passed a landmark law banning handguns. Gun rights advocates reacted by filing three lawsuits, two in federal court and one in state court, arguing that the ban violated both the Second Amendment and the Illinois State constitutional right to bear arms. As David Cole writes in *Engines of Liberty: The Power of Citizen Activists to Make Constitutional Law:* "The suits failed at every level. The U.S. Court of Appeals for the Seventh Circuit ruled, relying on Supreme Court precedents, that the Second Amendment had no applicability to state or local governments, and that in any event it 'extends only to those arms which are necessary to maintain a well-regulated militia.'"[15] From that point in the early 1980s until 2008, the Second Amendment had been a dead letter as a constitutional matter.[16]

Plan B: The NRA's State-by-State Strategy

After the unsuccessful challenge to the local handgun ban in Morton Grove, Illinois, the NRA constructed a state-based preemption strategy as a means of preventing such local gun ordinances from passing in the future.[17] This strategy was uniquely suited to advance the gun rights cause, because the geographic population distribution of most U.S. states tips in favor of gun owner preferences. When states consider the concerns of all of its residents, views often split between urban and rural voters. People who live in cities tend to favor tighter weapons restrictions because gun violence is a more pressing problem, and they also have more immediate access to police protection should they be threatened by someone with a gun. Whereas rural residents express a more urgent need to keep guns handy for self-defense.[18] They also are more likely to be gun owners who draw pleasure from using firearms, whether for duck or big game hunting or target practice.

Florida was among the first states in which the NRA successfully pressed for statewide preemption. Laws in the "Gunshine State" favor gun owners so heavily in no small part because of the efforts of Marion Hammer, the NRA's first female president and one of Florida's most influential lobbyists. A grandmother in her seventies who to this day carries a Smith and Wesson .38 Special in her purse,[19] Hammer delivered her first victory for the NRA in 1987, when Florida adopted a "shall issue" concealed carry law. The law specifies that, unless someone is prohibited from owning or possessing a firearm for reasons such as a criminal record or history of mental illness, alcohol, or drug abuse, the state shall issue a permit or license to carry the firearm. Over the next eight years, the NRA persuaded nineteen other states to follow Florida's lead; by 2012, the U.S. Court of Appeals for the Seventh Circuit struck down the last remaining state law prohibiting people from carrying concealed firearms.[20] Before the NRA became involved, the decision over whether to allow any individual to carry a concealed weapon in any town or city was often up to local authorities; since then it's a presumptive state right.

Today, due to the combined grassroots efforts of the NRA and other gun rights groups, the vast majority—forty-three out of fifty U.S. states—have preemption laws. These include Florida, Illinois, and Virginia (which we wrote about in the previous chapter, about the Charlottesville City Council being unable to pass more restrictive gun laws in the wake of the Orlando mass shooting of 2016). The majority of state preemption gun laws have been passed only since the NRA-ILA politicized in the 1970s; as of 1979, only two states had full preemption laws. By the mid-1980s, the NRA had made passage of state preemption laws its "top legislative priority,"[21] and today the overwhelming majority of U.S. states have them; only seven states have avoided them, including California, New York, New Jersey, and a handful of others.

All of that shoe leather worn down at state and local levels had another extremely far-reaching effect: It not only hampered the ability of local jurisdictions to act against gun rights, but it had federal influence as well. When the Supreme Court decided in 2008 the landmark handgun case, *Columbia v. Heller*, it ruled that the Second Amendment protects an individual's right to possess a firearm "unconnected with service in a militia for traditionally lawful purposes." In so doing, the Supreme Court affirmed the constitutional right for individuals to bear arms in its narrow 5 to 4 decision. Interesting, even by 2008, the NRA was still gun-shy about taking any Second Amendment cases to the Supreme Court, due in part to uncertainty about how the justices would vote.[22]

We believe it's in large part because of the extensive groundwork gun rights activists had painstakingly laid in courtrooms and courthouses across all fifty U.S. states that a new precedent had been set for the nation as a whole by the justices of the Supreme Court.

Smokeless States: A Winning Strategy for Tobacco Control

In our study of all the actors and initiatives that have contributed to cutting smoking rates in the United States down to 15 percent for adults and under 6 percent for youth, a few emerge as most instrumental to success. Certainly the grassroots non-smokers' rights movement that spread like wildfire with help from Americans for Nonsmokers' Rights was a key driver. Also important were other state-based advocacy efforts. These included the innovative approaches of several state attorneys general who mounted public interest lawsuits on behalf of their states against tobacco companies, and the Robert Wood Johnson Foundation, which backed the *SmokeLess States* Initiative and expanded the work of local coalitions that had been operating through the American Medical Association. The glue that cemented all of these various parts into a successful national movement was the Campaign for Tobacco-Free Kids, which orchestrated the whole affair by providing strong grass-tops federal energy while supporting and expanding the movement's state-based advocacy through its *networked* leadership structure.

Founded in 1995 by current president Matt Myers and then-president Bill Novelli, the Campaign's mandate was to provide a national "voice" for the tobacco control movement that could effectively counter the powerful tobacco industry lobby. Myers describes the Campaign's vision as three-fold: First, provide technical assistance to local coalitions enabling them to drive more sophisticated, nationally coordinated policy advocacy initiatives based on the most up-to-date information; second, infuse the movement with a savvy communications strategy designed to shift public attitudes and change the public debate and media coverage of tobacco issues at national, state, and local levels; and third, elevate the quality of tobacco control policy advocacy nationally.[23]

The Robert Wood Johnson Foundation (RWJF) seeded the Campaign with an initial $20 million.[24] As the largest single private contributor to the tobacco control cause, RWJF poured approximately

$700 million into the movement between 1991 and 2009.[25] In addition to the key contribution of underwriting the formation of the Campaign for Tobacco-Free Kids, the RWJF program that drew more funding than any other was *SmokeLess States: Statewide Tobacco Prevention and Control Initiative*, now called the *SmokeLess States®: National Tobacco Policy Initiative*, which the Foundation provided with more than $100 million in funding over the next ten years.[26]

The *SmokeLess States* Initiative built upon the earlier work of three large health volunteer nonprofits: the American Cancer Society, National Heart Association, and American Lung Association, which had joined forces in 1982 to create the Coalition on Smoking OR Health to advance national and, later, state-based control policies. In 1993, the RWJF board launched *SmokeLess States* and made grants to coalitions in nineteen states, including Alaska, Hawaii, and Washington. The coalitions worked to advance anti-tobacco policy levers known to reduce smoking—levers like increasing the price of cigarettes; reducing or removing tobacco advertising from the public environment; and restricting where cigarettes could be smoked and sold. These approaches were chosen over others because of the strong, rigorously researched evidence that proved these changes would lead to lower smoking rates.[27]

For instance, price control strategies proved particularly effective. Within the first few years of *SmokeLess States*, several states had increased their per-pack cigarette excise taxes to approximately $1.81.[28] By 2003, the state-based campaigns had played an influential role with the Campaign for Tobacco-Free Kids and others in support of increasing excise taxes in thirty-five states, as well as passing clean indoor air legislation in ten states and implementing local ordinances to restrict youth access to tobacco products in thirteen states.[29] Other states were then able to leverage those successes to secure similar legislative and regulatory controls.[30]

The importance of private funding to support state and local advocacy cannot be underestimated; it's the oxygen grassroots groups and coalitions need to survive. Financial support, coupled with the technical assistance and evidence-based strategies researched and supported by the Campaign for Tobacco-Free Kids, helped grassroots outfits knit together a coordinated strategy, paving the way to national success—much in the same way Freedom to Marry later helped orchestrate marriage equality campaigns on a state-by-state level.

What the Campaign for Tobacco-Free Kids did *not* do was create a top-down organization dictating policy strategies from inside the beltway, nor did it attempt to merge or roll up any of the local or statewide groups under their umbrella. Instead, the Campaign was structured to support and complement state and local efforts, while providing leadership at the federal level. While effective in the long run, this arrangement did not play out perfectly. Plenty of disagreements on strategy, authority, and campaign tactics persisted for years—including one excruciating fight in 1996 (which we explore in Chapter Four, "Reckon with Adversarial Allies"). But like other winning movements, it was effective *enough*.

State-Based Inoculation

The state-based tobacco control strategy was important for another reason: States became one of the most contentious battlegrounds in the tobacco wars. Just like the NRA and its gun industry allies, tobacco industry leaders recognized the states were a place they could gain traction for their cause—but in this case, anti-tobacco activists were ready for the fight.

It started with the grassroots efforts we explored in the previous chapter. As renowned non-smokers' rights advocate Stanton Glantz, professor at UCSF and author of the *Cigarette Papers* explains, tobacco controllers were winning at the local level. But they were less successful at the state level, where corporate financial contributions and lobbying prowess proved more powerful. So tobacco industry leaders mostly bypassed local efforts and pushed for tobacco-friendly preemption at the state level—just as the NRA was doing for guns. Preemptive statewide tobacco control legislation would effectively prohibit localities from enacting laws more stringent than the state law[31]— effectively rendering city councils and local health boards impotent. This was an effective approach for tobacco companies, because they had more leverage at the state level: Their lobbyists had more personal influence and their campaign contributions mattered more. Effective statewide preemption also had a secondary effect of dampening subsequent activism at the grassroots, because if local volunteers couldn't change anything in their home towns, what was the point of getting involved?

It was a savvy strategy, and by 2000, the tobacco industry had successfully passed some form of preemption in more than half of the U.S. states. But through the concentrated activism of state-based tobacco control coalitions supported and amplified by the Campaign for Tobacco-Free Kids, as well as other advocacy groups such as ANR, the preemption efforts were largely thwarted. As of 2016, more than a dozen states had rescinded their preemption rules, leaving just fourteen U.S. states with some form of state preemption regarding smoke-free air laws.[32]

Ultimately, the Family Smoking Prevention and Tobacco Control Act signed into law in 2009 would bring in some of the sweeping federal changes anti-smoking advocates had long fought for. But like every other winning movement we studied, that change came *to* Washington *from* the states, rather than the other way around.

Playing Hard and Smart Politics

For some movements, lobbying and litigation strategies were enough to win. In other cases, movement leaders had to deploy another weapon from the advocacy arsenal: influencing elections. In the cases of LGBT marriage and gun rights, it wasn't enough to mobilize the grassroots to lobby elected officials to change policies or to engage lawyers in mounting lawsuits. If they wanted to win, they would need to influence outcomes of elections as well. Freedom to Marry National Campaign Director Marc Solomon explains: "You have to play smart electorally. If people think you are going to cost them their seats, they'll vote your way. . . . It's so important to demonstrate your heft at state politics, and at local level, you must prove that [elected officials] *have* to be there for you."

The NRA's electoral strategy is well-known; the NRA rating system combined with its PAC, The NRA Political Victory Fund, can successfully raise millions nationwide and use it to both punish elected officials at the ballot box and help put others into office. What's interesting is that other causes, especially those not traditionally associated with politics and electioneering, have used this strategy equally effectively. Case in point: LGBT marriage equality.

Picking up at a critical point of the story in the opening to this chapter, once same-sex marriage equality advocates celebrated their newly won legal right to marry in Massachusetts with the 2003 Massa-chusetts Supreme Judicial Court Ruling, they realized the opposition was threatening a ballot referendum campaign that would put a consti-tutional amendment on the popular ballot that could potentially over-turn the court decision. In Massachusetts, any ballot referendum vote requires approval by the state legislature two sessions in a row over a four-year period. To ensure Massachusetts lawmakers didn't vote for a repeal, marriage equality activists realized they needed a majority of elected officials to be willing publicly to uphold their commitment to the marriage cause. And the only way to ensure that happened was to show politicians voters cared about the issue, too—and cared enough to vote on it.

Ensuring electoral support in the state of Massachusetts would be an incredible feat. Even though Massachusetts is known as one of the most liberal states in the United States, a majority of voters are Catho-lic, and Catholic Church leaders were protesting vigorously against gay marriage. The perceived wisdom in Massachusetts at that time was that an elected official in Massachusetts who supported same-sex marriage would lose his or her seat. So the marriage equality move-ment's hard-won legal victory in the state supreme court would be for naught if voters elected to overturn the ruling in the court of public opinion. Their main challenge was no longer legal or legislative. Their main problem was now *political*.

Enter Marty Rouse. A loquacious, funny, seasoned political cam-paign operative, Rouse was hired to be the campaign director for MassEquality—a loose knit coalition of state-based groups including ACLU, GLAAD, Human Rights Campaign (HRC), the Gay and Les-bian Political Caucus, and several smaller, regional progressive groups, including Freedom to Marry Massachusetts. To this group of largely legislative advocacy and litigious organizations, Rouse brought exten-sive background in political organizing, having worked on presidential campaigns and in local and state elections in New York and Vermont.

Rouse's first goal was to get a win, any win. "We have to defeat one bad person to prove we have political power," explained Rouse. "Then we did it, by hook or by crook. We helped candidates to run better campaigns, we got out the vote for them . . . we ran mail pieces. 'You need people to march in a parade?' We marched in their parade. We flooded campaigns with volunteers. We also did some very shrewd direct mail. . . . We did whatever it took," says Rouse. They also conducted rigorous research on sitting officials and candidates, unearthing information—whether helpful or compromising to the cause.

Under Rouse's direction MassEquality put top priority on grassroots organizing. They started by building a network of LGBT community members who were already "out" and who could help gay and lesbian couples come out and speak up. They also identified allies who would be sympathetic to the cause. "It wasn't something that people had done before. We were involving people who clearly had not been involved in politics before, and they were getting involved because they loved somebody." Rouse impressed upon them the importance of sharing their stories. Until that point, most same-sex couples maintained low profiles. They would stay in their suburb, mow the lawn, go to work, and generally keep to themselves, says Rouse. But now they were organizing and stepping out front, winning people over personally—capturing their hearts as well as their votes (a theme we explore in greater depth in Chapter Three, "Change Hearts *and* Policy").

The strategy worked. In 2004 MassEquality helped elect Carl Sciortino, a twenty-four-year-old gay man, defeating long-time Democratic incumbent Rep. Vincent Ciampa in his bid for state representative in the Massachusetts 34th Middlesex District. "The gays, they got Vinnie! They got Vinnie!" was the word on the street, recalls Rouse.[33] This was a game-changer for the marriage equality cause. If they could knock out Campia, they could displace others. And they did. Ultimately, Rouse raised more than $2 million for the fight for equal marriage rights in Massachusetts, and MassEquality organized and mobilized hundreds of volunteers and thousands of grassroots supporters to campaign for candidates who supported marriage equality—and won.[34]

Freedom to Marry and other organizations ultimately protected the right of same-sex couples to marry in Massachusetts and parlayed a similar strategy to win marriage in the state of New York, using that same combination of legislative, litigation, and electoral strategies. It was a gutsy combination of approaches that won the day in the end. None was easy, especially because most LGBT advocates fighting were not familiar with—or even comfortable with—political work. But they jumped into it because they saw the critical importance of winning at the ballot box as well as in courtrooms and in statehouses.

This ties back to the importance of having a networked leadership structure supporting advocates pushing for a 10/10/10/20 = 50 vision: By keeping the big picture in sight and providing support at local and state levels to advance the cause in ways that made sense for each of those communities, Freedom to Marry helped secure the outcome it desired nationally. And it helped shore up efforts by local jurisdictions that otherwise would have been lacking—and helped the movement succeed. It was painstaking, tedious, and exhausting work, which paid off in the end.

Rational-Nationalist vs. State-Based Strategies

Time and again, we saw how winning movements mounted targeted campaigns at the state and local levels, with networked leaders coordinating, cajoling, and supporting the organizations around them to move forward in a coordinated way. It wasn't clear the LGBT movement–backed candidates were going to win the elections they ran in, but Freedom to Marry realized they needed to at least try. Otherwise the opposition candidates would thwart their agenda. One of the biggest mistakes movement leaders made was pursuing a federally focused strategy when the opposition was taking the fight out to the state and local levels.

Gun control is one case in point. As the NRA-ILA was ginning up its state preemption gambit, the major national gun control groups had not built up the commensurate grassroots membership bases, and they had neither the money or leadership to stave off the NRA on state grounds effectively.[35] Certainly some state and local gun control groups were in operation, but they were fragmented, under-resourced, and largely local affairs, lacking much meaningful support from the large national groups that had far greater resources. It's not because the support wasn't available. The most important reason the gun rights movement was virtually unchallenged in the states was because the leaders of the dominant gun control groups *chose not to focus on the states*.

In her comprehensive review of hundreds of primary sources, including internal organizational documents and external media accounts of the gun control movement from the 1960s through 2006, author Kristin Goss in *Disarmed: The Missing Movement for Gun Control in America*, provides ample evidence of such choices. As state gun control groups were forming in the 1970s and 1980s, the Brady Campaign (then named the National Coalition to Ban Handguns) provided background support, for example, by offering educational materials and advice. "But it never pursued local or state policy change as its core political strategy." Similarly, the Coalition to Stop Gun Violence (then the National Council to Control Handguns), an association of mostly local organizations "did not want resources diverted to what it saw as basically ineffective state and local gun control initiatives,"[36] says Goss. "Elite leaders cheered on state and local initiatives, typically when the national landscape appeared particularly inhospitable; and in some cases, national groups contributed money. But they did not fully commit themselves to a grassroots-movement model over the long term."[37]

The national gun control groups were not making these choices naïvely. They had rational, evidence-based reasons to make the decisions they made. For instance, what was known back then as the gun control movement had suffered a crushing defeat of a handgun ban referendum in Massachusetts in 1976—which then was still one of the most liberal states in the United States. Of the approximately five hundred towns in Massachusetts, only about a dozen voted for the ban; even Boston rejected it by a wide margin.[38] The Brady Campaign (then named Handgun Control, Inc.) had provided financial support to the local efforts and was disappointed by the overwhelming defeat in the Massachusetts handgun ban referendum. Gun control leaders determined "[l]ocal and state handgun control laws have proven to be ineffective in the absence of a comprehensive national law."[39]

They decided to move away from membership drives, determining that mobilizing individual members at the local and state level for political activism had "proved to be the most difficult, time-consuming, expensive, and controversial undertaking of most national lobbies we're familiar with."[40] An internal memo detailed how local members have a "driving need for activity"; because national efforts come in "fits and starts," these activities use up resources, creating the need for more fundraising; and local activists become more focused on their own survival, causing a split with national activists.

The net result: While the NRA was doubling down on its aggressive state strategy, the Brady Campaign and other national groups were giving up ground in the states, in favor of focusing on national

legislative reforms. And for a time, gun control advocates were nota-
bly successful: In 1993 with Richard Aborn at the helm, Brady Campaign (then Handgun Control, Inc.) worked with a broad coalition
of nonprofits and community- and faith-based groups to gin up a
massive grassroots push, ultimately convincing Congress to pass the
Brady Handgun Violence Act, which established the National Instant
Criminal Background Check System for use by gun dealers; the following year the Federal Assault Weapons Ban was also enacted.[41]

Gun safety advocates clinched some major victories under this
nationally focused approach (although the Assault Weapons Ban
expired ten years later). But the Brady Campaign had also cemented a
political legacy that effectively ceded the vast majority of *state* wins to
the NRA. Today, with preemption laws in place in forty-three states
and the fact that most state constitutions have been amended to affirm
individual gun rights in accordance with the 2008 Supreme Court
decision, the NRA has effectively short-circuited most local gun control efforts for years to come.

Of course, this does not mean state gun laws today are unassailable. Since Everytown for Gun Safety was formed after the 2012 Sandy
Hook School shooting, half of U.S. states have enacted laws to keep
guns from domestic abusers. And gun violence prevention advocates
have blocked a range of bills proposed by the NRA over the past three
years, including preventing "permitless" carry in twenty states and
blocking bills in more than fifteen states that would allow guns on
campuses and in K–12 schools. "We've put the NRA on its heels in the
states," says John Feinblatt, president of Everytown for Gun Safety.[42]

However, the NRA has been sharpening its "10/10/10/20 = 50" for
several decades running, while gun violence prevention groups have
only recently stepped up their game. In this particular case of 20/20
hindsight, it's clear the NRA made savvy strategic choices early on
that have strengthened their position today.

Exceptions to the Rule

Admittedly, there are exceptions to opting first for state-based social
change campaigns—though rare. There are moments in history when
political, cultural, and economic events converge to allow a sweeping top-down change to occur. For instance, since the 1990s, one

of the most significant environmental advancements in the United States has been the reduction of acid rain. The feat was accomplished through amendments to The Clean Air Act of 1970, which in 1990 instituted a cap and trade market-based mechanism to allow businesses to effectively "pay to pollute" and get trade credits for reducing sulfur emissions.

This policy was signed into law by President George H.W. Bush, who wanted to distinguish himself as a more environmentally consciousness Republican than his predecessor, Ronald Reagan. The cap and trade provision lacked serious organized opposition from the conservative right or from business leaders; in fact, it was perceived by some as a pro-business measure because it was market-based. Paradoxically, some of the most virulent opposition arose from the environmental movement's left flank, as leaders like the late David Brower, former executive director of the Sierra Club, lambasted Environmental Defense Fund—the key architect of the cap and trade policy—for doing "deals with the devil."[43]

At that time, the ultra-conservative Tea Party wing of the Republican party had yet to materialize; science skeptics were not in place; and any grassroots opposition to such a cap and trade measure were largely dormant. So a top-down, paradigm-shifting change slipped through this rare portal of political opportunity. (Of course, to enact the original Clean Air Act of 1970 in the first place, intensive state-based grassroots fights for clean air and water were waged that led up to the federal law laying the foundation for commitment, which was then tweaked when a rare moment of political opportunity arose.)

In general, top-down gambits like this one are rare. Like the famed "unicorn" Silicon Valley investors salivate over—that one-in-a-million chance a business will break out to become the next Google or Facebook—federal game-changers are extremely unlikely and hard to predict. If such a window opens for a given movement, it's probably a once-in-a-generation opportunity and unlikely to open again. And for opponents, it's not worth waiting for a similar window to emerge under a new administration. As the saying goes, "What got you here won't get you there." Almost every cause in the modern U.S. political and social climate must settle for doing yeoman's work of incremental change, slogging it out in city councils and statehouses across the country.

Making the Case for States

The main reason some movements fail to deploy a "states first" strategy is practical constraints—they lack sufficient resources to effectively compete state by state. It is expensive, time-consuming, and incredibly tedious work, when compared to the power that can be unleashed by the stroke of a pen in the Executive Branch or by Congress. But limited resources are endemic to pretty much every movement, especially in the beginning, as all causes wrestle with tight cash, limited time, and leadership gaps. But in our analysis, a key pattern emerged among the successful causes: The victors *recognized* the importance of winning across the fifty states first, and they pushed the balance of resources they could muster in that direction. Then they didn't just pay lip service to it; they *acted*.

The first—most critical—step for movement leaders today is to *recognize* that a deliberate choice must be made to focus at the local and state levels, as marriage equality advocates did back in 2005 when their 10/10/10/20 = 50 vision came into focus. Then they must execute against that vision and channel every resource that can be mustered—money, grassroots energy, political connections, policy expertise, and organizing prowess—to lock in those desired wins at the state and local level. To do this effectively, movements must have the key building blocks in place: a robust grassroots base *and* a networked leadership structure with leaders who see their place as at the center of networks, rather than as commanding from above. They also must possess the ability to catalyze those around them to lead, a concept we explore more fully in the last chapter of this book, "Be Leaderfull."[44]

This approach works for national social change campaigns, but it can also be adapted and scaled up or down to advance causes at either the global or local level, too. When Rotary International set out to eradicate polio globally, they recognized they needed to raise money from major donors and convince World Health Assembly leaders and other influential international groups to join in common cause with them. But what has moved the needle on polio and pushed the world to the point of 99.9 percent elimination is the in-country advocacy by Rotarians, reaching out to members of Parliaments at national and regional levels across the 195 different countries in the world. Likewise, at the local level, these same strategies can be telescoped down and tailored to work in more modest community landscapes, as Kramer and Kania write in "Collective Impact."[45]

At the end of the day, this book is about how to drive wide-scale social change at a national or global scale. To advance a cause and win in the United States, there's no getting around one fundamental fact: Change makers must work within the confines of the system created by the framers of the U.S. Constitution, who purposely constructed a federalist scheme designed to vest very limited powers with the highest levels of government and push most authority out to the states. This was specifically designed to ensure that any major federal changes happened slowly and by consensus. To make change in a system like this, advocates must recognize the system they're in for what it is—one in which change rises up to the top, not the other way around.

Notes

1. Matt Coles. "The Plan to Win Marriage," in *Love Unites Us: Winning the Freedom to Marry in America.* Kevin M. Cathcart and Leslie J. Gabel-Brett (eds.). New York: The New Press, 2016.
2. "Winning Marriage: What We Need to Do." June 21, 2005, page 1. http://s3-us-west-2.amazonaws.com/ftm-assets/ftm/archive/files/images/Final_Marriage_Concept_Paper-revised_(1).pdf.
3. Marc Solomon, telephone interview, November 16, 2015, and Matt Coles, telephone interview, April 19, 2016.
4. Solomon, Mark. *Winning Marriage: The Inside Story of How Same-Sex Couples Took on the Politicians and Pundits—and Won.* Lebanon, NH: ForeEdge, 2014, page 95.
5. Matt Coles interview, April 19, 2016.
6. Matt Coles. "The Plan to Win Marriage," page 105.
7. *Ibid.*
8. "Winning Marriage," June 2005.
9. *Freedom to Marry.* Chapter 10, "Striking Down Federal Marriage Discrimination," page 21. http://www.freedomtomarry.org/pages/how-it-happened#section-11. Accessed February 29, 2016.
10. Barack Obama's acceptance speech at the Democratic National Convention, August 28, 2008. Transcript: http://www.nytimes.com/2008/08/28/us/politics/28text-obama.html.
11. Solomon interview, November 16, 2015.
12. Crutchfield, Leslie R., and McLeod Grant, Heather. *Forces for Good: The Six Practices of High-Impact Nonprofits* (2nd ed.). Hoboken, NJ: John Wiley & Sons, 2012, page 131.

13. Kania, John, and Kramer, Mark. "Collective Impact," *Stanford Social Innovation Review*, Winter 2011, page 38.
14. To oversee state-based projects, RWJF established the *SmokeLess States* national program office at the American Medical Association (AMA) in Chicago. Official Web site of Robert Wood Johnson Foundation, https://www.rwjf.org/content/dam/farm/reports/program_results_reports/2009/rwjf69101. Retrieved December 19, 2017.
15. Cole, David. *Engines of Liberty: The Power of Citizen Activists to Make Constitutional Law*. New York: Basic Books, 2016, page 104.
16. *Ibid.*, page 97.
17. *Ibid.*, page 106.
18. *Ibid.*, page 106.
19. *Ibid.*, page 105.
20. Cole, David. *Engines of Liberty*, page 108.
21. Winkler, A. *Gunfight: The Battle Over the Right to Bear Arms in America*. New York: W.W. Norton & Company, 2011, 2013, page 129.
22. Cole, David. *Engines of Liberty*.
23. Matt Myers, email exchange December 26, 2017.
24. Center for Public Program Evaluation. "The Tobacco Campaigns of the Robert Wood Johnson Foundation, 1991–2010," April 2011. https://www.rwjf.org/en/library/research/2011/04/the-tobacco-campaigns-.html.
25. Matt Myers, email exchange December 26, 2017.
26. *Ibid.*
27. Center for Public Program Evaluation. "The Tobacco Campaigns of the Robert Wood Johnson Foundation, 1991–2010." April 2011. https://www.rwjf.org/en/library/research/2011/04/the-tobacco-campaigns-.html.
28. Interview with Bill Novelli, 2016.
29. RWJF Retrospective, page 14.
30. *Ibid.*, page 20.
31. Preemptive state tobacco control legislation prohibits localities from enacting tobacco control laws that are more stringent than state law. State preemption provisions can preclude any type of local tobacco control policy. The three broad types of state preemption tracked by CDC include preemption of local policies that restrict (1) smoking in workplaces and public places, (2) tobacco advertising, and (3) youth access to tobacco products.
32. "History of Preemption of Smoke-Free Air by State." *Americans for Nonsmokers' Rights* (ANR), 2016. http://www.protectlocalcontrol.org/docs/HistoryofPreemption.pdf. Accessed February 1, 2017.
33. "Can you believe this man is making your laws?" MassResistance.org. November 15, 2004. http://www.massresistance.org/docs/a8a/sciortino/sciortino.html. Accessed April 22, 2016.

34. Cole, David. *Engines of Liberty,* page 48.
35. Goss, Kristin A. *Disarmed: The Missing Movement for Gun Control in America.* Princeton, NJ, Princeton University Press, 2006.
36. *Ibid.* pages 68, 159.
37. *Ibid.,* page 156.
38. Kopel, Dave. "Against All Odds." January 25, 2012. http://www.davekopel .com/2A/Mags/A1F/Against-all-odds.html. Accessed February 12, 2017.
39. Goss, Kristin A. *Disarmed,* page 69.
40. *Ibid.,* page 70.
41. Interview with Richard Aborn, August 1, 2017.
42. Email exchange with John Feinblatt, December 18, 2017.
43. Sale, K. "The Forest for the Trees: Can Today's Environmentalists Tell the Difference?" *Mother Jones,* 1986, *11*(8), 25–33.
44. Crutchfield, Leslie R., and McLeod Grant, Heather. *Forces for Good,* page 74.
45. Kania, John, and Kramer, Mark. "Collective Impact," *Stanford Social Innovation Review.* Winter 2011.

3

Change Hearts *and* Policy

"You don't have to change a thing. The world could change its heart."
—*Singer Alessia Cara, "Scars to Your Beautiful"*

TELL A TEN-YEAR-OLD you're writing a book about how big social changes happen—like how almost nobody smokes these days because we know it can kill you, but not so long ago nearly *everybody* smoked, *everywhere*, at the doctor's, in McDonald's, in the car. And the response might very well be like the one given by this author's 'tweenage son: "Oh, you mean like the cat video on YouTube?" Faced with a blank stare of non-recognition, he elaborated: "It's got all these funny cats and it says smoking's really bad because your cat can get cancer and die, too. It's got like *millions* of views!" (It was clear from his tone he was speaking to the only person on earth who had *not* seen this video).

We searched YouTube and immediately found #CATmageddon.[1] The fast-paced commercial was jam-packed with quirky clips of homemade-looking cat videos: A cat clad in a tiny pirate costume wielding a hook marches on hind legs; a cat "plays" the piano; a cat bats at a tablecloth trying to cover up a nasty-looking ashtray filled with grungy butts. The boldface punch line was simple: "SMOKING = NO CATS = NO CAT VIDEOS." It was brilliant. You couldn't not watch it. We replayed it over and over, giggling every time. Then we got sucked into searching for other random pet videos (which did not relate to how secondhand smoke causes cancer in cats).

77

But the point wasn't lost. Gen-Zers and Millennials can spend hours on YouTube every day. At this particular period in the social media world, cat videos—and stupid pet videos of all kinds—were hot. The anti-tobacco message worked for a variety of reasons. First, it didn't say, "Don't smoke." Instead, it said smoking causes cancer in pets. Young people care a lot about pets. And they love to watch silly cat videos on social media. This video went instantly viral with 110 million views.

The #CATmageddon commercial—and other edgy social media ads like it—is the reason why Truth Initiative gets major credit for helping slash teen smoking rates to their lowest level in modern history—under 6 percent in 2016. Truth Initiative (Truth) is a national campaign to curb youth smoking in the United States. Launched as the American Legacy Foundation, the nonprofit was established in 1999 under the Master Settlement Agreement between U.S. tobacco companies and all but four U.S. states (which had already settled).[2] The settlement endowed American Legacy Foundation with $1.5 billion and a mandate to help reduce and prevent youth smoking (the name was later changed to Truth).[3] One winning production was #CATmageddon—Truth's most viewed campaign at the time; its social metrics beat Truth's previous campaign in the first 90 minutes of going live.[4]

The Truth Initiative was modeled on the ground-breaking Florida "truth" campaign, an anti-tobacco marketing initiative mounted in 1998 by Florida's Office of Tobacco Control funded with settlement money. Instead of airing the same old, ho-hum, "just say no"-style PSAs public health proponents typically produced, Florida "truth" spun a fresh message—and spread it through pioneering *paid* media campaigns. Delving into the minds of teens and 'tweens just before the turn of the 21st century, they understood Gen-Xers were rebellious—skeptical of authority, bristling at being told what to do. So "truth" developed messages that tapped into their defiance. The campaigns portrayed corporate tobacco executives as profit-hungry, manipulative predators taking advantage of young people; the core message suggested young viewers rebel against the "corporate suits" trying to trick them into smoking. The $25 million advertising campaign included thirty-three television commercials, as well as billboards, print ads, and posters, all illustrating the idea that tobacco is an addictive drug promoted by the "adult establishment." In this alternative light, *not* smoking was now the hip, rebellious thing to do.

It worked. A study by Florida State University concluded that teen attitudes and behaviors related to smoking had dramatically shifted, and Florida's teen and 'tween smoking rate was cut to one of the lowest in the nation.[5] Other campaigns were mounted later building on the edgy "truth" model. One example is the Center for Disease Control's gut-wrenching advertising series "Tips from Former Smokers." These stark and disturbing spots feature noticeably deformed people whose mouths, faces, throats, and lungs have been mottled by cancer. Real smokers (not actors) speak through voice boxes inserted in stomas in their throats, their voices reverberating with that grating, creepy digitized tone.

Most recently, "truth" launched in 2014 its new "Finish It" campaign, which challenges the next cohort of fifteen-to-twenty-one-year-olds to be the generation that ends smoking for good. As Robin Koval, Truth CEO explains: "Gen Z and late-stage Millennials are less about 'rebellion for rebellion's sake' and more about taking collective action. They care deeply about social justice issues."[6] So the latest ads focus on how tobacco companies engage in racial profiling, targeting low-income minority communities to market and distribute cigarettes infused with menthol (85 percent of African Americans who still smoke choose menthol brands).[7] And just as in every previous generation, today's young people care a lot about relationships. So another truth ad simply states, "You're twice as likely to get 'left-swiped' on a dating app if your profile picture shows you smoking." Case closed.

Of course, clever advertising campaigns weren't the only forces driving down youth smoking rates to their lowest ever in U.S. history. Lots of other changes needed to happen in tandem. "It took tobacco control almost fifty years to figure out the right formula," explains Campaign for Tobacco-Free Kids founding president Bill Novelli. "You have to raise the price [of cigarettes]. You have to regulate. You have to provide adult smokers with cessation aids. You have to stop advertising to kids. And you also have to change the *environment*—change people's minds about what's acceptable, what's normal."[8]

To win the tobacco wars, anti-smoking advocates couldn't just push for FDA regulation of tobacco products or lobby to raise state excise taxes to jack the per-pack price high enough to put it out of reach for most cash-strapped teens and 'tweens. Tobacco control movement leaders realized they had to change the way young people *felt* about smoking. Making it hard to access or admonishing young people not to do something is a sure-fire way to entice them to do it. So tobacco control advocates had to change what youth believed to be *true* about tobacco companies. They recognized they had to change hearts, not just public policy or corporate practices.

Pulling Heartstrings

"Changing the rules never works unless you give people the idea that the change that you want is right," says marriage equality advocate Matt Coles. This insight applies to all the successful modern movements we studied. Whether the issue was tobacco use, drunk driving, same-sex marriage, gun rights, or others, the victors advanced their causes in state houses and court houses nationwide, *and* they influenced the court of public opinion. We believe a key reason why they won is because they *deliberately* and *persistently* acted to change hearts and minds, not just policy. They made a goal of reframing the way people viewed their issue and found ways to connect with the public in profound ways that resonated emotionally.

Take marriage equality. For decades, LGBT advocates had fought to change the way gays and lesbians were treated in society. After the first big window of opportunity for full and equal marriage opened in 1993, when the Hawaii Supreme Court ruled in *Baehr v. Lewin* that prohibiting same-sex marriage was unconstitutional, the marriage equality movement took off. The ensuing grassroots advocacy, litigation, and electioneering campaigns waged across all fifty states (as described in the previous two chapters) were geared to prove it was *illegal* to treat same-sex couples differently than straight couples as a matter of law and public policy. But LGBT advocates also had to sell the idea of homosexual marriage to the general public. This would take a wholly different kind of advocacy—one centered on debunking stereotypes about what it meant to be "gay" and shifting broad societal values and beliefs about same-sex relationships. They had to win in the court of *public opinion*.

The anti–drunk driving movement provides a textbook case of how to masterfully alter attitudes and behavior. While today, road safety advocates fight to combat each of the four D's—drunk, drugged, drowsy, and distracted driving—drunk driving remains the leading cause of death on roadways (although MADD has reduced them by half since the 1980s). When Candy Lightner launched Mothers Against Drunk Drivers (MADD), she was driven to change the way drunk drivers were handled by law enforcement and punished in the courts for doing something criminal, rather than be perceived as innocent perpetrators of unintended murder or injury. Lightner and her fellow MADD advocates realized they needed to first convince people a car crash caused by an impaired driver was indeed a criminal, punishable act—not some unavoidable "accident."

Evidence of MADD's early and relentless focus on changing hearts and minds is embedded in its founding mission statement: "to aid the victims of crimes performed by individuals driving under the influence of alcohol or drugs, to aid the families of such victims *and to increase public awareness of the problem of drinking and drugged driving.*"[9] Within five years, MADD had sharpened its mission: "To mobilize victims and their allies *to establish the public conviction that impaired driving is unacceptable and criminal,* in order to promote corresponding public policies, programs, and personal responsibility."[10] From the very beginning, MADD set out to change hearts and minds, *and* change policy.

The gun rights movement provides another extraordinary example of how tapping into emotions and deeply held cultural values and beliefs advances the cause. The NRA and its gun rights allies shifted the nation's focus beyond the specifics of gun use and ownership and tied guns to a fundamental American value: *freedom.* They persuaded members of the American public that their Second Amendment rights should be formally recognized as protecting an *individual's* freedom to exercise the right to bear arms (rather than as only *states'* rights to form militias). But NRA leaders were clever: They didn't attempt to merely prove their case in courts and legislatures. They played to the general public, conducting massive outreach with paid TV, radio, and print advertising and social media messages like this one:

"We, the people of the American Rifle Association, represent the very *best* of America's strength, and of America's character," says NRA EVP Wayne LaPierre in one widely viewed NRA YouTube spot, "We Are the NRA."[11] "In all of freedom's history, no other people have been so alert, so vigilant, so unafraid to take a stand and go out and fight for what's *good* and *right.*"

Owning the Internet

We first watched this "We Are the NRA" video on YouTube the same day we found the "Smoking = No Cats = No Cat Videos" ad. While we were searching online for other silly pet stuff, the NRA ad popped up on our video feed. It was arresting. Loud, invigorating guitar music thumped along as parades of people representing a rainbow of races, ages, and fashion preferences streamed by. The ad featured moms, dads, and babies, conventionally attractive and some unconventionally attractive people, all seeming to enjoy themselves while checking out rifles at gun shows, exploring gun shops, or out in the streets participating in mass demonstrations. Some frames were filmed at a staged NRA event, such as the one where LaPierre spoke (above). The commercial was clearly designed to be captivatingly positive; the vibe was upbeat, energizing, patriotic. The images also challenged conventional wisdom. If you happened to hold a stereotypical view of an NRA member as a big-bellied middle-aged white man clad in camouflage or biker gear, this video would quickly disabuse you of that notion.

The NRA spots linked to dozens of others. One starred famed country musician Charlie Daniels, others featured petite and pretty young women, one clad in black leather. There were pages after pages of links, many of them enticing you away from YouTube and to the NRA official Web site, which airs its own TV stations. After exploring these videos for a while, we decided to search YouTube for "gun control," curious to see what the opposition had to say about the issue. We got zilch. In fact, most of the links that appeared on the search list for "gun control" linked back to the NRA spots.

It was striking. On that particular summer day in 2016, in this particular YouTube feed, the NRA owned the Internet. The message that the NRA uniquely represented what was "good and right" about America went completely unchallenged.

Fighting Fire with Fire

Savvy social change makers understand that, if they want to achieve impact on their issues, they must shift social norms, not just reform policies and laws. Leaders of the winning movements we studied clearly recognized this—although some arrived at the insight later than others. Conversely, those movements that have struggled to gain the upper hand since the 1980s did not appear to be aggressively striving to change the way society perceived or felt about their issue. Or if they did, they didn't back it up with the kinds of robust marketing and advertising campaigns designed to win over hearts and minds.

The importance of changing people's *attitudes* about an issue cannot be over-emphasized—and it's especially true for movements that face for-profit industry opponents with enormous, entrenched economic interests at stake. Whether companies are peddling fattening and hard-to-resist foods; cancer-causing tobacco products; driving-impairing spirits; or deadly firearms, they have vested economic interests in selling their goods and services. And they put hundreds of millions, and in some cases billions, of dollars behind marketing their products. Companies also invest in less tangible, but even more valuable assets: They build powerful, aspirational *brands* behind their products. Activists featured in this book have fought against some of the most iconic, recognizable and, yes, *beloved*, brands: Marlboro Man, Joe Camel, Smith & Wesson, Remington. These brands represent something larger than simply the products they are associated with; they are aspirational, emotional projections of how consumers imagine themselves to be perceived in the world.

As a result, social change makers must work doubly hard to counteract those iconic images and match them with their own compelling brands and equally well-funded promotional campaigns. They must *fight fire with fire*. It's hard, because advocates are often trying to persuade consumers to do *exactly the opposite* of what companies want them to do: Activists aim to convince people to stop smoking or never start. Or not buy or use guns. Or drink just enough to quench your thirst for alcohol—but not so much that you're too tipsy to drive. Convincing consumers to stop or not do things that give them pleasure, safety, or myriad other perceived benefits is daunting. To win, social change advocates must give their target audiences even *more enticing* appeals than what their opponents offer.

Successful movement leaders also recognize that they can't simply mount a clever advertising blitz to win. Triumphant campaigns take into account the need to change the purchasing environment, so accessing and buying the opposition's products is more difficult, illegal, or in other ways put out of reach. This entails lobbying for policy change to influence pricing, such as raising taxes on a product. It also can involve pushing for regulatory changes, so corporate options are more limited as to how, where, and to whom they can market their products. And it involves creating smoke-free environments, which limits smoking and exposure to secondhand smoke. "You need the full vaccine," explains Truth CEO Robin Koval. It's not enough just to air a bunch of cool social media ads—no matter how clever or viral. Advocates must pull all of the different levers of social change—policy lobbying, litigation, electioneering, as well as social marketing—to achieve the desired attitudinal shifts and, ultimately, the behavioral changes they seek.

Social Marketing 101

Winning movement leaders are savvy *social marketers*. Social marketing is different from the traditional discipline of marketing employed by for-profit companies to sell products and services. The term "social marketing" was introduced by Philip Kotler and Gerald Zaltman and is generally associated with efforts to influence behaviors that improve health, prevent injuries, protect the environment, and contribute to community well-being in a variety of ways.[12]

Social marketing is more than simply creating Madison Avenue–style advertising campaigns to promote social causes; it's about selling *behaviors*. Tobacco control advocates were striving to convince smokers and non-smokers to adopt a whole range of behaviors, including accepting new ones (view smoking as uncool rather than cool or as more harmful than pleasurable); modify current behaviors (don't smoke in public or around children); reject potential new behaviors (don't start smoking in the first place); or abandon old behaviors (quit smoking).

The key to effective social marketing is to understand that the practice centers around changing a consumer's behavior and perceptions, not on "selling" a product or solution. Social marketers talk *to* the consumer, not *about* the product.[13] Social marketing shifts the emphasis from transactions to relationships—an essential element of systems thinking (see Figure 3.1).

While the goals and measures of success are different in commercial versus social marketing, many of the same strategies and tactics are

	Commercial Marketing	Social Marketing
Product	Goods and services	Desired new behaviors
Goal	Earn profit	Create social impact
Target Market	Greatest profitable sales potential	−Prevalence of problem −Ability to reach the audience −Readiness for change
Marketing Mindset	Sell the product	Listen to the consumer
Competitors	Other similar brands	Current behaviors and their perceived benefits
Trade-offs	Money, time	Giving up behaviors that offer pleasure, safety, comfort, or other perceived benefits

Figure 3.1.   Commercial vs. Social Marketing

Based on Philip Kotler and Nancy R. Lee. *Social Marketing: Influencing Behaviors for Good*. Thousand Oaks, CA: Sage, 2008.[14]

employed in conducting both kinds of marketing. For instance, both commercial and social marketers: (1) place a high value on consumer research, (2) understand the importance of audience segmentation, and (3) deploy strategies that span the full marketing mix across all four P's—product, price, place, and promotion.

For tobacco control, this is how the movement delivers the "full vaccine" against smoking. Tobacco control has involved the invention of alternative *products* to supplant smoker's needs—goods and services like smoking cessation aids such as Nicorette™ gum and quitters hotlines; *prices*—higher excise taxes (or "sin" taxes) designed to raise the price of cigarettes beyond reach for most teens and tweens; *placement*—banning smoking in public and in private places where workers and non-smokers are exposed to harmful secondhand smoke; and *promotion*—advertising and communications campaigns designed to raise awareness and influence attitudes and beliefs about tobacco. (Other chapters in this book address how winning movements approach the first three P's; this chapter focuses mostly on the fourth.)

Adding yet another layer of complexity when it comes to driving wide-scale systemic societal change, an additional dimension of marketing comes into play. Again, as Bill Novelli notes, "You also have to change the *environment*—change people's minds about what's acceptable, what's normal."[15] Novelli is getting at a very important idea: the difference between influencing *individual behaviors* and shifting wider *societal norms.* While the two are related, they are distinct. "Social norms" are behavioral rules constructed and shared by a group; they are different from individually held beliefs or attitudes, explains marketing expert Alan Andreasen.[16] A social norm is made up by one's beliefs about what others do, and by one's beliefs about what others think one should do.

The most effective social change marketers are firing on all of these cylinders—they attempt to influence individual behaviors and social norms in tandem through differentiated yet coordinated strategies. For instance, influencing a peer group's social norms around a behavior through social marketing messages—suggesting teen smokers are stooges of the tobacco industry or that young smokers looking for love on Internet dating sites get "left swiped" twice as often as non-smokers—can be a powerful influencer on individual behavior. And the more individuals change their behavior (that is, quit smoking or never start), this, in turn, influences social norms.

Let's look now at how some of the savviest modern social movements marketers figured out how to win over people's hearts and minds, change individual attitudes and behaviors, and flip entire social norms in the process.

The Day Love Won

One of Freedom to Marry founder Evan Wolfson's favorite quotes comes from a passage in the case decided by U.S. District Court for Utah in which LGBT partners won the right to marry. The judge in the Utah case wrote: "It's not the Constitution that has changed. It's our knowledge of what it means to be lesbian and gay."[17]

This explanation of how courts came to view same-sex marriage differently in the 21st century than they had during the 1900s is telling. It was as much a testament to the savvy *social marketing* campaigns LGBT activists employed to advance their cause as it was to their litigation and lobbying prowess. The right for gay couples to marry was won in large part because a majority of people in the United States became more aware of just how many LGBT couples committed to long-term partnerships were out there. Secondly, many straight people came to understand that same-sex couples loved each other in the same way they loved their different-sex partners. As President Obama said after the announcement of the Supreme Court ruling recognizing same-sex marriage, "Love is love."[18]

The core message of "love" was not always at the center of the marriage equality platform. LGBT advocates arrived at it after many decades of taking different paths, fighting mainly in the courts and legislatures to establish the legal right to marry for same-sex couples. The movement faced some of its most daunting setbacks less than a decade before the U.S. Supreme Court ruling. First, in 2008 when the California Supreme Court reversed a previous ruling and rescinded the right to marry when Proposition 8 received a whopping defeat at the ballot box. And later in Connecticut, where the state supreme court created an unprecedented "separate but equal" category of marriage specifically for same-sex couples, conferring all of the legal rights, protections, and responsibilities of traditional marriage—except it wasn't full marriage.

Freedom to Marry National Campaign Director Marc Solomon says these setbacks presented a "wake-up call" to marriage equality movement leaders, who began to realize they needed to stop talking so much about rights and benefits and legal protections and start talking about marriage as something people wanted to do because of a deep sense of love and commitment.[19] "It was a galvanizing point for how we [talked] about marriage, and how we [made] our case to the public. It led to a real shift in our messaging approach," recalls Solomon.

The idea to shift the campaign message specifically from "rights" to "love" hatched with an insight that emerged during one of the many rounds of polling and other forms of market research conducted by major LGBT groups. One Oregon poll was particularly influential. In that survey, designed to take the temperature of "average" Americans on the idea of same-sex marriage, respondents were asked why people in general want to get married. The most common answer was "love and commitment." Then they were asked, "Why do you think gay people want to get married?" The most common answer was, "I don't know." A few hazarded guesses that it might have something to do with hospital visitation rights or other health benefits–related reasons.[20]

That's when the light bulb went off. Gays and lesbians wanted to marry because they *loved* their partners and desired to make lifelong commitments to each other, just like straight couples. "The reason people get married is not 'the goodies.' It's because they're in *love*," says Solomon. In the same way gun rights advocates shifted the debate to focus on fundamental American values such as freedom and individual rights (and away from the human harm guns can cause), gay marriage activists found a way to connect with universal human values. They put love at the center of their campaign.

Spreading the Love

It's one thing to have a game-changing idea like "love" pop. It's another to put that idea into practice and mobilize a norm-changing campaign behind it. Marriage equality advocates set out to do just that—starting with their ground game.

In Massachusetts, MassEquality coalition Campaign Director Marty Rouse developed a new grassroots game plan, centered on identifying and organizing gay and lesbian couples in long-term relationships who'd be willing to come out and speak up. As noted in "Sharpen Your 10/10/10/20 = 50 Vision," the campaign involved people who'd previously not been "political." As Rouse said, ". . . most same-sex couples would stay in their suburb, mow the lawn, go to work, and generally keep to themselves." Rouse's team plied them with arguments like, "If you want to get married, stay married, protect your family, you need to know who your legislator is, and meet your legislator . . . show them your personal side."

Turning its grassroots gold, MassEquality conducted massive signature campaigns and collected piles of postcards expressing voter support from key state legislators' districts. Then their love-focused social marketing strategy put the icing on the cake: A lesbian couple would hand-deliver to their local elected representative the towering pile of postcards, tied with a ribbon and affixed with a picture of them with their adopted child they had been raising together.

MassEquality also played mainstream media very well, understanding what would resonate in the unique context of Massachusetts culture, where the two dominant cultural institutions were the Catholic Church and professional ice hockey. Rouse found a student who was an all-star hockey player being raised by two moms. "These women were like a typical Massachusetts couple. All they did was take care of their son, drive him to hockey practice at five o'clock in the morning, cheer him on at games, and he was the star." The two women agreed to appear in a TV commercial and were filmed celebrating together with their son on the ice after a big win. It was a heartstrings moment. Countless others like them helped the LGBT advocates win over the public in Massachusetts. They were successful because they put love at the center of the message and demonstrated that gay and lesbian parents were just like straight parents. It was countless numbers of individually inconsequential but collectively powerful acts that helped "normalize" gay and lesbian relationships, shifting them closer to the mainstream.

Changing Environmental and Individual Attitudes

Many other factors contributed to shifting social norms around gay marriage. Some were specifically engineered by LGBT marriage equality movement leaders; others were more spontaneous. Evan Wolfson explains how, as Freedom to Marry began to embrace the "love is love" message, they realized the key attitude they needed to shift was not held by LGBT community members, but the *straight* community. So when they created commercials and social media spots, the star of the spot was often not gay, but a relative or friend of someone who was gay or lesbian, such as a straight dad or aunt or childhood family friend. The straight person would talk about how he or she came around to the idea of a child or friend being in love with someone of the same gender. Wolfson says that Freedom to Marry got pushback from some LGBT groups for this approach: Why weren't gay people being featured centrally in these ads? Weren't we the ones suffering from discrimination and unfair treatment? But Wolfson had the long game in mind: If LGBT advocates wanted to win the freedom to marry, they needed to win over the hearts and minds of straight people. So they put non-gay people at the center of the story—protagonists with whom the vast majority of people in America could identify. Freedom to Marry saw the forest for the trees.

Other factors helped tip the country in favor of same-sex marriage, including many that were more happenstance. There's the *Will and Grace* effect: Vice President Joe Biden credited the long-running sitcom, which centers around the friendship of a gay man and straight woman, with helping him come around to the idea of gays and lesbians tying the knot.[21] Other pop culture influences, like the mockumentary family sitcom *Modern Family* and Lady Gaga's platinum ballad, "Born This Way," as well as countless other entertainers, helped tilt societal norms around LGBT issues. And when social media became more ubiquitous starting in the early 2000s, suddenly members of the younger, more Internet-facile generations took up the marriage equality cause. In one clever scheme, the Human Rights Campaign, starting in 2013 when the U.S. Supreme Court first began to debate the topic, urged people to change their Facebook profile pictures to the now-famous pink equal sign (=) over a Valentine-red backdrop to show their support. That and other social media campaigns like it went viral.

Love Trumps Hate

A final reason we believe that "love won" the marriage equality movement is that marriage equality advocates put behind them some of the more cantankerous tools of social change—angry protests, defiant marches, and vitriolic shouting against the other side. While such tactics were critical to advancing the LGBT movement in earlier waves of activism, more recent advocacy efforts turned to more peaceful, non-confrontational approaches. For instance, when marriage equality proponents lost their first ballot referendum vote in Massachusetts, LGBT activists were devastated by the setback. But during the highly charged mass demonstration outside the statehouse the day of the vote, MassEquality Campaign Director Rouse recalls: "We were outside singing 'God Bless America,' we were singing patriotic songs, holding the [American] flag. We were not screaming 'gay rights.'"

This approach was different from the strident approach embraced in the first wave of the modern gay rights movement, when LGBT people were coming out in the 1960s and 1970s in the wake of the Stonewall Riots and other demonstrations. At the time, many LGBT community members were palpably angry and hostile toward the straight population, understandably so given the legal and social discrimination they had endured for so long. But in the more modern era of marriage equality since the 1980s, LGBT advocates have largely struck a more harmonious note. "It was about persuasion—listening carefully and engaging with skeptics—and it was about winning versus blaming," explains Solomon. "We didn't want to call people bigots or haters, although there were a lot of people who wanted to do that, and some who did. . . . We needed people to come to their own conclusion about what this was, and recognizing same-sex marriage represented *the best* of who they wanted to be."[22]

Persuasion, deep listening, encouraging people to adopt to new attitudes and behave differently: This is social marketing at its height.

Get People "MADD" About Your Cause

What works for some movements doesn't necessarily work for all. Case in point: the anti–drunk driving crusade sparked by MADD founder Candy Lightner. Bereaved over the death of her young daughter and enraged at the lax ways police and judges treated drunk drivers, Lightner would have had little patience for the painstaking "persuade people to evolve" strategy that worked so beautifully for the modern same-sex marriage campaigners. Instead, Lightner launched an all-out, knock-down, pull-all-punches war to awaken people to the fact that drunk driving crashes were not tragic, unavoidable "accidents," but were in fact *criminal* acts—and preventable 100 percent of the time.

At the point in U.S. history when Lightner was launching MADD, drunk driving was glorified—not criminalized—in pop culture: "Lovable drunks" starred in hit films like Dudley Moore's *Arthur*, the sympathetic (though pathetic) drunken millionaire tooling around in his Rolls-Royce while completely plastered. Other movies like *Animal House* helped equate extreme drunkenness with humor. And while public health advocates tried to counter these popular images with messages to the contrary—the National Highway Traffic Safety Administration had long sponsored cautionary public service announcements warning the public with messages like, "Don't Drink and Drive"—drunk driving rates were climbing to their highest point by the late 1970s.

Americans also held diametrically different views on who the "victims" were in drunk driving tragedies at that time. In typical newspaper articles covering drunk drivers' trials before 1980, it would often be reported that the judge had let the offending driver go with a simple admonishment, not even a fine. In one case in Wisconsin, a driver killed seventeen-year-old John Turk and pled no contest. The judge gave him "the customary slap on the wrist—probation." Paraphrasing the reasoning in *One for the Road*, "After all, it wasn't intentional and it was an accident. We can't bring John back—and the defendant has suffered and will continue to suffer."[23]

So Lightner and her fellow MADD crusaders faced serious challenges: They needed to change laws and policies to protect the true victims of a drunk driving crash—the people killed or injured—and ensure the perpetrators of the crime were prosecuted. But they also realized they needed to flip social norms and attitudes around drinking and driving, that is, to make it socially unacceptable. By the time MADD was launched, it already was illegal to drive drunk (although the level of alcohol in the body that qualified someone as "drunk" was higher than it is today). Judges and law enforcement knew it was wrong; drivers knew it was wrong. But few people were *doing* anything about it. That's why Lightner didn't start by trying to reform only laws and policies—the rules were already set in MADD's favor. Instead, she set out to change the *narrative* around drunk driving and tap into people's *emotions* and *beliefs* and challenge what they were willing to accept.

As we explored in Chapter One, "Turn Grassroots Gold," changing the narrative started with the grassroots—mobilizing the people with the lived experience of the problem. From the beginning, MADD put victims at the center of its crusade. MADD staff and volunteers supported and counseled victims and their families and connected with other families and friends going through a similar grieving process. They also armed them to advocate on behalf of drunk driving victims and work to ensure perpetrators were punished for their crimes. From its very start, MADD was about helping victims and their surviving families and friends cope with their losses and mobilizing them to take action in their local jurisdictions.

In Lightner, MADD also had a ready-made vehicle to take the anti–drunk driving message national. An attractive, articulate, confident public speaker, Lightner was a camera-ready spokeswoman who could convey with emotional vigor and moral authority the need to correct the injustices in the law enforcement system that favored drunk drivers over victims. By 1983 she had catapulted to national recognition when her personal story was portrayed in an NBC made-for-TV movie, *The Candy Lightner Story*, and she appeared on popular shows like *Phil Donahue* and was invited to testify on Capitol Hill, among other high-profile events.

Through its state-based chapter structure and grassroots advocacy efforts (as we explored in the previous two chapters), MADD also presented a ready-made vehicle to disseminate social marketing messages geared to change individual behavior and social norms. "Friends Don't Let Friends Drive Drunk" was originally introduced by the U.S. Department of Transportation and the Ad Council,[24] and the "Designated Driver" solution was an idea hatched in Scandinavia and adopted in Canada in the mid-1980s. MADD embraced these messages and helped spread them virally across the United States. Because MADD had hundreds of chapters nationwide, and at least one in every state, it had a built-in distribution and communications network to take these campaigns viral—long before social media made it effortless. So while the dangers of drunk driving had been well-documented and government authorities had been promoting "Don't Drive Drunk" messages for decades, it wasn't until the MADD-led grassroots movement focused deliberately and relentlessly on changing attitudes and behaviors that these campaigns gained traction.

Strange Bedfellows

It's interesting to note, in the case of the anti–drunk driving movement, that there was no entrenched corporate interest leading relentlessly, resisting from the other side. While some companies did fight back against some of MADD's policies, unlike the tobacco wars—which pitted public health advocates squarely against the tobacco industry—in the case of drunk driving, alcohol was not the ultimate "enemy." Of course, some alcohol companies balked at MADD's strident rhetoric, but Lightner made it clear that MADD wasn't fighting the alcohol industry; they were fighting the criminal act of driving while drunk. In fact, MADD early on accepted a $175,000 offer of support from Anheuser-Busch; it ultimately received only $50,000 but MADD still drew harsh criticism.[25] Later MADD changed its sponsorship policy and no longer accepted support from alcohol companies (although its "MADD's Virgin Drinks" line received a portion of sales from Heineken N.V.). Regardless, in the grand scheme, the alcohol industry was a minor financial contributor to the organization.

More important to the cause was the in-kind social marketing support MADD received from alcohol companies, which generally promoted "drink responsibly" messages to demonstrate their commitment to social responsibility. Lightner made a point of saying she still drank alcohol and it wasn't prohibition she was after. This made MADD, RID, and other anti–drunk driving groups' policy fights often easier. Without an entrenched, well-funded, powerful opponent industry fighting it at every single turn (as tobacco and gun industries did against their opponents), MADD was able to change laws and policies and to simultaneously flip widely held social norms in a matter of decades. By the mid-2010s, drunk driving rates had been cut to their lowest point ever—despite the fact that a much higher numbers of drivers were on the road.[26] It was one of the most remarkable social shifts in U.S. history—and a textbook case of social marketing prowess.

David vs. Big Tobacco

Unlike their anti–drunk driving analogues, tobacco control advocates encountered an enormously powerful, deeply entrenched, abundantly resourced opponent in the tobacco industry. Public health scientists had proven that any amount of smoking increased one's chances of dying or suffering from the myriad diseases caused when inhaling the more than forty known carcinogens absorbed with every puff of a cigarette. That message was backed by influential government figures such as the U.S. Surgeon General, the Centers for Disease Control, and progressive leaders like David Kessler, who as FDA Commissioner under President Clinton sought to bring nicotine-laced tobacco products under the jurisdiction of the FDA as "drug delivery devices," given that nicotine was proven to be an addictive substance. It took modern tobacco control more than fifty years of relentless policy advocacy, litigation, and public awareness-raising, with the help of federal agency leaders—Congressional and state policy officials often at their side—to ultimately reach its smoking cessation goals.

The movement started to gain significant national traction with the creation of the Campaign for Tobacco-Free Kids in 1996, which, with financial backing from the Robert Wood Johnson Foundation, engaged in serious social marketing warfare. Tobacco control activists confronted the tobacco industry head-on with Madison Avenue–quality anti-smoking advertisements and awareness campaigns, created under the direction of Campaign for Tobacco-Free Kids founding president

Bill Novelli, who was a renowned pioneer in the social marketing field, having founded one of the first commercial firms to conduct social marketing campaigns, Porter Novelli.*

It was a fierce fight. The tobacco industry had unparalleled political leverage, particularly in tobacco-growing states in the U.S. South. But it also had other powerful weapons on its side: the rugged, sexy, independent Marlboro Man and the cool, kid-friendly Joe Camel cartoon, plus actors and actresses in movies; models in glossy magazine ads; and doctors, nurses, and other professionals who all smoked. Until a couple of decades ago, smoking was everywhere—just watch an episode of *Mad Men* to see how ubiquitous it used to be.

Founders of the Campaign for Tobacco-Free Kids knew what they were up against. Nancy Kaufman, then vice president of the Robert Wood Johnson Foundation, who seeded the Campaign, recognized that tobacco control needed a forceful national counter to the powerful tobacco industry lobby. Kaufman had funded a critical tranche of research when the attorneys general state lawsuits were heating up in mid-1990s. "I noticed that all of the [tobacco] stories always ended with a Tobacco Institute quote, and there were never any national organizations quoted from the other side," recalls Kaufman. "So I said, 'We're going to fund a tobacco institute for the good guys.'" That nugget materialized as the Campaign for Tobacco-Free Kids (the Campaign), which RWJF launched with $20 million in seed funding. To run it, Kaufman recruited as senior vice president Matt Myers, a seasoned lawyer with a long history in tobacco control, and Bill Novelli, the renowned advertising guru.[27]

The idea of an "ad man" serving as president of this new national group rattled some tobacco control activists, especially those operating at the grassroots. "Why the hell did they hire him?" asked one advocate. "He's a PR guy."[28] But RWJF could see more clearly what others in the movement might have missed: Tobacco control had an opportunity to parlay its growing grassroots ground game and state-by-state litigation and policy advocacy approach into a powerful voice inside the beltway and also nationally to combat the marketing messages put out by tobacco companies.

* Full disclosure: Novelli is a Georgetown University professor and founder of the Global Social Enterprise Initiative, where author Leslie Crutchfield serves as executive director; GSEI provided significant financial support for this book.

"There was the public health way of looking at public relations—slow and plodding. And then there was the Madison Avenue way," explains Kaufman. "[Bill Novelli] had stature and connections in the PR world. The tobacco companies were flabbergasted and started flipping out when they saw there was such a senior person in charge." National tobacco control advocates were gearing up to fight fire with fire.

Delivering the Full Vaccine

Novelli and Myers were quickly tested when the Campaign for Tobacco-Free Kids was brought in by tobacco companies and the attorneys general to help negotiate a proposed global settlement agreement. The following year, the Master Settlement Agreement was ratified, which imposed a range of restrictions on tobacco companies, including curtailing corporate marketing activities and ceasing all tobacco product marketing to minors. Tobacco companies were also required to pay at least $206 billion in the first twenty-five years and into perpetuity to the states to help recover lost revenues due to Medicaid expense. Some of those proceeds launched the American Legacy Foundation, which mounted the Truth Initiative—producer of highly effective campaigns like #CATmaggedon, described at the outset of this chapter, and other award-winning ads.

Of course, even the hippest, most creative advertising campaign won't do the trick alone. Every movement needs a range of tools—litigation, grassroots organizing and mobilization, policy advocacy, education, protests, and more. Through these approaches, tobacco control advocates put together campaigns that incorporated all four P's in a full marketing mix: They made the price of cigarettes too expensive through higher taxes; prohibited marketing directly to minors; banned smoking in public and severely restricted where people smoked in private; and engaged in myriad other changes. But the glue that seems to have held it all together, and helped push smoking rates to their lowest ever in U.S. history, was the all-out assault on social norms and individuals' beliefs and behaviors. In less than a generation, tobacco control advocates had managed to turn smokers from being admired and emulated into social pariahs.

Mixed Messages

Social marketing expert Philip Kotler says the traditional behavior change paradigm has held that people *think-feel-do*. Neurobiology shows a different order of action; people *feel-do-think*. In this reverse view, emotions are the *precipitators* of behaviors, not the other way around. The best social change makers realize they must make people *feel* something before they will do anything else—whether the goal is to get them to change their minds about an issue or to stop or never start a harmful habit. Having visceral emotional reactions awakens people to alternative possibilities—it's what motivates them to act.

The problem is, too many social change campaigns are predicated on the traditional mode of marketing. Leaders think: If people could just see the data or proof, they will feel enraged or inspired or empathetic and they will simply come around to our way of thinking. In other cases social change advocates presume the population already agrees with them, so they don't need to focus as much on emotional ploys to change minds, and they dive straight into policy and legal reform work.

This seems to be one of the foibles of the gun control movement from the 1980s until very recently. Norm change was historically seen as largely a distraction by the prominent gun control players like the Brady Campaign and the NCSV. "From its start in the late 1960s, the gun control 'movement' was . . . not going to focus on non-legislative goals such as changing social norms, nor was it going to build policy from localities upward," writes Kristin Goss in *Disarmed: The Missing Movement for Gun Control in America*.[29] That shifted in 1999, when Donna Dees-Thomases pushed for a grassroots movement with the Bell Campaign and other groups to mount the Million Mom March Across America. Deploying the "MADD model" Bell Campaign founder Andrew McGuire says he based the campaign's chapter structure on the same chapter approach embraced by MADD in the 1980s when Bell Campaign and Dees-Thomases' group merged. But as revealed in the previous two chapters, the Million Mom March (MMM) chapters soon lost momentum when they were folded into the Brady Campaign (then named Handgun Control, Inc.).

Since then, the established gun safety groups only recently seem to have shown a lot of interest in trying to change public attitudes and opinions at an emotional or visceral level—which has changed in recent years. For instance, Everytown's Be SMART campaign raises public awareness about the dangers of having guns in the home. Brady's ASK campaign, which launched in 2000 at the Million Mom March, promotes similar messages. And a new nonprofit, Sandy Hook Promise, aims to raise awareness to prevent school-based gun violence tragedies from happening in the first place. Founded and led by several family members of students and educators killed at Sandy Hook Elementary School on December 14, 2012, Sandy Hook Promise works nationally to protect children and prevent loss of life by training students, educators, and school administrators to recognize and act on warning signs of violence—*before* a shooting occurs. In one chilling social media video created with advertising agency BBDO New York, "Tomorrow's News," community members speak to reporters about what they will say about the disturbing behavior patterns they saw in the shooter, but ignored, when a school shooting happens the next day.[30]

The NRA, however, had been investing in social marketing and traditional media campaigns long before the newer gun violence prevention groups embraced them. And it was purposefully and persistently spinning the yarn that law-abiding gun owners are what is "good and right" about America and intentionally connecting the fundamental American value of freedom to owning and using guns. The NRA's message is reinforced by the fact that guns are ubiquitous. There are more gun shops in the United States than there are McDonald's and Starbucks *combined*, and guns are glorified in popular culture from blockbuster action movies rated R for violence to children's video games. Like gay rights and tobacco control activists, gun rights proponents have stirred together just the right marketing mix of the four P's and parlayed them to promote a culture of gun-loving patriotism that is uniquely American.

At the other extreme, some causes seem to have the opposite problem as gun control. Instead of emphasizing policy and ignoring social norm change campaigns, the emerging Black Lives Matter movement and the recent Occupy Wall Street uprising provide two counter-examples of the opposite issue. Black Lives Matter leaders have caught the attention of the nation and the world, rising up in protest and demonstrating in anguished, bereaved, and angry outbursts at each subsequent police shooting of an unarmed black man. They have a strong message, and they have a willing and mobilized grassroots base. But they don't appear to have coalesced around a common policy or litigation strategy that can translate their protests into concrete changes. In this case, they're changing hearts, but the big question for movement leaders is: What are the policy and other systemic barriers that must be changed so the world changes for the better?

Similarly, for Occupy Wall Street, "occupiers" captured the world's attention with their "We are the 99 Percent" rallying cry. It became a key platform in the 2016 Democratic primary race embraced by contender Bernie Sanders. And it has lent credence to the national "Fight for 15" living wage campaign, among other economic equity causes. But beyond the message, there are not yet many concrete law and policy changes that would indicate this idea has been converted into concrete reforms. We delve into possible reasons why in Chapter Six, "Be Leaderfull."

The point is, social marketers need to get the "marketing mix" right. And the mix doesn't just involve clever advertising campaigns or even social media stunts that suddenly go viral. The most effective change makers realize they need to change hearts and minds, *and* they need to change policies and laws. They can't do just one or the other. If they want to win, they must do both.

Notes

1. Truthorange. #CATmageddon https://www.youtube.com/watch?v=tLtschJxRy8. Published February 10, 2016. Accessed August 2016.
2. The attorneys general had sued the major tobacco companies to recover billions in healthcare costs their states had absorbed to care for people dying or suffering from diseases caused by smoking. Part of the settlement required tobacco companies to curtail their marketing practices—including ceasing all marketing to minors—and pay out to U.S. states at least $206 billion over the next twenty-five years.
3. The MSA also exempted tobacco companies from private tort liability regarding harm caused by tobacco use, and the settlement dissolved the tobacco industry groups Tobacco Institute, the Center for Indoor Air Research, and the Council for Tobacco Research.
4. #CATmageddon was Truth's most successful campaign as of 2016 in terms of cultural impact and changing teen attitudes toward smoking. Following its

launch, the #CATmageddon campaign drove 3.18M owned-channel social engagements, 110k mentions, and 110 million views—Truth's most viewed spot ever. It is credited with successfully reframing the risks of smoking and changing perceptions in teen audiences. Youth and young adults exposed to truth ads were almost 2.5 times more likely to agree with anti-tobacco attitudes and 70 percent less likely to intend to smoke cigarettes in the next year. There also was a 21 percent increase in agreement with "Tobacco companies make me angry" among those aware of #CATmageddon, and a significant increase in knowledge and change in attitudes about secondhand smoke. Data excerpted from the Official Web site of the Shorty Awards. http://shortyawards.com/9th/catmageddon. Retrieved November 6, 2017.

5. Hicks, Jeffrey J. "The Strategy Behind Florida's 'Truth' Campaign." Tobaccocontrol.com. Available at http://tobaccocontrol.bmj.com/content/tobaccocontrol/10/1/3.full.pdf. Retrieved November 14, 2017.
6. Robin Koval, Truth. Interviewed November 2, 2017.
7. Bach, Laura. "Tobacco Use Among African Americans" Fact Sheet. Campaign for Tobacco-Free Kids. https://www.tobaccofreekids.org/assets/factsheets/0006.pdf. Published June 21, 2017. Accessed November 6, 2017.
8. Interview with Bill Novelli, 2016.
9. MADD Web site, http://www.madd.org/about-us/history/. Accessed February 7, /2017.
10. Ibid.
11. NRA. "We Are the NRA." https://www.youtube.com/watch?v=P2WW-Brq-BZs. Published April 1, 2016. Accessed August 2016 and February 14, 2017.
12. Kotler, P., & Zaltman, G. "Social Marketing: An Approach to Planned Social Change," Journal of Marketing, 1971, July, 35, 3–12.
13. Kotler, Philip, and Lee, Nancy R. Social Marketing: Influencing Behaviors for Good. Thousand Oaks, CA: Sage, 2008, page 7.
14. Ibid., page 14.
15. Interview with Bill Novelli.
16. Andreasen, Alan. Marketing Social Change. San Francisco: Jossey-Bass, 1995.
17. Interview with Evan Wolfson, 2017.
18. NBC News Web site, Friday June 26, 2015, "Love Is Love." Accessed November 5, 2017. Nbcnews.com.
19. Interview with Marc Solomon, November 16, 2015.
20. Ibid.
21. Biden, Joe. Interview with Chuck Todd, Meet the Press. NBC, May 6, 2012.
22. Marc Solomon interview, 2015.
23. Lerner, Barron H. One for the Road: Drunk Driving Since 1900. Baltimore: The Johns Hopkins University Press, 2011, page 74.
24. Ibid., page 87.

25. *Ibid.*, page 109.
26. Michael Barnes interview, former MADD board member and Congressman from Maryland, July 11, 2016.
27. Author's note: Novelli is a Georgetown University Professor and sponsor of the initiative which underwrote the research for this book.
28. Interview with an individual who requested anonymity given sensitivities within the tobacco control field.
29. Goss, Kristin. *Disarmed: The Missing Movement for Gun Control in America.* Princeton, NJ: Princeton University Press, 2006, page 40.
30. "Tomorrow's News" video. Sandy Hook Promise official Web site https://www.sandyhookpromise.org/tomorrowsnews.

4

Reckon with Adversarial Allies

"In all matters of opinion, our adversaries are insane."

—Oscar Wilde

SQUABBLES OVER WHO gets credit for the march, which outstripped all expectations. Secret calls to major donors telling them to pull your grant. Accusations of arrogance and ignorance. Feuds over who "owns" the contact lists. Power struggles between big national groups with deep pockets and scrappy local groups with strong grassroots connections. Wrangling over who will testify before the Congressional committee; speak on stage at the protest event; appear on prime-time TV. *Contretemps* between board and staff. Fallouts over personal vendettas, romantic dalliances, and other superfluous issues. Rampant sexism, racial tokenism, ageism (both ways). Genuine disagreements over policy solutions and campaign strategies.

Sound like your movement? You're not alone. Whether wildly successful or frustratingly stuck, every cause is plagued with struggles over power, credit, money, and personality. It takes a big ego to believe you can change the world, and every cause has its egomaniacs. But rarely is a cause blessed with one clearly defined, unarguably correct way to move forward. The stuff of social change is complex—messy, conflict-ridden, shape-shifting. All sides genuinely believe they are "right." Often leaders within a field find themselves violently disagreeing over how to move forward, but in vehement agreement about who

103

is the enemy. Other times, leaders disagree over who or what they are actually fighting against. So they attack each other, rather than focus on a larger shared goal. They lose the forest for the trees.

This fate is common across winning movements and struggling movements alike—no cause we studied in this book was spared inside strife. Take tobacco control: It's the most successful public health movement in modern U.S. history; no other societal shift has saved more lives or prevented more disease than the anti-smoking crusade. Yet wounds are still so raw, feelings so bruised, and animosity runs so deep in parts of the tobacco control field that one prominent activist refused to speak with us for this book. She felt so much lingering distrust and lack of respect for the other leaders we'd interviewed— colleagues who sat on *her* side of the cause. As one major funder surmised, ". . . this is a movement that eats its own."[1]

Power struggles can't all be attributed to simple personality clashes. In most fields, the divides cut much deeper than that, although asynchronous personalities can amplify the animosity. Every movement we studied had leaders with deep philosophical differences— fundamental disputes over end-goals, policy solutions, or campaign strategies. Some overcame these disagreements and forged a common path. Others plowed ahead in spite of their differences, and these movements lurched in fits and starts, sometimes progressing forward and other times collapsing from the combined blowback of enemies *and* would-be allies.

This chapter won't offer any easy answers or rules of thumb; we have no checklist summarizing the "Five Ways to Overcome Adversarial Allies." It's never that simple. What we can offer, however, are reflections on what seemed to differentiate winning movements from others in terms of how they coped with the divisions within their ranks. And although we're keenly aware that what works for one movement will not perfectly translate to another cause, there do appear to be some commonalities. As Mark Twain said, "History doesn't repeat itself, but sometimes it rhymes."

One thing we looked at closely was how movement leadership was structured. In Chapter Two, "Sharpen Your 10/10/10/20 = 50 Vision," we wrote about how winning movements shared in common a *networked* leadership structure. In causes like LGBT marriage equality, gun rights, and tobacco control, the leaders who most significantly defined the outcomes of the movement either actively cultivated coalitions or put their grassroots members and chapters at the top of their organizational hierarchies. The most effective movement protagonists we studied seemed to perceive their leadership roles as influencing others from behind and in tandem with them, rather than leading primarily from the top down. They saw success would be achieved by supporting and persuading the myriad organizations and individuals who made up their fields to move in a common direction and embrace a unified purpose. They didn't tell others exactly what to do or how to do it, but they provided direction and helped others see and aspire to a common vision. It doesn't mean some leaders didn't have sharp elbows or big egos; leaders of each cause we studied alienated at least some key constituencies over the courses of their campaigns. But on balance, the victorious leaders persuaded more people to move forward together than tear each other apart.

The best movement leaders can be called systems leaders.[2] They focus on how to get the various parts of their fields working in alignment. It goes back to the systems frame we explored in Chapter One, "Turn Grassroots Gold." A functioning system is a group of independent things that are inter-related, in which no part can alone achieve the goal without others doing their parts. Winning movement leaders figure out how to get the various parts of their "systems" to work together—not necessarily all of the time, but more often than not. It's an extremely difficult feat. Many movements fail at it. But a few have figured out how to make it work. Let's look now at how they did it.

Fifty Shades of Same-Sex Marriage

When Andrew Cuomo proudly made his bid for governor in 2010, he proclaimed at an Empire State Pride Agenda event: "I don't want to be the governor who just proposes marriage equality. . . . I don't want to be the governor who fights for marriage equality. . . . I want to be the governor who signs the law that makes equality a reality in the state of New York."[3] This promise of support from the then-attorney general and soon-to-be governor helped catapult the same-sex marriage campaign toward victory in New York. But it was a different sentiment expressed by Cuomo that ultimately sealed the fate of the same-sex marriage cause in New York State.

Just one year prior, marriage equality advocates had faced a crushing setback when their marriage bill failed to pass the New York Senate. After winning the gubernatorial election, Cuomo asked to meet in private with a handpicked group of leaders from some of the major LGBT advocacy groups, including Empire State Pride Agenda, Freedom to Marry New York, Human Rights Campaign, and Log Cabin Republicans. Cuomo was concerned that lack of coordination among these disparate groups was part of what contributed to the 2009 loss,[4] and he didn't want a repeat performance. As Marc Solomon writes in *Winning Marriage*, "'I am prepared to lead,' Governor Cuomo said. 'I am prepared to make it a personal top priority. But,' he continued . . . 'I need all of you to work together, to do all the things that need to happen to create the best, most conducive environment to win.'"[5] Put more bluntly, Solomon translated Cuomo's message as: "You guys need to get your shit together and work together."[6]

The governor's public promise of support for gay marriage was both a buoy and a gauntlet: He had no patience for the in-fighting endemic among LGBT advocates in New York. Using the governor's challenge as a fulcrum, Freedom to Marry Campaign Director Mark Solomon brought leaders together to create New Yorkers United for Marriage, a coalition that included the two main LGBT groups in the state plus Freedom to Marry. Each agreed to raise $250,000, jointly hire a communications teams, and mount a joint marriage equality effort. "Everything we did from then on, we did through New Yorkers United for Marriage," recalls Solomon.

How they did things from that point forward is just as important as *what* they did. LGBT advocates had to find a way to trust one another and work collaboratively, rather than competitively. One of the keys was that Freedom to Marry encouraged each group to sign a Memorandum of Understanding (MOU). The MOU addressed the majority of thorny issues that frequently prevent nonprofit groups from working effectively together. It spelled out how much money each organization was to put into the campaign, how the donor and supporter lists would be managed, and what would happen to those lists at the end of the campaign—as well as how any remaining money would be divvyed up.

The MOU also detailed how decisions were going to be made and what the campaign would do—as well as what it *would not* do. This innovation paved the way for better working relationships, because it neutralized many of the toxic things members of coalitions frequently fight over: VIP contacts and donor lists, staff time, and decision-making authority. Now advocates could focus on winning the war for marriage equality in New York, not tussle with each other over scarce resources like money, credit, and power.

With a workable coalition agreement in place, New Yorkers United for Marriage was poised for success. With the money groups put into the coalition, HRC hired thirty field organizers, who created shirts emblazoned with "New Yorkers United for Marriage." Working under this common banner, advocates from all groups targeted and took on re-election bids of policymakers who were weak on their issue, knocking out multiple anti-gay politicians in the 2010 elections. They mounted a fierce grassroots ground game, with field organizers vigorously mobilizing constituents and encouraging them to speak to lawmakers. They stood around grocery stores, shopping centers, and train stations, asking voters to "stop and dial"—literally taking the organizer's cell phone and calling the lawmaker "right then and there."[7]

New Yorkers United for Marriage Equality ultimately succeeded in helping Governor Cuomo make good on his campaign promise. Cuomo signed the New York State Marriage Equality Act into law in 2011 with a Republican-controlled State Senate looking on. To accomplish this feat, gay marriage advocates did all the things we've written about in the previous three chapters—from turning grassroots gold to changing hearts *and* policy. Who does the credit for the win go to? Not any one of the organizations behind the campaign, but *all* of them. With Freedom to Marry's MOU to guide them, they'd collectively reckoned with their adversarial allies.

Dealing with the Devil You Know

What works for certain causes, however, won't necessarily work for all. Sometimes, the personalities of the players involved, the veracity of the opposition, or the polarizing nature of the issue itself make it difficult for allies to collaborate. Case in point: tobacco control—the movement that "eats its own."

The tobacco control "movement" in fact is more aptly named "movements," because so many disparate, often disconnected, sometimes warring factions comprise the modern anti-tobacco crusade that has transpired over more than fifty years of U.S. history. One pivotal player came on the scene in 1995, The Campaign for Tobacco-Free Kids (the Campaign), a 501(c)3 nonprofit seeded with start-up funds from the Robert Wood Johnson Foundation and other supporters such as the American Cancer Society, American Medical Association, and American Heart Association, among others. The Campaign was created to be the "national voice" for the anti-tobacco community and function as a visible, forceful counterpoint to the Tobacco Institute, the tobacco industry's lobby.[8] Led by Matthew Myers, a seasoned lawyer, and Bill Novelli, a PR and social marketing expert, the Campaign represented a powerful coalition of public health and anti-smoking advocacy groups—including some of the largest and most influential health charities in the United States, with millions of members dedicated to their missions of curing and preventing cancer and heart and lung disease.

The roots of the modern tobacco control movement were planted well before the Campaign sprouted up. Back the 1970s, the first local grassroots efforts were taking form across the country. Influential leaders such as University of California professor Stanton Glantz and community organizer Julia Carol were among many "true believers" in the anti-smoking cause and took up arms on behalf of non-smokers who were vulnerable to the ill effects of secondhand cigarette smoke. Building on campaign models established in other states, they helped launch the non-smokers' rights movement in California to enact local non-smoking ordinances; the organization morphed into Americans for Nonsmokers' Rights (ANR) as they took the strategy nation-wide.[9]

By the mid-1990s, these and other camps of the anti-tobacco crusade came crashing together as a perfect storm brewed, one that would derail the tobacco control movement from achieving many of its goals for several years.

A Perfect Smoking Storm

Here was the scene: In 1994, a set of lawsuits was under way, led by Attorney General Mike Moore who, along with five other state attorneys general, was suing tobacco companies to recover hundreds of millions in state Medicaid costs caused by smoking-related diseases. This innovative legal tactic introduced a new angle for public health advocates; previously, lawsuit plaintiffs were *individuals* and their family members pressing for damages, but now entire *states* were holding tobacco accountable for the expenses shouldered by taxpayers and state-backed public health systems. Also in 1994, a whistleblower from the tobacco company Brown & Williamson leaked documents that showed its executives knew nicotine was addictive and smoking was unhealthy. This directly contradicted what the chiefs of seven major tobacco company had said—under oath and on live television—at the famous Waxman Hearings on Capitol Hill.

Tobacco industry stocks nose-dived, as the mounting state lawsuits, the freshly exposed lies, and unrelenting legislative pressure forced the corporate executives into a defensive crouch. The industry was facing pressure at every level—local, state, and federal, as President Clinton had named Dr. David Kessler as FDA commissioner. Kessler was a well-regarded pediatrician who'd declared tobacco use a "pediatric disease" and boldly asserted the FDA should have regulatory authority over tobacco. Since nicotine was then classified as a drug, Kessler argued, cigarettes should be regulated as "drug delivery devices."

In response to the lawsuits and under this cloud of new regulatory threats and a nasty public relations disaster, tobacco industry leaders proposed to strike a deal. They suggested a series of discussions with the attorneys general, which would lead to a proposed Global Settlement Agreement. The tobacco companies said they would pay billions in damages to settle the lawsuits, and they would even succumb to comprehensive federal regulation of their products. But in exchange, they wanted some form of protection from further legal liability.

The attorneys general wanted the lawsuits to advance public health goals, and they requested help from the tobacco control community to negotiate effectively with tobacco industry leaders. Says Matt Myers, president of the Campaign for Tobacco-Free Kids (formerly executive vice president and legal counsel): "They needed the support of public health leaders because they faced strong political opposition to bringing these cases and needed guidance from the tobacco control community about how the tobacco industry worked and what needed to be changed." An anti-tobacco insider, Myers represented the Coalition on Smoking OR Health, an organization comprised of the American Cancer Society, the American Heart Association, and the American Lung Association; from there he'd led the lobbying campaign that persuaded

Congress in 1984 to improve the contents of the warning labels on cigarette packs. So the attorneys general asked Myers and the Campaign leadership to join them during the negotiations.

As it turns out, Myers had entered into an untenable position—and the Campaign was caught in the eye of one of the most vicious internecine wars the likes of which most movement leaders had not witnessed. One key point of conflict came down to the issue of immunity: The tobacco industry wanted exemption from future lawsuits, in exchange for agreeing to FDA regulation and paying billions in damages. To some public health advocates, this could advance their cause because it would severely limit how tobacco manufacturers marketed their deadly products and provide billions to underwrite public awareness campaigns, smoking cessation programs, and other pro-health activities.

But to true-believing activists, the settlement did not go far enough. Detailed analyses of the proposed terms led them to conclude that the settlement simply would not work, given its many loopholes and open concessions to the industry. Also, they were wary of doing a "deal with the devil." As anti-settlement tobacco control activist Stanton Glantz notes, "The way to beat [big tobacco] is to beat them, not make a deal with them. . . . I have never found a single instance anywhere, anywhere, where a compromise with the industry served the public health. Never."[10]

Meanwhile, others were torn. As Nancy Kaufman of RWJF recalls, "I was very conflicted . . . part of me was saying, 'Yeah! The benefits [of a global settlement] would be terrific.' And the other part of me was saying, 'But why would you ever dance with the devil?'"[11] The global settlement proceedings were forcing fault lines into the tobacco control movement that hadn't previously been as visible.

The various camps in the anti-tobacco movement soon splintered, and all-out warfare was waged when it was leaked to *The Wall Street Journal* that the negotiations were taking place. (A detailed account of these events and the conflicts that surrounded them can be found in tobacco control advocate Michael Pertschuk's *Smoke in Their Eyes: Lessons in Movement Leadership from the Tobacco Wars*.[12])

Ultimately, the settlement terms were packaged into a bill that required passage by Congress, but the bill failed to pass for a variety of reasons. One key facet, among many others, was the lack of unified outside support from the grassroots public health advocacy community.

Myers says it was the most depressing and wrenching point of his entire career.[13] He had devoted much of his professional life to fighting the tobacco industry. He'd started out as a trial lawyer, and while working on the FTC under the Carter Administration, investigated tobacco cases. He became involved with the Campaign because he believed so strongly in the cause. "I was captured . . . mostly the rightness and wrongfulness of it, and the magnitude of the issue," Myers said.[14] "Rarely are issues so clearly black and white." Myers admits he did not anticipate "the ferocity, the nastiness, the viciousness." It was not the industry opponents who surprised him, recalls Myers. "It was the people and organizations whom I assumed were allies."[15]

20/20 Hindsight

Tens of thousands of book pages are devoted to documenting and analyzing the details of the tobacco wars—including Richard Kluger's Pulitzer-prize-winning *Ashes to Ashes*, David Kessler's *A Question of Intent*, and Michael Pertschuk's *Smoke in Their Eyes*, among others.[16] Each of these authors wrestles with the question of how various events, personalities, and policies played out in the incredibly complex tobacco control movement. Even the most scrupulously researched tome offers no easy answers to how movement leaders could have done things differently. One thing is clear: There was no one right path forward, no single solution that would have galvanized the many disparate factions around one answer to the tobacco settlement debates.

It's also clear that what works for one movement or cause doesn't always neatly translate to other issues. For instance, in the fight for marriage equality, even though a contingent of the LGBT community was vehemently opposed to traditional marriage, overall there were more gays and lesbians who wanted to get married than those who did not.[17] So some natural consensus could coalesce, and the Freedom to Marry campaign cleverly concocted a strategy that allowed each camp to work on what it saw as the best path forward—some for marriage, some for civil unions, and some to simply fight discriminatory laws in various states (see Chapter Two, "Sharpen Your 10/10/10/20 = 50 Vision").

In tobacco, there were policy and ideological fault lines that just couldn't be bridged. It was impossible for some of the movement's "true believers" to let go of their conviction that tobacco companies knowingly allowed their products to harm people, and so they should not have been immune to paying damages and lawsuits. Tobacco killed people; companies should pay. In some regard, these activists are like ultra conservative and libertarian activists, who promote their small government, anti-regulatory screen to every issue. These "purist" views are not compatible with what moderates propose.

This brings into stark relief the reality that movements are messy. They are enormous, unwieldy beasts of change comprised of passionate individuals and strident organizations agitating at the grassroots and grass-tops, splintered across a spectrum of policy preferences, each elbowing for advantage. Given how many ways things can go awry, it seems miraculous that any movement gets its act together enough to accomplish real change. If one thing about miracles is true, it's that they are rare.

Inside Emerging and "In-Progress" Movements

We've looked closely at the complex intra-field dynamics of several movements that won their wars—although their paths were not linear and setbacks were plentiful. What lessons can be applied to issues struggling to move forward? Certainly, the gun violence prevention movement could take a page from the marriage equality and tobacco control crusades. The nature of the gun safety issue is in many ways similar to tobacco control—they both face an entrenched, financially and politically powerful enemy with deep financial stakes in not facing more regulation or other measures of control.

Largely missing from the gun control movement is a central group or coalition playing the *networked* leadership role. Groups like Freedom to Marry in the LGBT marriage movement and the Campaign for Tobacco-Free Kids in the tobacco wars played unique roles: They were central but equal players in the larger ecosystem providing "grass-tops" support to a range of organizations through robust coalitions. Conversely, the gun control movement landscape appears to be dotted with a few big players and lots of local and regional groups, but no single "backbone" organization ensuring all—or at least a majority—of the groups were united in common cause. Over many decades, at times gun control groups appear to have been working independently of each other and at other times in direct competition, or even conflict.

This seems to be changing, with the advent of Everytown for Gun Safety, which came on the scene with $50 million from billionaire former New York City Mayor Michael Bloomberg, and other new groups such as the former Arizona Congressional Representative Gabby Giffords's Americans for Responsible Solutions. These and leaders from the major gun control groups report working now in much closer coordination.[18] It remains to be seen whether they can orchestrate and coordinate their movement alliances in the same effective ways Freedom to Marry and the Campaign for Tobacco-Free Kids were able to for same-sex marriage and tobacco control. But if gun safety advocates want to gain ground, they must try.

Another movement that may be ripe for re-set is the climate change segment of the environmental movement. Interestingly, when environmentalists advocated for the 1990 Clean Air Act amendments that helped reduce acid rain and laid the groundwork for the ozone-protecting Montreal Protocol, they had joined together in a working coalition dubbed "Project 88." This nonpartisan, cross-sector group was spearheaded by Senators Tim Wirth and John Heinz and directed by Harvard professor Robert Stavins. It included dozens of environmental advocates, scientists, and corporate leaders joining together to find innovative solutions to major environmental problems. Their report, "Project 88: Harnessing Market Forces to Protect the Environment,"[19] contained thirty-six recommendations for an incoming presidential administration, many of which proposed to employ economic forces to achieve heightened protection of the environment at lower cost to society. When George H.W. Bush won the presidential election in 1990, environmentalists fixated on lobbying the White House for a series of reforms to help save and protect U.S. land, water, and air.

Almost two decades later, another cross-sector coalition formed as pro-environment groups advocated for the Waxman-Markey carbon bill, this time under the coalition, USCAP. While it appeared the groups were employing a networked leadership approach at the grasstops, the efforts fell flat because the grassroots were not effectively mobilized or deeply engaged in the fight. (For an in-depth analysis of the gambit, see Theda Skocpol's "Naming the Problem."[20]) Further clouding the situation was the fact that the environmental movement has become increasingly polarized since the 1980s, with intra-field conflicts intensifying as new "extremist" groups arrive. Earth First!ers have since boldly chained themselves to old-growth trees and Greenpeace activists are tracking whaling ships—putting themselves directly in the line of fire between hunters and their prey.

Meanwhile, more moderate groups like the Environmental Defense Fund and Natural Resources Defense Council have been moving toward the center—and even to the right—with their business-friendly cap and trade proposals, which essentially allowed harmful industries to "pay to pollute" in exchange for overall environmental gains. When activists on one extreme believe companies should not be allowed to operate if they produce environmentally harmful products or hurt the environment through other practices, and, on the other hand, more moderate advocates are willing to let companies do *some* harm in the near term in exchange for greater good in the long run, there is no common ground. Like the true believers in tobacco control, for the most extreme eco activists, compromise is not an option.

Further complicating matters, just as groups like Environmental Defense Fund move toward the center and extremist environmental groups move out to the farthest left fringes, ground is shifting on the right as well. With the Tea Party comes an itinerant coterie of climate skeptics, stretching even further to the right the extreme *opposition* to environmentalists' carbon-cutting agenda. Climate skeptics depart from the global scientific consensus that global warming is real and human activities are heavily exacerbating the problem. And although they represent a small minority, climate skeptics are a vocal and influential block. Their views are embraced by the larger populist movement and amplified through conservative circles on social media and via *Fox News* and other right-leaning media platforms. With such raucous, vehemently opposed groups screaming at each other, online and off, it seems the environmental world could soon burst at the seams. "Things fall apart; the center cannot hold; Mere anarchy is loosed upon the world." Yeats was writing *The Second Coming*, which sounds a lot like the world today.

Reckoning with Adversarial Allies

The environmental movement is just one of the many causes we studied that faces profound levels of tension and pressure. In some cases, like the movement for marriage equality, enough common ground was staked out between opposing camps within the LGBT community that the cause could move forward united. In other cases, like tobacco control, the movement collapsed under its own weight at various points, but ultimately frog-marched forward. In gun control, the lack of a central *networked* leadership group seemed to contribute to the inability to gain traction. It appeared to us that the answer to dealing with adversarial allies was to operate within a movement structure that was flexible enough to withstand some pressure coming from both within *and* outside the field.

Think of a *networked* leadership structure as a suspension bridge. Unlike traditional board bridges, which are rigid and can crack or implode under pressure, suspension bridges are designed with *flexibility* in mind. While suspension bridges are upheld by mighty towers of immovable steel and concrete, they are rigged with interlocking systems of cables and other supports that *rely* on the forces of compression and tension working together to hold up the bridge span. There's a lot of "give" built into these marvels of engineering, which enables them to withstand the relentless forces of gravity, extreme weather events, and the pressure built up by millions of people and vehicles incessantly trucking stuff to and fro.

Like a well-designed suspension bridge, the best movements have some slack built into the system. This helps them absorb shocks coming from within *and* outside the field, and even sometimes channel some of that excess energy toward a common goal. Whereas movements that fail or struggle don't have as much "give" built in, and therefore can't adapt as easily. A common mistake struggling movement leaders make is to reject their adversarial allies—either discounting them as unimportant or ignoring them altogether. Other problems arise when movement leaders attempt to force consensus where none can be reached. There are points at which no possibility for compromise exists on some issues. For instance, despite White House Chief of Staff John Kelly's recent misguided comments about the U.S. Civil War, there was no point of compromise between anti-slavery Union forces and separatist Confederates.

But most causes aren't totally black versus white; there are some grey areas in how to move forward on issues like climate change, guns, and public health concerns such as drunk driving or obesity control. For leaders who want to move the dial on their issues, the trick is to figure out a workable way for various constituents to fit together—as marriage equality advocates did by drawing up a simple MOU between previously sparring LGBT groups. This gave a working structure for allied but opposing groups to collaborate; it forged consensus and built trust. It takes time to put pieces like these in place—but sometimes to go fast, it's necessary to go slow. By taking the time to improve their internal relationships, movements dramatically increase their chances of success.

As the Africa proverb suggests, "If you want to go fast, go alone. If you want to go far, go together."

Notes

1. Nancy Kaufman interview, March 9, 2015.
2. Kania, John, Hamilton, Hal, and Senge, Peter. "The Dawn of System Leadership." *Stanford Social Innovation Review*, Winter 2015.
3. Solomon, Marc. *Winning Marriage: The Inside Story of How Same-Sex Couples Took on the Politicians and Pundits–and Won*. Lebanon, NH: ForeEdge, 2014, page 171.
4. *Ibid.*, page 176.
5. *Ibid.*, page 176.
6. Marc Solomon interview, November 16, 2015.
7. *Ibid.*
8. The Campaign for Tobacco-Free Kids was originally named The Center for Tobacco-Free Kids. RWJF Retrospective, page 17.
9. Julia Carol stayed on to become co-director of ANR; Glantz left the organization, but remained a strong, though unaffiliated, presence in the tobacco control movement, using his command of complex scientific data to produce potent anti-smoking messages the public could easily grasp.
10. Kennedy School of Government Case Program. "Dealing with the Devil," page 11.
11. *Ibid.*, page 12.
12. Pertschuk, Michael. *Smoke in Their Eyes: Lessons in Movement Leadership from the Tobacco Wars*. Nashville, TN: Vanderbilt University Press, 2001.
13. Matt Myers interview, January 5, 2015.
14. *Ibid.*

15. Kennedy School of Government Case Program. "Dealing with the Devil," page 28.
16. See bibliography under Additional Resources for recommended readings on the tobacco movement and other causes featured in *How Change Happens*.
17. Interviews with Carol Rose, March 17, 2016, and Lee Swislow, April 8, 2016.
18. Interviews with Brian Malte of Brady Campaign and John Feinblatt of Everytown for Gun Safety.
19. Stavins, R. N. "Project 88: Harnessing Market Forces to Protect the Environment." Available at https://scholar.harvard.edu/files/stavins/files/project_88–1.pdf. Retrieved November 12, 2017.
20. Skocpol, Theda. "Naming the Problem: What It Will Take to Counter Extremism and Engage Americans in the Fight Against Global Warming." January 2013. https://www.scholarsstrategynetwork.org/sites/default/files/skocpol_captrade_report_january_2013_0.pdf.

5

Break from Business as Usual

"A business that makes nothing but money is a poor business."

—Henry Ford

"Power concedes nothing without a demand."

—Frederick Douglass

SLASHING CARBON EMISSIONS tops today's environmental climate action agenda. But rewind just a few decades in U.S. history and recall a time when sulfur dioxide and nitrogen oxides posed the gravest earthly threats. Midwestern coal plants were spewing the stuff, turning clouds—and rainfall—acidic. Foul precipitation corroded everything it touched. Acid rain poisoned lakes. In New York's Adirondack Mountains, low pH waters killed fish, and in turn, starved loons and other fish-eating birds. Acid leached calcium from soils and robbed plants of key nutrients, choking off New England's sugar maples; trees that would have lived four hundred years were dying at sixty-five or seventy.[1] The acidic fallout also eroded structures—from private cemetery headstones and mausoleums, to public statues and monuments, to car paint jobs across much of the northeastern United States and into Canada. Frustration ran so deep that Canada's prime minister bleakly joked about "declaring war on the United States."[2]

Today in the United States, acid rain is mostly a problem of the past. Stemming from the 1990 Clean Air Act Amendments, which

119

included a cap and trade provision to combat acid rain, by the 2000s, sulfate and nitrate in precipitation had decreased by some 40 percent. In 2007, for the first time, SO_2 emissions from power plants had fallen below the long-term annual emission cap target of 8.95 million tons— three years earlier than the statutory requirement. The Environmental Protection Agency found that acid deposition had declined significantly and lakes and streams were showing significant signs of ecosystem recovery.[3] These dramatic results were achieved at a fraction of the predicted cost, and far ahead of schedule. How could one of the worst environmental scourges of modern U.S. history have been cleared up so decisively in just a decade or so?

The crux of the solution emerged during Christmas week of 1988, when an eclectic group of environmentalists huddled in the New York City headquarters of the Environmental Defense Fund (EDF) to hash out a plan to tackle the mounting menace of acid rain. Timing was important: President-elect George H.W. Bush was preparing for office and keen to realize his "environmental president" campaign pledge. Congress had considered more than seventy acid rain bills during the two preceding Reagan administrations; all had floundered. One of Bush's aides, C. Boyden Gray, had read a *Wall Street Journal* op-ed by EDF president Fred Krupp that introduced the idea of the environmental movement's "third wave." If the first wave was led by Teddy Roosevelt–era land and wildlife conservationists, and the second came in the 1970s with Earth Day activists protesting pollution and other industrial harms, the third wave, Krupp proposed, would employ "market-oriented incentives" to achieve greater environmental and social benefits.[4] So EDF's group of earth advocates gathered during their would-be holiday break to spec out an air pollution reduction program that would somehow tether capitalist forces to better environmental ends.[5]

The planning crew's composition was also important: The group consisted of two lawyers with extensive environmental policy advocacy and litigation experience, Joe Goffman and Jim Tripp; one widely renowned atmospheric physicist, Michael Oppenheimer; and a senior economist, Dan Dudek. This concoction of lawyers mixed with a physicist and an economist was emblematic of EDF's cross-disciplinary approach to tackling environmental issues. For much of the 1960s and 1970s, the green movement was dominated by NGOs alternately protesting, advocating against, and suing polluting industries. EDF was among them—its public interest lawyers brought several of the first lawsuits against the spraying of the toxic pesticide DDT, acting in concert with other green groups on the heels of author Rachel Carson's ground-breaking *Silent Spring*. Although EDF's informal motto in its early years was "sue the bastards," the group was quietly pursuing another, more counterintuitive strategy.

It started in 1975, when EDF California office head Tom Graff hired Zach Willey, the first Ph.D. economist to work full-time at an environmental group.[6] Graff and Willey began tinkering with market-based systems to make water rights transferable in California. Instead of building new dams on the state's remaining wild rivers, irrigation districts could sell excess water to thirsty communities in Los Angeles and use the money to finance more efficient irrigation systems and boost agricultural yields.[7] When Fred Krupp took the helm at EDF in 1984, he saw an opportunity to expand on the group's market-based reform ideas, recognizing that the command-and-control regulatory approaches environmentalists who supported the Environmental Protection Agency (EPA) in enforcing were slow and often ineffective. Krupp set out to hire an economist in New York, and Dudek sold Krupp on his ideas: "Instead of having government trying to figure out the best technology, which either missed the best approach entirely or froze in place technologies that were becoming obsolete," explained Dudek, he advocated for a scheme that would allow companies to *compete* to invent better ways to conserve natural resources and clean the air and water. They would harness two driving forces of capitalism—competition and innovation—and tether them to environmentally positive outcomes.

The Environmental Defense Fund team came up with an emissions trading scheme widely known today as "cap and trade." The novel approach entailed allowing businesses to buy and sell the "right" to pollute—and to profit from doing so, which sparked major controversy. Cap and trade still became national law in 1990 as part of the Clean Air Act Amendments signed by President Bush, despite powerful resistance—including from the utilities industry and the Environmental Protection Agency. Federal bureaucrats were hesitant to surrender their regulatory power to the marketplace, and they'd seen some previous emissions trading pilots go awry. Perhaps the most vociferous opponents were other major green groups. David Brower, the late Sierra Club head, had declared "Economics is a form of brain damage," and the National Clean Air Coalition comprised of most major green groups made a motion to censure the 1990 emissions trading law. They were furious because EDF had committed two sins: going behind their backs to work with Republicans, and pursuing market solutions instead of command-and-control.[8]

Ironically, less resistance arose among Republicans. President Bush was eager to distance himself from his predecessor, Ronald Reagan, on the environmental score. Two influential Bush aides, C. Boyden Gray and Bill Reilly, had embraced the innovative, market-based, centrist scheme in hopes it would succeed where past reform attempts had failed. Gray called up Krupp and challenged EDF to come up with a fresh plan to combat acid rain, which sent the green group scrambling to turn what had largely been economic theory into workable practice. The gambit worked. Despite vociferous resistance from a few Republican leaders, such as John Sununu, Senate Minority Leader Mitch McConnell (R-KY) joined a majority of members of the Senate and House to vote in support of cap and trade in the 1990 Amendments. By 1995, when the trade cap took effect, acid rain emission fell by three million tons—well ahead of the schedule required by law.[9]

Today, most Adirondack lake fish stocks are replenished. New England air is largely free of sulfur contaminants, and sugar maples are prospering. Car finishes are no longer demolished after heavy rains. And the environmental movement has evolved as well. Although first vilified by its green peers, EDF's move from simply "suing the bastards" to "finding the ways that work" became a new norm. Even members of hardline activist groups like Greenpeace—renowned for intercepting whaling vessels on the high seas and skydiving off smokestacks—came to accept centrist approaches. "We now believe that [tradable permits] are the most straightforward system of reducing emissions and creating the incentives necessary for massive reductions," said a Greenpeace research director in The Wall Street Journal.[10]

The injection of market forces into the environmental solutions equation marked a paradigm shift for eco-activism from that point forward. Going into the 21st century, business would now be seen as responsible for creating environmental solutions, not just attacked as the source of the problem.

Business as Unusual

As we studied acid rain reduction in North America in the 1990s and considered how environmental advocates, policy makers, and industry leaders thought differently about business's role in creating change, we began to ask ourselves: What was the place of business in other movements of our time?

The traditional role cast on corporations by progressive activists has been "enemy." Certainly, industries explored in this book have directly caused, or at least contributed to, some of the most pressing social and environmental problems of modern times: Cigarette, gun, and coal-fired power plant industries produce or emit products and substances that can kill people and wreak havoc on the environment. These industries—and many others—are core targets, and are the subjects of the traditionally antagonistic relationship between progressive activists and the private sector. Of course, when viewed from the conservative right, these same companies are seen not as foe but as friend. Members of the National Rifle Association (NRA), the U.S. Sportsmen's Alliance, and the Safari Club International each embrace their Second Amendment rights to bear arms to defend themselves or hunt big game like moose, elk, and deer; shoot fowl; or simply collect firearms for pleasure. Coal-fueled industries for more than a century have provided jobs and income to U.S. Rust Belt workers. And many smokers chafed at the "nanny state" chastising their right to choose to consume their daily pack of Marlboro Reds.

This friend or foe, black versus white construct of corporate roles was the dominant view of progressive reformers of the 1960s and 1970s. But as we looked more closely at movements peaking or emerging during the 1980s through today, we began to see the role of business in a different light. We saw evidence of corporations participating in societal change in counterintuitive ways, breaking from more conventional, that is, contentious, frames. The injection of market forces into the environmentalist acid-rain tool kit was a groundbreaking moment. While allowing businesses to "pay to pollute" under the 1990 Clean Air Act was unexpected —and repugnant to many—it *worked*; it resulted in more rapid reduction of acid rain than any activist group or regulator had planned.

It also laid the groundwork for other advancements, including the Montreal Protocol, which protected the earth's ozone layer from contaminants, and other further-reaching reforms. Carbon trading markets have since been established in dozens of countries, including in the United States, where California is home to the largest domestic carbon-trading market. So even as the United States failed to pass the federal Waxman-Markey carbon emissions reduction bill and President Trump more recently rejected the Paris Climate Agreement, today cap and trade is thriving. Case in point: China president Xi Jinping announced plans to build the world's largest market for carbon emissions permits.

As we reflected on how capitalist forces have been harnessed to help *solve* environmental problems, not just create them, we began to think about other ways business contributes to societal change. Across almost every issue, we found examples of commercial innovation yielding new products and services designed to help advance the causes featured in this book. To cut smoking rates, GlaxoSmithKline sells Nicorette™ gum to help smokers quit; other smoking cessation aids have come online in the form of patches, sprays, tablets, and quitters hotlines. To help slash drunk driving rates, ignition interlock devices help prevent inebriated drivers from starting their cars. New "smart gun" technologies deploy fingerprint sensors, biometrics, and other authentication devices to ensure only the gun owner can fire the weapon.

We also observed businesses influencing movements by reforming their *policies* and *practices*, initiating employment and consumer rule changes within their companies. One striking example is when corporations in the finance, technology, and entertainment industries across California started to recognize employee same-sex partners as eligible for health benefits and other perks in the same way as heterosexual partners. This "business as first policy mover" helped pave the way for later public policy reforms on a broader, systemic scale. The approach flies in the face of the traditional notion that business is largely resistant to change—or reactive and merely attempting to comply with regulatory or policy changes mandated by law. Here we saw business as a *driver* of change, not a defender of the *status quo*.

Another way we saw business playing an unexpected role was as educator and promoter of causes, as evidenced by Rotary International, the network of business leaders who joined in a collective global quest for polio eradication. They leveraged the assets built up as respected business owners and employers in countries around the world to advance the cause. This approach went beyond the traditional role of business as philanthropic supporter. Certainly, many nonprofits continued to approach companies as potential funders for their causes (when clear conflicts of interest didn't exist), and the role of corporation as charitable sugar daddy continues to this day. But as noted in *Do More Than Give* (Wiley, 2011), companies can reach beyond checkbook philanthropy to catalyze change by engaging in advocacy and education to advance causes in systemic ways. Often, the value of their non-financial assets—clout, connections, and cache—is greater to advancing a cause than any level of cash donation.

Finally, just as we saw business's role in proactively driving change evolve in exciting ways, during this same period we also observed business's defensive stance shift as well. For just as economists were infiltrating the ranks of green groups like Environmental Defense Fund, pushing their pro-capitalist solutions, a new form of far-left activism was jacking up anti-corporate sentiment through extreme actions mounted *directly* against the industries. No longer content to march on the grounds of Capitol Hill protesting and demanding greener policies, new hardline leftist groups such as Greenpeace and Earth First! mounted creative campaigns of extreme activism, staging high-profile "actions" on the front lines of industry operations.

"The time has come to . . . place our bodies between the bulldozers and the rainforest; stand as part of the wilderness in defense of herself; clog the gears of the polluting machine; and with courage, oppose the destruction of life," proclaimed David Foreman, who co-founded Earth First! in 1980. "We must stop playing the games of political compromise the industrial power brokers have designed for us."[11]

Anarchistic Earth First!ers climbed trees and camped in the canopy to prevent loggers from cutting down old growth forests. Zealous Greenpeace volunteers dared to skydive off power plant smokestacks and motored modest rubber boats onto the high seas, putting themselves directly in the line of fire of the liarpoons (a type of harpoon) launched from massive commercial whaling fleets. These life-risking actions were recorded and amplified by news media, placing offending industries directly in the crosshairs of a glaring and unforgiving global spotlight.

Waves of Creative Destruction

"The perennial gale of creative destruction . . . incessantly revolution-izes the economic structure from within, incessantly destroying the old one, incessantly creating a new one."[12] While the Austrian economist Joseph Schumpeter was writing about capitalism and the ceaseless churn of free markets, his insights might just as easily apply to today's genuflecting social change movements. As we explored how change has happened during the course of the past few decades, we found our-selves alternately amazed, transfixed, and at times confounded, by the counterintuitive and sometimes paradoxical phenomena we observed.

Consider that, just as free-market solutions were drawing environ-mentalists and business leaders closer toward the center, anarchistic activists were stretching the edges of the movement to frighteningly far frontiers. This simultaneous push inward to the center and outward toward the edges challenged us to look again at each of the movements under our historical microscope and to reconsider the role business has played, searching for clues as to how industry sometimes helped advance movements in innovative ways, while at others played "true to type" as enemy. As we looked more closely at the unusual as well as the more predictable interactions between business and social move-ments leaders since the 1980s, we saw four distinct paths to breaking away from business as usual.

Four Roles of Business in How Change Happens

1. *Policy first movers.* While government policymaking is painstaking and time-consuming, private companies can make or switch poli-cies more nimbly. Private-sector organizations can quickly respond to the interests of their various stakeholders, which include cus-tomers and investors, but also employees and community mem-bers. By modifying or introducing policies that advance social and environmental goals in the workplace, as well as at investor and consumer levels, businesses have achieved both immediate and more far-reaching ripple effects.
2. *Allies in advocacy and education.* Businesses can contribute a lot more than money to advance a cause. While trust in all U.S. institutions has declined, corporate leaders still maintain clout,

connections, and know-how in areas like innovation, management, marketing, and finance that can be leveraged to influence change. All of these assets—financial and non-financial—can be deployed to impact causes.

3. *Product innovators.* The things businesses manufacture and sell, the services delivered, and the practices employed can also contribute to how societal change happens. Business leaders see profit potential in making technical products and designing new services that can help advance social and environmental goals—from electric cars and interlock ignition breathalyzer devices, to "smart" guns, and Nicorette™. They rarely are "silver bullets," but they contribute to the larger ecosystem of change through their presence in the marketplace.

4. *Hyper-exposed targets.* Business's traditional role as the "enemy" has come into sharper focus in recent decades, as bolder, more sophisticated, and extreme activists take their crusades to the front lines of industry operations. These actions expose wrongdoing by companies ranging from coal-fueled utilities to whaling, forestry, and tobacco enterprises, and they amplify the message through all forms of media—print, television, and social. The result: greater awareness of certain industries' roles in fueling societal problems, with the aim to shame businesses into stopping or curtailing practices that harm people and the planet.

These four categories aren't mutually exclusive, and not every movement we studied demonstrated activity in all of these areas. But we couldn't help but notice that in each of the successful movements we studied, business played an important role, whether conspiring in cross-sector coalitions to help lead the charge, supporting change efforts from behind, or battling from across enemy lines. Let's look more closely at some examples of how they did it.

1. Business as Policy First Mover

Influencing business policy was a primary strategy for California-based LGBT marriage equality movement advocates from the get-go, according to ACLU Legal Director Matt Coles: "It was a calculated philosophy to ultimately get business and California manufacturers to recognize [same-sex partners]. Once we had 80 percent of the substantial employees in the state with access to benefits, we could say [public officials], 'We've got all your people covered under different laws and requirements, wouldn't it be clearer if they all had equal access to these benefits?"[13]

It started with a push in the 1970s to pass domestic partnership laws and a focus at the municipal level on opening up health plans for city employees' same-sex partners. Coles and fellow LGBT advocates created a registry, which allowed city employees in same-sex partnerships to register their relationships. They set up the policies so businesses could employ them as well, and these were later used very heavily in the film industry, as well as in banking and computer technology. "By the mid-1980s, you begin to see affinity groups in business, with LGBT groups at Bank of America and Wells Fargo," recalls Cole. "Our theory of change was [that] we will start with these fairly modest and business-based plans. It was not litigation-focused; it was a bottom-up approach."

The bottom-up, business-centric advocacy play worked. By the time the California Supreme Court ruled in 2008 to remove the state gay marriage ban, the vast majority of working Californians were already employed by companies that recognized same-sex partners. What was once a fringe concern had now been made mainstream, "normalized" in the routine course of doing business.

Marriage equality advocates parlayed the success in California into a national campaign. Freedom to Marry Campaign Director Marc Solomon recalls how advocates pushed to get forty of the *Fortune* 100 companies to support the cause, including big, iconic, and often conservative-leaning American corporations like Procter & Gamble, Eli Lilly, and Conagra—powerful, consumer-facing companies located away from U.S. coasts. "Once we had so many of them on board, it helped our ability to argue that there was a consensus and businesses were in synch with us."[14] Big companies weren't the only players; local businesses jumped on board as well. Freedom to Marry Campaign Director Marty Rouse recalls how, when equality advocates successfully pushed a same-sex marriage bill into law in New York in 2011, clothing stores across SOHO featured fashionably-dressed, same-sex mannequin "couples" in window displays.

Smokeless Skies   Another striking example of how businesses took the first steps toward policy changes can be found in tobacco control. Airline industry workers pushed for the first ban on smoking in flights. It's hard to imagine today, but until 1988, smoking was allowed on most airplanes. The smoke filled the lungs not only of the smokers themselves, but those of other passengers, attendants, and pilots; it permeated hair, clothes, and luggage, and could cause cancers in lungs, mouth, and nose. As evidence-backed studies came out demonstrating the dangers of smoking and inhaling secondhand smoke, flight crews were listening. Flight personnel suffered from all of the problems created by secondhand smoke, up to and including deadly diseases like lung cancer. The flight attendants' union began fighting for a smoking ban in the late 1960s, as this was a workplace issue for them.[15] By the late 1980s, efforts to ban smoking in workplaces had intensified with the 1986 Surgeon General's Report on Involuntary Smoking. Flight attendants, working with advocacy groups, including Americans for Nonsmokers' Rights, as well as the American Lung Association, American Cancer Society, and American Heart Association, generally through the Coalition on Smoking OR Health, played a critical role in an ensuing campaign to ban smoking on all domestic airline flights. Eventually Congress passed a ban on smoking for all flights by 1989. Similar changes occurred in bars and restaurants, where workers' health was similarly compromised by secondhand smoke.

2. Allies in Advocacy and Education

Just as businesses can change policies that influence customer and employee behavior and attitudes, they can also impact causes by leveraging their clout, connections, and know-how as business leaders to advocate for causes. And they can use their extensive marketing reach, brand recognition, and consumer influence to raise awareness and educate the public about issues. While businesses' embrace of cause-marketing campaigns has had significant impact on many issues in modern times, it can come at a cost. The conflict of interest between a business's bottom-line mandate to sell more product or services and its interest in advancing social and environmental issues can result in mixed or diluted messages. But across many of the issues we studied, we saw examples of companies that appeared to be trying to "do the right thing."

Take drunk driving. Ever since prohibition laws were lifted in the 1930s, liquor, beer, and wine businesses and related hospitality companies actively promoted responsible drinking messages. These companies had to walk a fine line between social acceptance of drinking and its dangers and didn't want to step out of bounds or risk losing their licenses to sell booze and stay in business. The Distilled Spirits Institute, a lobbying group established by the liquor industry in 1933, urged companies to use the slogan: "We who make whiskey say: drink moderately."[16]

When anti–drunk driving advocacy groups like MADD and SADD came on the scene in the 1980s, alcohol and hospitality companies attempted to forge delicate relationships—as long as the activist campaigns stayed focused on combating *drunk driving*, not *drinking*. They found a willing partner in MADD founder Candy Lightner. She encouraged industry leaders to join coalitions and be part of anti–drunk driving advocacy and educational campaigns. She believed businesses *should* have a seat at the table, because they could help advance many of MADD's anti–drunk driving messages.

By 1991, Miller Brewing Company was spending millions of dollars urging drinkers to "Know your limits," a sister campaign to Anheuser-Busch's "Know when to say when." Anheuser-Busch executives liked to say, "Good business and good citizenship go hand in hand." The Century Council was formed by distillers as a nonprofit organization to discourage underage drinking and it supported many of the initiatives favored by anti–drunk driving activists.[17] (Century Council later changed its name to Foundation for Advancing Alcohol Responsibility, or Responsibility.org.) Today, AB InBev*, which became the world's largest brewer after acquiring Anheuser-Busch, promotes Global Smart Drinking Goals designed around programs "that measurably shift social norms and behaviors around harmful alcohol use."[18]

In another controversial move, Lightner also agreed to allow donations to MADD from the industry. In 1983, MADD accepted a

---

* Full disclosure: Georgetown GSEI received a commitment of financial support from AB InBev Foundation to work on an anti–underage drinking campaign.

$175,000 offer of support from Anheuser-Busch; MADD ultimately received only $50,000.[19] MADD and Lightner were comfortable working with the industry because of shared beliefs: both groups placed the blame on the alcoholic driver, rather than the alcohol itself or unsafe cars. But taking money from the "enemy" (as some activists perceived the alcohol industry) resulted in complications and deep divides—which only intensified after Lightner left MADD in 1985 and joined a lobbying firm that represented the hospitality industry. Critics accused her of going to the "dark side." Critics included former MADD board member Andrew McGuire, whom Candy Lightner recalls introduced MADD to Anheuser-Busch and arranged and attended a meeting with the brewing company.[20] This did not bother Lightner, even though her new consulting gig did put her on the opposite side of policy solutions from MADD. In the 1990s, the push to lower the blood alcohol concentration or BAC limit down from .10 percent to .08 percent was vociferously opposed by alcohol and hospitality executives.

While evidence showed the increased public health benefit from lowering the limit, Lightner felt the focus should be maintained on drivers with *severe impairment*, seriously blotto drivers like the one who killed her daughter. And while the National Restaurant Association was a frequent opponent to MADD and other advocacy proposals, on certain issues they could boost the cause, such as being an active partner on the Designated Driver Campaign. These and other specific policy disagreements could pit the industry against groups like MADD. But on a broader level, the industry put its heft and marketing muscle behind the core thrust of the anti–drunk driving crusade to reduce levels of drunk driving, which it could enforce with messages of "drinking in moderation."

Corporate Marriage Equality   Another example of how industry leaders raised their voices to advocate for legal reforms and educate the public on causes can be found in recent marriage equality campaigns. Just as LGBT advocates were persuading companies to include same-sex partners in their employee benefit packages and act as "policy first-movers," Freedom to Marry and its coalition members were courting businesses to help advance the cause in advocacy and litigation spheres as well. One pivotal moment came after the controversial passage of the Defense of Marriage Act (DOMA), which President Bill Clinton signed into law in 1996, and California's Proposition 8 gay marriage ban. Advocates convinced corporate leaders to sign onto two amicus court (friend-of-the-court) briefs related to the Supreme Court arguments over challenges to the DOMA and Proposition 8. Hundreds of employers, large and small, including Google, Apple, Verizon, Walt Disney, Viacom, Nike, Morgan Stanley, and Microsoft signed. "Big corporations want same-sex couples to be allowed to marry because they believe gay marriage is *good for business* [emphasis added]," claimed one *PBS NewsHour* report. "They want their LGBT employees to be able to focus on their jobs, not on dealing with the stigma and inequality that creates problems for their families."[21]

Selling Guns   In the case of gun rights and expanding access to firearms, there is, of course, scant daylight between the gun industry and advocacy groups like the National Rifle Association. Gun companies invest heavily in the advocacy, litigation, and awareness-raising strategies of NRA and other groups. While gun companies contribute only a percentage of the overall NRA budget, they benefit from the NRA's lobbying heft on Capitol Hill and in state houses and courtrooms across the country. At the grassroots level, gun companies promote awareness and inure gun rights supporters to the cause through myriad commercial and community-based activities; they sponsor gun shows, sell through gun shops, and support marksmanship trainings and shooting ranges. Through efforts like these, gun companies promote their products, boost sales, and at the same time ensure the right to purchase and use firearms.

On the other side, gun safety groups have tried to lure businesses to their side of the divide. Moms Demand Action launched "Skip Star-bucks Saturdays" in protest of open carry laws, building on a campaign started by the Brady/MMM chapters in 2009, which resulted in a ban on open carry in California in 2011. Protests like these have persuaded companies like Starbucks and Target to post signs that encourage customers to "please leave guns outside." (Walking a fine line, however, these businesses did not actually ban guns on the premises.[22]) Businesses often become the first frontier in which societal battles are fought, and angry consumers can shut down a business much more readily today thanks to social media, forcing businesses that aren't otherwise connected to an issue to take a stand or risk losing sales.

3. Product Innovators

While new devices and product innovations are not "silver bullets"—they alone cannot solve any major societal problem—commercially manufactured and marketed items have certainly influenced progress for every cause examined in this book. The invention of polio vaccines, including the first injectable invented by Dr. Jonas Salk in 1955 and the oral version created by Dr. Albert Sabin in 1961, were the fulcrum of Rotary International's push to eradicate polio globally.

In other fields, definitive cures have proven more elusive. What cigarette smoker struggling to quit hasn't wished for a single shot that could instantly cure tobacco addiction? But an array of smoking cessation products—from nicotine-laden gum and patches to inhalers, lozenges, and tablets—have been proven to help people quit when combined with the hard work of behavior change. Nicorette™ is the most widely recognized brand of smoking cessation gum. Marketed by GlaxoSmithKline in the United States and Johnson & Johnson globally, the idea for this product was hatched in the late 1960s by Swedish inventor Dr. Ove Fernö, "founding father of modern smoking pharmacotherapy." He began experimenting with nicotine gum when a colleague shared with him how submariners and aviation crews substituted chewing tobacco and snuff for cigarettes when on board. The innovation wasn't simply adding nicotine to gum; the breakthrough came with a new time-release mechanism. Dr. Fernö figured out how to affix nicotine to an ion exchange resin that, when inserted into chewing gum, enabled the chewer to control the rate of release.[23]

In drunk driving, breathalyzers are simple devices used since the 1950s for estimating blood alcohol concentration (BAC). Newer innovations deployed to reduce incidents of drunk driving include ignition interlock devices, breathalyzers adapted for vehicles so a car won't start if the driver's BAC is too high. By the 2000s, MADD and a new consortium of driver safety advocates, Driver Alcohol Detection System for Safety (DADSS) are investing in two new technologies, a touch technology that can read blood alcohol concentration (BAC) through fingertips and an air-sampling system that can test and isolate the air exhaled by only the driver.[24] Autonomous or self-driving vehicles are also of great interest to road safety advocates for fighting against all kinds of unsafe driving—whether drunk, drugged, or distracted by text or other mobile devices.

In the push for reduction of acid rain, a variety of means were employed to cut the amount of sulfur dioxide released from coal-burning power plants. One option was for companies to install scrubbers on smokestacks to remove the sulfur dioxide before gases escaped into the atmosphere. Another was to switch to different sources of energy— although it would take decades for alternative, renewable energy solutions like solar and wind to move from being obscure "off the grid" fringe solutions to more widely available and affordable options. Even so, by the mid-2010s, wind and solar still provided less than 5 percent of U.S. power.[25] The massively complex challenge of changing the power-purchasing and production lines of a quarter of a billion people in an $18 trillion economy will take more than the existence of alternative energy sources; if you build it, they won't come unless there's a system that makes it easy and affordable to access it.

4. Hyper-Exposed Targets Action

Mounting extreme guerrilla-style actions has been the tactic of choice for edgier eco-activists in recent decades. Greenpeace—self-described as "the world's most visible environmental group"—was founded in 1971 with a small cohort of advocates who set sail from Vancouver to an island near Alaska attempting to stop a U.S. nuclear weapons test. Soon Greenpeace was targeting the commercial whaling industry, commencing with a voyage to confront a fleet of Russian whaling vessels. The commercial hunters were headed for a pod of sperm whales swimming off the coast of California, about fifty miles due west of Eureka. As the hunters on one of the Russian catcher boats hurled a 250-pound liarpoon toward the pod, two Greenpeace activists lodged their small rubber sailing craft between the boat and the whales. Fitted with a grenade head, the liarpoon gouged through 20 inches of whale blubber and detonated. As a *New York Times* writer noted, "In itself the event was not unusual. Thousands of whales are killed this way every year for their oil and meat." What *was* different was that, for the first time, environmentalist activists had put themselves directly in the line of fire—risking death or injury. And this time, the world was watching.[26]

Since then, "direct action" exploits have been deployed by multiple groups for a range of causes. The first Earth First! "tree-sit" was staged in 1985 in a grove of old-growth Douglas firs in the Willamette National Forest in western Oregon. Members of Earth First! and another environmental group were trying to block logging in the forest. "No logger, the thinking went, would cut down a tree with a person in it."[27] It was not an easy climb. Old-growth fir trunks are bare for the first 50 or 60 feet. Fortunately, Earth First! activist Mike Jakubal was an experienced rock climber. So he hammered nails into the trunk every few feet to hang his climbing gear and scaled the massive trunk, stopping around 60 feet up to spread out a porta ledge, where he sat until nightfall.

Since this maiden ascent, hundreds of activists have taken up residence high in trees, usually to protest clear-cutting. These edgy, controversial, "monkey wrench" tactics were highly dramatic and visually arresting—and therefore well-suited for stopping the immediate alleged infraction in the short term, and often for putting the brakes on industry practices over the long term by turning a media spotlight and consumer and voter awareness to the cause.

Needless to say, targeted corporations have not welcomed this glaring attention. And not all green groups have embraced these "direct action" tactics. Extreme activist stunts contrasted sharply with the more moderate, pro-business, market-based "third wave" solutions that have been simultaneously fomenting since the 1980s. These disparities have created a level of cognitive dissonance not previously experienced in environmental movement history. Green group activists were furious with Fred Krupp and Environmental Defense Fund colleagues for working behind the scenes and "doing deals with the devil" with business executives and Bush Administration officials on the cap and trade fix for acid rain. As we explored in Chapter Four, "Reckon with Adversarial Allies," every movement contains colorful casts of characters who often viciously disagree on the strategy and tactics to advance their cause, even if they agree on the ultimate outcomes.

Extremist actions also work for other causes outside of the environmental realm. For example, tobacco control activists targeted cigarette manufacturers in their quest to stop or prevent teens from smoking. In one gritty video spot, "Body Bags," the camera tracks a white delivery truck pulling up to a busy, cacophonous street corner. The lens then pans up a towering glass-and-steel office building, and the words "Outside a major tobacco company" flash across the screen. Young people unload white sacks marked "body bag" in black letters, eventually piling up twelve hundred bags. A black man dressed in winter coat and knit cap shouts into a megaphone, "Do you know how many people tobacco kills every day? . . . We're going to leave this here for you so you can see what twelve hundred people actually look like." The white bags pile up as the street noise from cars and passersby intensifies and a helicopter buzzes overhead. The affect is jarring—gritty, raw, and uncomfortable.

This scene was created by Truth, the anti–teen smoking campaign funded by the American Legacy Foundation, widely credited with helping bring teen smoking rates to under 6 percent—their lowest in recorded U.S. history. The ads were highly controversial. In the first takes, they targeted specific corporations: In an earlier version of the "body bags" ad, the gleaming office tower was identified as "Philip Morris Headquarters." (Later Truth modified the subtitles to read "outside a major tobacco company.") But the point would not be lost on viewers. Tagging tobacco companies as evil manipulators marked a departure from how teens had traditionally been marketed to; as we explored in Chapter Three, "Change Hearts *and* Policy," the ad campaign rejected traditional PSA approaches that chastened kids not to smoke. Truth instead tapped into young people's activist, rebellious spirits. It also marked a departure in how companies themselves were used as the bull's eye for activism.

Toward Better Business Behavior

As we examined the mind-boggling multi-faceted ways in which businesses have shaped—and been shaped by—modern movements, we started to reflect on the broader context in which business and society relate. Stepping back from seeing business in these four roles, we began to think about the underlying trends fomenting across the private, public, and social sectors during the past few decades. During this same time, a blurring of boundaries was starting to occur between profit-motivated companies and public-good groups, as illustrated by EDF's embrace of market-based environmental solutions.

During the 1980s the early seeds of the social entrepreneurship movement were sown, as Ashoka founder Bill Drayton created the first venture-style NGO providing funds exclusively for budding "innovators for the public." Business principles had taken a firm hold in the social sector by the late 1990s, as professor J. Gregory Dees laid out the social enterprise spectrum in *Harvard Business Review,* and the social entrepreneurship movement took off, as new social enterprisers attempted to blend profit with purpose and create self-sustaining businesses that could also yield better social and environmental outcomes. By 2011, strategy gurus Michael Porter and Mark Kramer proposed to "reinvent capitalism," goading large global companies to engage in "creating shared value" and driving social and environmental impact through their core business strategies.[28] No longer the purview of the progressive entrepreneurial set like Ben Cohen and Jerry Greenfield or the hippie founders of Whole Foods, today many *Fortune* 500 companies compete to be featured on the more exclusive *Fortune* 50 Companies Changing the World list.

This blurring of private, public, and nonprofit boundaries was new. Historically, the lines between business, nonprofit, and public sectors were much starker in the United States. Prior to the timeframe of the movements in the book (1980s to present), it was largely assumed that making a profit was the goal of business; making a difference was the domain of nonprofits; and government would step in to close gaps when markets failed or nonprofits lacked resources or authority. If ever society was so neatly divided, it isn't today.

Part of what has made manifest the more nuanced modern approach is that society's relationship with business is always evolving—perhaps more rapidly since the 1980s, when significant shifts began. In the face the 1960s and 1970s activist movements for civil rights and greater protections for the environment, workers, and consumers, business was forced to respond. Industrial manufacturers were no longer able to ignore the "negative externalities" their products and processes heaped on the planet and human health.

Tragedies such as the Love Canal environmental disaster laid bare what massive toxic industrial waste dumping could do to an average community. Residents were shown to be suffering from increased rates of cancers, nervous disorders, and miscarriages, as well as giving birth to deformed children. The irrefutable evidence of the impact of acid rain was etched on rotted cars, crumbling cathedral spires, and dead lakes. These ravages could not be ignored, whereas today the threat of global warming and the effects of carbon emissions can be more easily denied because the damage is not immediately palpable. But because of the observable, undeniable harm acid rain caused people and the earth, air, and water in the United States and Canada, businesses were forced to respond.

During the period since the 1980s, with the global supply chain revolution opening up markets and flattening trade, the corporate social responsibility movement was spawned. Businesses with operations that clearly hurt the environment or exploited workers—adults as well as children—suffered under a newly intensified global media glare and were goaded into adopting more environmentally and socially responsible ways. As Frederick Douglass observed, "Power concedes nothing without a demand."

Meanwhile, some forward-thinking businesses moved out front, electing to put social and environmental goals at the top of their agenda. Groups like Businesses for Social Responsibility and Social Venture Network, led by Ben & Jerry's and The Body Shop, Starbucks, and Timberland, were pioneers in trying to blend profit with social and environmental progress. The focus on the triple bottom line grew stronger, underscored by thought leaders like Jed Emerson and enterprising investor groups like Calvert. Globally, the mission-investing movement started to gain traction. Inspired in part by C.K. Prahalad, who saw a "fortune at the bottom of the pyramid"[29] and who challenged global business leaders to find ways to help emerging market economies bootstrap out of poverty, rather than continue to rely on traditional philanthropy and government aid. Now leaders of major multinational companies are jumping aboard the bandwagon with commitments to creating "shared value," prodded by strategists Michael Porter and Mark Kramer, who observe companies embedding social and environmental goals into business strategy and operations, value chains, and across clusters.[30] Meanwhile

Millennials and Next-Gen consumers and workers say they want to buy from and work for companies that "do well by doing good." Where they actually shop and what they actually buy is not always aligned with that value, but the sentiment has become a driving force in business.

As a result, the arc of business history over the last two decades has bent toward greater social and environmental responsibility—whether corporations have been pushed into it by angry activists or pulled by the lure of profiting from socially and environmentally positive lines of business. When viewed through the lens of the modern movements studied for this book, we saw four distinct ways that business changed the world—for better or for worse—depending on where one stands on the issues. The challenge for today's movement leaders going forward will be to find ways to harness market forces to drive social and environmental progress and to no longer simply treat business as the enemy, but also as a potential force for good.

Notes

1. "Sugar Maples Sicken Under Acid Rain's Pall." *The New York Times*, May 15, 1991. http://www.nytimes.com/1991/05/15/us/sugar-maples-sicken-under-acid-rain-s-pall.html.

2. Conniff, Richard. "The Political History of Cap and Trade." *Smithsonian Magazine*, August 2009. https://www.smithsonianmag.com/science-nature/the-political-history-of-cap-and-trade-34711212/.

3. "Progress Report on the EPA Acid Rain Program." Official Web site of the Environmental Protection Agency. Available at https://nepis.epa.gov/Exe/ZyPDF.cgi/P1001ES8.PDF?Dockey=P1001ES8.PDF. Retrieved November 14, 2017, and January 28, 2018.

4. Krupp, Frederic D. "New Environmentalism Factors in Economic Needs." *The Wall Street Journal*, November 20, 1986. Available at https://www.wsj.com/articles/SB117269353475022375.

5. Pooley, Eric. *The Climate War: True Believers, Power Brokers, and the Fight to Save the Earth*. New York: Hyperion, 2010, pages 81–82. https://play.google.com/books/reader?id=DbSZAAAAQBAJ&printsec=frontcover&output=reader&hl=en&pg=GBS.PT71.w.1.2.22. Accessed September 30, 2017.

6. Krupp, Fred. "The Making of a Market-Minded Environmentalist." *Strategy + Business*, June 10, 2008, *51* (originally published by Booz & Company). https://www.strategy-business.com/article/08201?gko=97ea9. Accessed September 20, 2017.

7. Krupp, Fred. "The Making of a Market-Minded Environmentalist."
8. Pooley, Eric. *The Climate War*, pages 82–83.
9. Conniff, Richard. "The Political History of Cap and Trade."
10. *Ibid.*
11. Foreman, David. "It's Time to Return to Our Wilderness Roots," *Environmental Action*, (December/January 1984), 15(5), pages 24–25, as quoted in Phillip Shabecoff, *A Fierce Green Fire*. Washington, DC: Island Press, 1993.
12. Schumpeter, Joseph A. *Capitalism, Socialism, and Democracy*. New York: Harper Perennial Modern Classics, 1942, page 83.
13. Matt Coles interview, April 19, 2016.
14. Marc Solomon interview, November 16, 2015.
15. Sharkey, Joe. "What Flying Was Like Before the Smoke Cleared." *The New York Times*, February 23, 2015. https://www.nytimes.com/2015/02/24/business/what-airlines-were-like-before-the-smoke-cleared.html?_r=0.
16. Lerner, Barron H. *One for the Road: Drunk Driving Since 1900*. Baltimore: Johns Hopkins University Press, 2011, page 20.
17. *Ibid.*, page 126.
18. AB inBev. http://www.ab-inbev.com/about-us.html. Accessed October 2, 2017.
19. Lerner, Barron. *One for the Road*, page 109.
20. Interview with Candace Lightner, December 11, 2017.
21. Badgett, M.V. Lee. "The Economic Benefits of Gay Marriage," March 29, 2013. *PBS NewsHour* Web site. http://www.pbs.org/newshour/rundown/the-e/. Accessed December 20, 2016.
22. Tim Markis interview, October 4, 2017.
23. Wikipedia.com. *Nicorette*. https://en.wikipedia.org/wiki/Nicorette. Accessed October 2017.
24. MADD Web site https://www.madd.org/the-solution/drunk-driving/secure-the-future/. Accessed October 9, 2017.
25. Environmental Defense Fund Web site, Climate and Energy, https://www.edf.org/climate. Accessed October 9, 2017.
26. Flowersaug, Charles. "Between the Harpoon and the Whale." *The New York Times* Archives. August 24, 1975, page 192. http://www.nytimes.com/1975/08/24/archives/between-the-harpoon-and-the-whale.html?mcubz=0. Accessed September 25, 2017.
27. Fountain, Henry. "Rising Above the Environmental Debate." *The New York Times*, June 18, 2006. http://www.nytimes.com/2006/06/18/weekinreview/18basic.html?mcubz=0. Accessed September 30, 2017.
28. Porter, Michael E., and Kramer, Mark R. "Creating Shared Value: How to Reinvent Capitalism and Unleash a Wave of Innovation and Growth." *Harvard*

Business Review. June 25, 2013. http://www.creativeinnovationglobal.com.au/wp-content/uploads/Shared-value-Harvard-business-review.pdf.

29. Prahalad, C.K. *Fortune at the Bottom of the Pyramid: Eradicating Poverty Through Profits*. London: Dorling Kindersley Pvt Ltd., 2006.

30. Disclaimer: The author of this book is affiliated as a senior advisor with FSG, the social impact strategy group co-founded by Michael Porter and Mark Kramer, and co-authored the book *Do More Than Give* with Mark Kramer and John Kania of FSG.

6

Be Leaderfull

"My theory is, strong people don't need strong leaders."

—Ella Baker

MADD FOUNDER CANDY LIGHTNER is one of the most recognizable and heralded leaders of all the modern movements we studied for this book. Her organization is synonymous with the triumphant anti–drunk driving crusade. Lightner founded MADD in 1980 in a fit of grief—and rage—after one of her young daughters was killed by a drunk driver while walking down a bicycle lane to a church carnival. Lightner was both anguished and incensed because she learned her daughter's killer—a repeat offender—would likely not do any jail time. Within five years, Lightner had built up MADD from a scrappy California-based group into a $13 million national organization with more than 450 local chapters and two million members and donors nationwide.[1] Teaming up with Cindi Lamb and other bereaved mothers of children harmed or killed by drunk drivers, Lightner and her MADD crusaders convinced Ronald Reagan to initiate a Presidential Commission on Drunk Driving, and governors nationwide established task forces. A comely, articulate, impassioned spokeswoman, Lightner was an instant media darling: She appeared on popular TV shows like *Phil Donahue* and NBC premiered the made-for-TV movie, *Mothers Against Drunk Drivers: The Candy Lightner Story* which made MADD a kitchen-table name. The Smithsonian National Museum of American

History has memorialized Lightner, holding in its archives her vanity license tags, "I AM MADD," among other personal effects.

When viewed through a different lens, however, Lightner is also one of the more *controversial* leaders of the modern movements we studied for this book. Lightner left the organization in 1985 as the result of a contract dispute. "I was burned out, it was time for me to go, and I realized I really hadn't grieved for my daughter," recalls Lightner. "I had dealt with the anger of her death by founding MADD. But I hadn't dealt with the pain of her death."[2]

The board and staff also had concerns about Lightner's leadership style: in one study, Lightner had been accused of being autocratic, egocentric, erratic, and conflict-prone.[3] No matter. Lightner proudly embraced her strong leadership approach. "I ruled the roost," said Lightner. "They called me 'Mother Superior,' which I found rather funny. I was not one to run back to the board [on every decision]. When it came to drunk driving policy issues, I did it without board approval. If a legislator would call me, I made those decisions on my own. I didn't have time to set up a board meeting or a conference call," explains Lightner. "There were a lot of people who ended up disagreeing with me on issues. But what I said *went*." Lightner didn't see herself as the leader of some bureaucracy—or even as the CEO of an organization: "I was an *advocate*, an *activist*. Dealing with bureaucrats like my executive director or board was just not in my nature."[4]

MADD's founding history serves as a go-to case study of the contrast between movement versus organizational leadership. Lightner's story is an archetypical illustration of the clash that can occur when a charismatic, visionary founder confronts the mundane challenges of managing an increasingly bureaucratic organization. When Lightner left in 1985, it seemed that MADD might be at risk of succumbing to Founders Syndrome—a fate that afflicts organizations unable to function without a powerful founding leader. Except in this case, the organization *did* manage to move forward. MADD not only survived the departure of its founder, but it *thrived*.

The impact MADD had while Lightner was leading it, and has continued to have during the decades after she left, has been astounding: During the five years Lightner was running MADD, more than seven hundred state anti–drunk driving laws were enacted, and the number of fatalities from drunk driving crashes dropped 20 percent.[5]

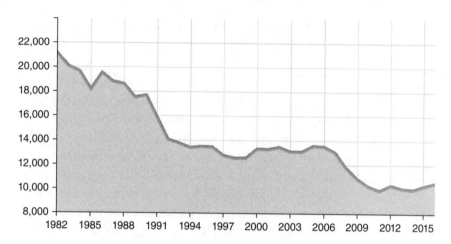

Figure 6.1 Drunk Driving Death Rates (1982–2016)

Source: MADD Web Site[6]

After Lightner's exit, drunk driving death rates climbed temporarily and then declined to the point that, today, they're less than half their peak in the early 1980s (see Figure 6.1). Moreover, it's now widely accepted that drunk driving is not only a punishable crime, it's totally *socially unacceptable*—MADD executed a complete flip in social norms in less than a generation.

How is it that a leader with some apparent flaws could create an organization that so masterfully advanced its cause? We believe it is because, first, Lightner never set out to build an *organization*. She was on a mission to build a *movement*—to make drunk driving a criminally prosecuted, socially unacceptable act. And second, the movement she catalyzed was *leaderfull*.

Leaderfull Movements

Building movements is like capturing lightning in a bottle. Successful leaders don't so much create movements out of thin air as tap into energy that percolates around them. They give that energy shape, channeling it toward a common cause. Leaders like Lightner give voice to grievances and concerns that many people have, but who may not possess the conviction, courage, or capability to speak out publicly and personally initiate change.

The fundamental lesson of MADD's success is not that a movement needs a charismatic, courageous, outspoken leader in the style of Candy Lightner. Although she possessed many exceptional qualities, we also observed equally powerful movement leaders whose styles were quite different. In interviewing leaders for this book, we encountered extremely varied characters who were by turns circumspect, measured, and introverted, as well as the classic charismatic, emotionally effusive types. What united the successful leaders—what seemed to separate them from the rest—was that their movements were "leaderfull."

What does it mean to be leaderfull? In our research, we found three fundamentals: First, leaderfull movements empower local leaders to step forward. Leadership begins at the grassroots, and lots of power resides there. And while national campaign leaders like Lightner push for change from the grass-tops, they recognize that giving local organizations and individuals the resources, incentives, and platforms to work together in common cause is key to success. Second, a leaderfull movement centers on coalitions of like-minded allies *and* unusual suspects—and it's not led by a lone individual or organization calling the shots, always demanding center stage. Successful movement leaders bring diverse coalitions together under a "big tent." Third, a hallmark of leaderfull movements is the people with the *lived experience of the problem*—the individuals most directly affected by the cause—are empowered to speak and act on behalf of the organization. If some grassroots constituents don't initially have the innate ability to speak, grass-tops leaders groom them. Leaderfull movement leaders give the grassroots the tools and roadmaps to success—not commands or detailed instructions that must be followed.

At the end of the day, winning movement leaders realize that, to succeed, they need everyone *around them* to succeed. They embody the philosophy of the great civil rights organizer Ella Baker: "I have always thought that what is needed is the development of people who are interested not in being leaders as much as in developing leadership in others."[7] In essence, leaderfull movement leaders employ each of the best practices we've written about in the previous chapters in this book: They turn grassroots gold. They push for change across all fifty states guided by a "10/10/10/20 = 50"–type vision and work in *networked* leadership structures at the grass-tops. They break from business as usual, partnering with unlikely allies as well as usual suspects—including industry leaders when expedient. And they change *hearts* as well as policies, putting people with the *lived experience of the problem* at the center of their campaigns. It's what differentiates the best movements from the rest.

Leaderfull Leadership at MADD

Let's examine more closely how Lightner launched MADD, and in the process managed to spark one of the most successful public health crusades in modern U.S. history.

Interestingly, there is little in Lightner's background to portend she would go on to launch such a successful social change campaign. Naïve, with experience in neither nonprofits or politics, Lightner had worked in real estate before she quit her job to create MADD. So she approached friends and colleagues on how to get started, "trying to figure out who's who and what's what," as she put it. One meeting was with a member of the Attorney General of California's team, Steven Blankenship. "He said, 'What you need to do is start chapters and start them in the neighborhoods where the legislators are in California, and then they can impact their legislators. [That is how you] change the laws," recalls Lightner.[8]

So that's what Lightner did. She first created a handful of chapters in California, and within two years MADD had spawned ninety chapters across the country.[9] What *fueled* the chapter explosion was the way Lightner conceived of relationships with other victims and activists in the field. When local advocates contacted MADD and asked, "What can we do?" MADD answered: "Start a local chapter."[10] MADD did not dispatch field organizers or try to establish direct control at the local level. Instead, MADD sent study guides and encouraged victims and their supporters to learn about the advocacy process, decipher the motor vehicle code in their towns, monitor court cases, and meet with law enforcement officers, prosecutors, judges and legislators.[11] Most crucially, MADD let local chapter leaders *lead*.

Meanwhile, back at MADD's headquarters in California (which were later relocated to Texas), Lightner and her colleagues focused on advancing state legislative reform proposals the grassroots could get behind and pushing for federal policy changes. To do this, Lightner's first instinct was to gather a broad range of allies, including established figures but also unusual suspects. "Early on, it became clear that I must seek broad and strategic alliances for MADD to be successful. I turned to law enforcement officials, restaurateurs, legislators, and civic organizations. It was only by building broad coalitions of such highly influential constituents that MADD, during my tenure, was able to initiate a sweeping change in public attitudes and laws against drunk driving."[12]

This "big tent" philosophy roiled some seasoned policy wonks and advocates. Lightner recalls when she was trying to introduce a mandatory jail sentencing bill in California on drunk driving first offenses. To draft the bill, she told colleagues she'd planned to invite all the lobbyists who had worked on this issue, pro or con, to meet. Lightner recalls, "They said 'no, you don't do that. You don't invite your opposition to have a meeting before you introduce the bill! You just get your supporters together.'" Lightner persisted: "I really wanted to know who'd oppose it, and I really wanted to know why, and what [they'd oppose]. I wanted to learn more."[13] She held the meeting in the back of a church, and in attendance were representatives from ACLU, the California Attorneys General, law enforcement, the alcohol industry, and "whoever else had opposed anything related to drinking in the past," said Lightner. She talked about what MADD wanted. Law enforcement officials and other potential opponents told her what would fly, what wouldn't. Lightner tailored the bill, proposed it, and it passed.[14]

While spawning local grassroots chapters and working to change state laws, MADD was simultaneously agitating on the national stage. One of Lightner's first moves in 1980 had been to call on then-governor of California Jerry Brown to form a task force, and MADD supporters marched on the state capitol. Lightner's daughter, Serena, had launched SADD (Students Against Drunk Driving) in California and picketed, too. MADD went on to stage a high-profile, nationally focused protest in which victims and survivors marched around the White House carrying placards. The protest received tremendous press coverage, with assistance from the National Highway Traffic Safety Administration (NHTSA) press office. MADD articles began to pop up in places like the *Los Angeles Times* and *Family Circle*, and Lightner was invited to appear on national television as a guest on shows such as *Today* and *Phil Donohue*. With momentum building at the national level, soon Lightner and the MADD team were sparking legislative changes across the country and the Presidential Commission was established.

Amidst all of these high-profile national activities, MADD was doing something else that would prove vital to its long-term impact: supporting the victims of drunk driving crashes and offering solace to survivors and their friends and loved ones. Although its bereavement groups and other victim support services have been less well-known to the public, MADD's commitment to serving its core constituents was perhaps the single most important factor that would define the long-term success of the movement. Support circles forged bonds of trust and mutual obligation between individuals at the local level and cemented a formidable grassroots army of ready-made soldiers fired up to do battle in small towns, big cities, and entire states. The support groups also ensured a growing membership for MADD.[15] Lightner was smart to focus what resources she could muster on chapter support groups from the outset; when MADD received its tax-exempt status in 1981, Lightner soon raised $100,000 in private donations and $60,000 from NHTSA specifically to support chapter development.[16]

MADD's chapters were the bulwark of the organization; in 1983, Lightner put a new governance structure in place so a majority of the board was made up of chapter leaders. Under this structure, the president of MADD (*always* a victim or survivor of a drunk driving crash) could serve as national spokesperson and a professional nonprofit leader would serve as CEO and handle the administrative duties. As a result, MADD would be forever led essentially from the bottom up.

This approach has its inherent challenges—MADD undoubtedly could be more efficiently run if it had adopted a more tightly controlled, top-down governance and leadership structure, along the lines of what many corporations and some more traditional nonprofits employ. But that's the difference between leading an organization and building a *leaderfull movement*.

Being Leaderfull

The "leaderfull" movement idea we explore in *How Change Happens* was prompted by the concept of "leaderless" organizations explored in *The Starfish and the Spider: The Unstoppable Power of Leaderless Organizations*. Authors Brafman and Beckstrom compare two seemingly similar but surprisingly different biological creatures to illustrate how technology-driven decentralized companies—think Wikipedia,

YouTube, and Napster—operate differently than centralized, command-and-control corporations. Rather than being led by a single, all-powerful CEO, decentralized companies are relatively "leaderless," and as such, are often more resilient to shocks and adaptive to competitive threats. The authors compare traditional companies to a spider, which has a brain that functions as "central command" and controls the movements of its various parts—eight legs, multiple eyes, and internal organs. Whereas the starfish has no brain—or head, for that matter. Starfish operate as neural networks of cells. Their major organs are replicated throughout each arm, which can regenerate if one limb is cut off. In order for a starfish to move, scientists believe an arm somehow "signals" the others to join in.

Starfish-like organizations operate as decentralized networks without a strong central command; each part makes its own decisions and acts independently, but also coordinates with the others. Examples include Alcoholics Anonymous and the Apache Nation. Spider-like organizations, on the other hand, include traditional corporations, military units, and large government agencies, which have centralized command centers led by a visible head, authorized to issue orders down to the ranks.[17]

Successful social movements have a lot more in common with starfish than with spiders. They win because their power is spread across a sprawling network of many individual parts—grassroots activists, local- and state-based chapters, coalitions at local, state, and national levels. Winning movements also have strong national groups with central headquarters, critical to developing strategies, raising resources, and helping coordinate across networks. So in one sense they possess a "brain" or central unit. But these central bodies don't have *absolute* power—they can't "command" their counterparts to act. There is no one "chief in charge."

The best social movements, however, aren't entirely "leaderless" either. Visible, charismatic figures such as MADD founder Candy Lightner, Freedom to Marry founder Evan Wolfson, and NRA executive vice president Wayne LaPierre are clearly powerful, influential players. But none of these individuals is solely responsible for success. That credit goes to the armies of grassroots activists and members they embolden and to the coalitions and alliances they foster, as they enable diverse leaders at local, state, and national levels to come together in a common cause. Although they may have titular authority, successful movement leaders realize that ultimate power is amassed by empowering others. They see their own success as inextricably linked with the success of those around them. The more we studied various movements and their individual leaders, the more we began to see that the successful ones were actually not "leaderless," but instead were "leaderfull."

The leaderfull notion is not original. It echoes the thoughts and writings of civil rights activist Ella Baker. Arguably the most influential woman in the U.S. civil rights movement, Baker deeply believed in the power of grassroots organizing; her approach entailed empowering people who suffered from disenfranchisement to advocate for themselves: "My theory is, strong people don't need strong leaders."[18] Baker's philosophy is evident in many of the surging movements today, such as Black Lives Matter (BLM), sparked by Patrisse Cullors, Alicia Garza, and Opal Tometi, who were joined by countless other activists protesting the 2012 acquittal of George Zimmerman, who shot and killed Trayvon Martin, an unarmed young black man. While BLM is often described as leaderless, BLM principals say that's a misnomer: "The Black Lives Matter movement is a leaderfull movement,"[19] composed of many local leaders and organizations including Black Youth Project 100, the Dream Defenders, the Organization for Black Struggle, Hands Up United, Millennial Activists United, and the Black Lives Matter national network. ". . . We demonstrate through this model that the movement is bigger than any one person."[20]

Of course, Ella Baker was organizing long before the rise of social media and technology-driven organizing platforms that can instantly elevate movements like BLM. But the principles of effective organizing are the same: Build trust between individuals and work through networks, whether online or offline, to create a whole greater than the sum of the parts. The power of any network lies in the infinite connections that exist *between* individuals, and rather than the power of any one singular individual, as we explored in Chapter One, "Turn Grassroots Gold." That's how movements ignite.

Let's look now at the traits of some of the leaders who either ignited or elevated the successful movements we studied for this book and examine what qualities they share in common that might explain why they pursued a "leaderfull" approach to social change.

The Origins of Leaderfull Leaders

To understand more about the makeup of leaders profiled in this book, we conducted interviews; read articles and books; and asked their allies, opponents, and peers about them. As we collected more and more information, four interesting patterns began to emerge that seemed to distinguish leaderfull movement leaders from others. Some of these patterns seemed counterintuitive to us; others were more predictable. But together, these traits appear to distinguish the best movement leaders from the rest.

"Leaderfull" Movement Leaders

   I. Hail often from unlikely backgrounds

   II. Listen to the point of transcendence

   III. Let go of ego

   IV. Relentlessly pursue impact

I. Unlikely Backgrounds

Consider the background of this leader who has elevated one of the most successful movements in the last thirty years: While a college student, he believed he would pursue a teaching career. He was neither an outspoken advocate or activist, although he liked politics: While other college students protested the Vietnam War, he interned with a New York state legislator.[21] After graduation, he worked as a substitute special education teacher. One *New York Times* profile revealed this about him: "Interacting with children who were not only developmentally disabled but also poor had a dramatic impact. . . . 'I concluded that a lot needs to be done to give those kids hope.'"[22] People who know him well describe him as subdued and thoughtful, "He is more professor than a leader. [He is a] [v]ery mild mannered person," observed a former spokesperson for his organization.[23] "He's one of the shyest, kindest, most unassuming, total lack of ego, nonconfrontational—he hates confrontation—individuals I have ever met," shared one board member.[24]

The leader described here is Wayne LaPierre, executive vice president and chief executive of the National Rifle Association (NRA). Wildly revered by gun rights supporters—and deeply reviled by gun control advocates—LaPierre is famous for riling up his base with combative, bellicose defenses of gun rights and Second Amendment freedoms. Contrary to his private personae, one of the most roiling public dust-ups was sparked by his now infamous direct mail appeal line, in which LaPierre accused federal agents from the Alcohol, Tobacco, and Firearms (ATF) agency involved in the Ruby Ridge and Waco assaults of being "jackbooted thugs" who [had] power to "take away our constitutional rights, break in our doors, seize our guns, destroy our property, and even injure or kill us." His polarizing claims generated widespread backlash, including prompting President George H.W. Bush, a lifetime member of the NRA, to resign his membership in 1995 in the wake of the Oklahoma City bombing. LaPierre eventually apologized. But this admission was an unacceptable display of weakness to NRA hard-liners.[25]

LaPierre would not make that mistake again. Just days after the Sandy Hook shooting in December 2012, in which twenty-six grammar school children and their educators were shot and killed by a man with a semi-automatic rifle, LaPierre refused to concede guns were part of the problem. "The only thing that stops a bad guy with a gun is a good guy with a gun," he proclaimed. Skewered by the left as a "gun nut" and in the media as the "craziest man on earth," his tone-deaf response was appalling to millions. But no matter. In the wake of Sandy Hook, with LaPierre's leadership, the NRA went on to secure even *more* gun rights victories, not fewer.

Unusual Suspects
LaPierre makes a fascinating study as one of the most unlikely movement leaders of our time. As a teenager growing up in Roanoke, Virginia, LaPierre reportedly had no apparent interest in hunting or guns. He earned an early professional reputation as being more shy and studious than ideological, accumulating stacks of yellow legal pads filled with detailed notes.[26] He first worked for the NRA in 1977 as a twenty-eight-year-old lobbyist, was soon named the NRA-ILA's director of state and local affairs, and then became executive director of the NRA-ILA in 1986. In 1991, LaPierre was named EVP and chief executive, and since has received credit for "[having] done more to expand gun rights than perhaps any other official in NRA history."[27]

What's most fascinating about LaPierre is not the dissonance between his muffled private personae and his bellicose public image. It's the fact that he doesn't seem to have had a life-long, ingrained passion for guns. One PBS documentary profile pinned LaPierre as " more comfortable on K Street than in a duck blind." And while he did buy his first gun, a .38-caliber revolver, after college for target shooting, NRA colleagues chide him as a clumsy marksman.[28] "Wayne is not a gunny, he's not ex-military, he's not a hunter, he's not a trapper," said former NRA Director of Public Education John Aquilino in one media profile.[29] "He represents a real departure for the NRA," said Osha Gray Davidson, author of *Under Fire: The NRA and the Battle for Gun Control*. "He's the first leader for the NRA who doesn't come from the shooting-sports and hunting area. He's a politician."[30]

Political skill turns out to be more important than marksmanship. But LaPierre is not the conventional inside-the-beltway kind of a lobbyist or policy wonk. LaPierre leads the NRA more like a political *campaign*. Since becoming EVP and chief executive in 1991, LaPierre week after week, year after year, has traveled across the country, tirelessly showing up at gun shows and hotel ballroom fundraisers and NRA gatherings—including those at nights and on weekends—and sometimes making multiple stops in a single weekend.[31] He glad-hands with NRA members, constantly shining the limelight on local activists. In one media account, a supporter who helped host a "Friends of the NRA" fundraiser in Cape Girardeau, Missouri, recalls: "We've got one guy on our [fundraising] committee, he's seventy-two years old, he's got a two-foot-long gray ponytail, and twice Wayne has picked him out at the national convention to give him a hug, to say, 'You're my trouper.'"[32]

LaPierre was busy canvassing the country bootstrapping an army, rather than leading from on high at NRA headquarters in Fairfax, Virginia, and simply hobnobbing with policy elites. Within four years, LaPierre managed to turn around a declining membership and drive it to a record high. He also promoted an award-winning gun-safety program for children, shored up NRA lobbying efforts, and built the gun association up to 550 employees and an annual budget of $100 million.[33] Since then, LaPierre's grown the NRA budget to nearly a quarter of a billion dollars and attracted nearly five million members.[34] The power of this massive grassroots membership has propelled the

NRA to victory in almost every major national or federal legislative battle on guns since LaPierre took the reins.

Despite his unlikely personae and his sketchy shooting abilities, LaPierre succeeds because he's built a movement that's *leaderfull*.

More and Less Likely Leaders

As we examined the leaders from a diverse set of successful movements, we found an interesting pattern: They were just as likely to come from non-traditional backgrounds as predictable ones. This challenged conventional wisdom, which portrays movement leaders as passionate, charismatic, and deeply connected to the cause. Of course, some of the leaders we studied certainly fit the traditional mold: Take Evan Wolfson, the same-sex marriage crusader who wrote his law school thesis on the right for same-sex couples to marry and volunteered on legal cases until finally convincing his first employer, Lambda Legal, to start a marriage project. Wolfson was a leader in the marriage equality crusade for thirty years before the 2015 Supreme Court ruling made it the law of the land. Wolfson is persuasive, persistent, relentlessly optimistic— and inextricably identified with same-sex marriage as an impassioned, charismatic gay man fighting for LGBT rights his entire adult life.

Or take Bruce Aylward, the intrepid medical doctor and public health expert who fearlessly led the Global Polio Eradication Initiative for more than two decades, relentlessly pushing for polio elimination in 99.9 percent of the world. Likewise, Candy Lightner fits this profile, as a bereaved mother anguished by the death of her daughter killed by a drunk driver and propelled into action.

But in other ways, the leaders we studied hailed from backgrounds more *unlikely* than likely. When Lightner was thrust into the unwanted position of parent of a drunk driving victim, she had no activist or organizing experience. A former real estate worker who apparently didn't even vote prior to founding MADD, there is nothing in Lightner's background that would portend spearheading a phenomenal social change campaign that would profoundly shift federal and state laws and fundamentally alter social norms and behaviors around drinking and driving.

Or take the key catalysts of the worldwide polio eradication movement—members of Rotary International. Rotarians were unlikely protagonists in the polio cause; they were business leaders, not scientists.

It was Dr. Jon Sever, a Rotarian who'd worked on eradicating polio in the Philippines, who proposed a global eradication push around the time of Rotary International's 75th anniversary, when the organization had been casting about for ideas for a unifying cause the whole global membership could get behind. While Severs was an MD, most Rotarians knew next to nothing about vaccines or public health systems. But it turns out they had what it takes to trounce a global public health threat: vast international networks with boots on the ground capable of mustering the political will and government resources to drive the polio campaign with Rotary's 33,000 chapters and millions of members worldwide.

As often as we observed leaders with temperaments and life experiences that would appear to make them well-suited to lead a social change movement, just as often, we didn't. What we found instead was they all shared a common instinct to build movements that were *leaderfull*, so we began to think perhaps their personal profiles didn't much matter. Then we asked: What makes a leader inclined to engender action and leadership in others around them, rather than try to shore up power for themselves or control things from the top? Two key traits emerged: an abiding interest in listening to others and a willingness to let go of ego.

II. Transcendent Listening

"The most important thing . . . is to really get into their shoes and understand their viewpoints. Listening doesn't really explain it. The word 'transcend' comes to mind," said Environmental Defense Fund (EDF) President Fred Krupp. He was speaking of the myriad constituencies that could either ally with or oppose EDF's stances, including fellow environmentalists, labor groups, and corporations, among others who had a stake in the gambit EDF espoused to reduce acid rain in the United States through an innovative, market-based cap and trade approach. "It's hard to make change until you really understand the perspectives of all the players."

Krupp was influenced by the writings of the Jesuit theologian Father John Dunne, who explored the phenomenon of "passing over"—deliberately entering into the experience of others and understanding what they believe with complete empathy. "Passing over is a shifting of standpoint, a going over to the standpoint of another

culture, another way of life, another religion," wrote Dunne. "It is followed by an equal and opposite process we might call 'coming back,'
coming back with new insight to one's own culture, one's own way of
life, one's own religion."[35] Dunne practiced "passing over" with people
who held religious beliefs different from his. Far from dissolving his
own religious commitment, he held that this practice helped him see
his own beliefs more clearly.

As we interviewed movement leaders for this book and studied
what has been written and said about them by others, a key theme kept
popping up: the ability to listen. Great movement leaders were able to
not only hear, but deeply internalize and empathize with the others
around them, both their closest allies as well as their adversaries and
enemies. This was not the case 100 percent of the time, but it was a
pattern that emerged in interview after interview.

Evidence of "crossing over" was perhaps most prevalent in the
marriage equality movement. One major "cross over" moment came
in 2009, when leaders of the same-sex marriage crusade had hit a wall.
They'd just lost the right to marry in California and another fight in
Maine. And although by the early 2010s LGBT activists had built a
hairsbreadth majority of support, with just 51 percent of people in
America expressing support for same-sex marriage, it wasn't strong
enough to withstand the onslaught of more than a dozen anti-gay ballot measure campaigns brewing. Culling through polling data trying
to understand how to move the needle on their cause, Wolfson says a
light bulb moment occurred as they suddenly realized the need to put
"love" at the center of their message, rather than "rights" (as described
in detail in Chapter Four). LGBT activists came to this insight by
deeply listening to and genuinely trying to understand the views of
non-gay people. This exercise gave same-sex marriage advocates deeper
insight into why LGBT couples wanted to marry. Love then became
the cornerstone for the next round of state-focused campaigns.

Marriage equality activists also realized they needed to make it possible for unconverted but potential supporters to make a similar journey
and "cross over" to their way of thinking. One way of doing this was to
uplift gay and lesbian couples, encourage them to outwardly display and
speak about their love in public and with legislators and other influencers. This would help "normalize" same-sex partnerships. One high-profile
example of a personal conversion story is that of Vice President Joe Biden.

In April of 2012, Biden was invited to meet with HBO executive Michael Lombardo and his husband, architect Sonny Ward, in their tony Los Angeles home. The couple had been together for twelve years and were raising two children. As Freedom to Marry National Campaign Director Marc Solomon writes in *Winning Marriage*, Biden came in and said a quick, gracious hello to the hosts "and then completely lit up when he greeted Josie and Johnny."[36] Biden gave the children two stuffed-animal German Shepherds he'd brought and started showing them pictures of his grandkids and his dog Champ. Later Biden was ushered into another room to meet with a larger group of LGBT advocates. After his speech, during the question-and-answer period, Biden said: "I came in. I saw these two kids. I saw this family . . . [and] it's hard to be against gay marriage." Biden went on, "It's about changing hearts and minds. It's about people meeting. It's undeniable." While Biden has publicly credited the show *Will and Grace* for helping him come around to the idea of gay marriage, it's likely an intimate encounter like this one convinced him more than anything else.

But this was not as effective a strategy for the more skeptical audiences. "We wanted to reach the reachable, but not yet reached," explained Wolfson. "And they needed to hear the non-gay people like them, hear their journey stories and why they had changed their minds."

Another hallmark of transcendent listening is being genuinely interested in what others have to say—especially adversaries. In the opening story to this chapter, we shared how MADD founder Candy Lightner built coalitions of unlikely allies to advance the anti–drunk driving crusade, often including unusual suspects who sometimes made for strange bedfellows alongside drunk driving crash survivors and victim family members. Lightner reached out to law enforcement officers—who historically had been weak on enforcement of drunk driving laws—and alcohol companies, which many advocates shunned as what they deemed "instigators of the problem." Lightner was genuinely interested in what the other side believed.

Also, it's key to note that Lightner wasn't on an anti-*drinking* crusade. She was on an anti–*drunk driving* tirade. Far from being a teetotaler, Lightner was an unapologetic consumer of alcohol. MADD's very origins can be traced back to a night when a grieving Lightner and her sister and some friends were having a drink at a bar and spoke about creating some sort of organization to combat drunk driving, and

Lightner's friend suggested she name it, "Mothers Against Drunk Drivers." [MADD later changed that word "Drivers" to "Driving."] In the movie, *The Candy Lightner Story*, the actress playing Lightner often appears with a glass of wine in hand. To MADD, the enemy was *drunk driving*, not drinking, and Lightner was often criticized by adversarial allies—those on *her* side of the cause—for not distinguishing between the two. But by having alcohol companies in her camp and seated at the bargaining table, MADD could leverage their vast corporate branding and marketing reach to share its "responsible drinking" messages. It later played into MADD-led campaigns such as "Friends Don't Let Friends Drive Drunk" and other messages that went "viral" (long before the Internet age). Lightner was no purist. She was a pragmatic activist.

This ability to listen—and hear and internalize—many competing perspectives was also essential for the Environmental Defense Fund, the green group responsible for advancing the cap and trade policy solution to reduce harmful sulfur dioxide emissions and curtail acid rain in the Northeastern United States. The Environmental Defense Fund developed a proposal for President George H.W. Bush's Administration to pass amendments to the Clean Air Act in 1990, which created a market for trading pollution permits, combined with emissions caps, or "cap and trade." Under the system, utilities such as coal-fired plants that reduced emissions by more than the required amount earn credits, which they could bank for future use or sell to companies unable to meet their targets. For the first time on a national scale, businesses were allowed to employ market-based approaches to regulating their emission output.

The importance of this innovation cannot be overstated. After years of regulation, which was expensive, painstaking, and often did not yield the best results, cap and trade was based on principles that harnessed a business's core capability to innovate. It let them come up with the best solutions for their unique contexts, then allowed them to trade and continue to compete. As a result, acid rain was cut *faster* than predicted. The cap and trade system became a key example in the framework of the 1996 international Kyoto Protocol.[37]

EDF leaders realized that environmentalists were never going to put "business out of business." So they committed to trying to understand what drives business and asked: "How can market forces be harnessed to advance environmental goals?" The fact that EDF was able to listen in this way was unique—and we believe they did so in large part because of the unique makeup of their leadership team. EDF recruited environmentalists and scientists and advocates, but also economists. This cocktail of expertise: economists who understood what drives business interests; PhDs in environmental sciences like biology, engineering, and life sciences who understood organisms and ecosystems; and policy analysts and advocates who understood the political environment, enabled EDF to lay out a vision for the third wave of the environmental movement—one that unearthed and exploited the interests and capabilities of corporations and harnessed them to drive environmental goals.

Interestingly, the ability to listen may tie back to the fact that Krupp himself was an unlikely leader of this environmental group. Not only was he young—just thirty years old when he became president of the Environmental Defense Fund—but he wasn't a "dyed in the wool" environmentalist schooled in the adversarial politics of prior environmental activist waves. "He was the only major environmental group leader from a non-environmental background," recalls Ashoka founder Bill Drayton, a former senior EPA official under President Carter who pushed for innovative market-based approaches to reductions rather than command-and-control regulatory schemes. Perhaps this is what made Krupp more open to seeing a different path forward.

III. Letting Go of the Ego

Related to the practice of "passing over" is the ability to "let go." This involves allowing oneself to be subsumed by the movement, to give oneself over to the mission or the cause. This almost always means subordinating personal and organizational identity to the interests of broader coalitions and alliances. Rather than grab the spotlight, control the agenda, or lead with a ham-fisted approach, successful movement leaders find that by stepping aside, allowing others to lead, extending credit to those around them, and sometimes blending entirely into the background, they are able to effectively move a cause forward. It seems counterintuitive and goes against traditional ideas of competition, which hold that leaders should vie for power, authority, and credit and continually strive to build up brand recognition and value at the expense of others. But this is where leaders dedicated to making social change depart from leaders of corporate organizations dedicated to making money: They win not by competing, but by collaborating, and by leading from behind, rather than out front.

An excellent example of this is Rotary International, which for the past thirty years has pushed the polio eradication cause forward—mostly from behind the scenes. Rotarians enticed Bill Gates Jr. and leaders of WHO to join them in a common cause, raising $250 million and launching the global polio elimination crusade. Since then, Gates has poured in billions, with plenty of media recognition, while hundreds of thousands of Rotarians were the boots on the ground, volunteering to administer polio vaccines on the front lines and convincing government leaders to join the cause. The most poignant example of their ability to "let go" is during the last-mile push to eradicate it in one of the few regions in the world where polio persists, Pakistan. There the polio push is stuck in a war-torn area where distrust of Western aid and U.S. officials in particular is very high. While tens of thousands of Rotarians volunteer all around the world, they wear their red stickers emblazoned with *"End Polio Now."* But in very high-risk areas of Pakistan, they don't. Any sign of an American organization—its logos, anything written in English—puts volunteers at serious risk. In 2016, fifteen people were killed in a bomb attack on a vaccination center in the southwestern city of Quetta. Islamist militants oppose vaccination, viewing it as a Western conspiracy to sterilize Pakistani children.

Undeterred, UNICEF asked Rotary to take the stickers off their vaccine equipment and erase all visible signs of Rotary or Western involvement. "They were absolutely gracious about it," recalls Sherine Guirguis, senior communications manager of polio eradication at UNICEF. "More gracious than [state] government, which did not go so far." Rotary put the cause ahead of the organization; they subsumed their organization's name, brand, and credibility to deliver the vaccines without harm to volunteers or the local police who protect them.

A similar strategy was put in place in New York, where LGBT advocates and their allies successfully pushed for marriage equality. Freedom to Marry helped pull together a coalition with two other main groups at the center, Human Rights Campaign and Empire State Gay Pride Agenda. "We came up with the name 'New Yorkers United for Marriage,' each agreed to raise $250,000 so they could jointly hire a communications team and have a joint campaign to manage the effort," explains Freedom to Marry Campaign Director Mark Solomon. The coalition wasn't called "Freedom to Marry." Similar tactics were used across the country, as Freedom to Marry made manifest its new focus on "love," described earlier. "We shifted the emphasis so that they [non-gay potential supporters] would be hearing what they needed to hear. We propagated through the movement, the media. We were sharing the data and analysis, video, recalibrating messaging that we had created and they were using it as their own." Freedom to Marry was extremely effective at getting people to work together. And they built the tools other organizations could use and shared them freely. Explains Wolfson: "We built the back end, and we ran the social media for their organizations. We would produce the stories, we created this drum beat, created a shared Web site. But it would be under their banner." It was a win–win.

This ability to let go of the ego emanated from the grass-tops. Wolfson recalls a critical moment in the movement's history when a handful of LGBT leaders had gathered in Jersey City to retrench and adapt their strategy after a slew of devastating setbacks. They came up with "The Plan to Win Marriage" with the 10/10/10/20 strategy to capture all fifty states, which Matt Coles wrote (see Chapter Two). As the recognized architect of the marriage equality campaign and one of the most passionate and persistent marriage equality advocates, Wolfson could have demanded he write the strategy. But Wolfson explains: "Matt was viewed as a thoughtful [leader], and also a very good writer, so he took on the role of writing the concept paper, rearticulating that strategy and [sounding] the call to arms." Wolfson stepped aside and asked Coles to write it because he recognized it might be received better than if it came straight from Wolfson himself.

By way of analogy, Wolfson recalls a scene from *1776*, the musical about the founding of the United States, in which John Adams encourages Thomas Jefferson to write the Declaration of Independence, rather than do it himself. Adams recognized he was "obnoxious and disliked." It would be best if the document were to be authored by a respected Virginian. Similarly, Wolfson acknowledged other LGBT leaders often perceived him as "obnoxious. . . . I was viewed as a mono-maniacal single-issue guy pushing, pushing, pushing, marriage, marriage, marriage."

This ability to let others lead, to step aside so others take center stage, to see the forest for the trees, are hallmarks of great movement leaders. They echo the same characteristics of nonprofit leaders profiled in *Forces for Good: The Six Practices of High-Impact Nonprofits*, only amplified across coalitions and broad membership groups rather than contained within one organization. They are also the opposite of the traits exhibited by less-effective movement leaders. Lower-level performers tended to grab the limelight, to demand their organizations be credited for success, that *they* be featured on the dais at the march and highlighted as the keynote speakers. Whereas the effective movement leaders did the opposite: They put their members and citizen advocates—the people with the lived experience of the issue and the most passion—up on stage, and they put their allies out front to receive credit. They built coalitions and led from behind.

IV. Relentless Pursuit of Impact

The final characteristic of successful movement leaders we observed runs to the core of what drives them, and what enables them to so effectively transcend to others' views, to listen, and to let go of the ego. That trait is the relentless focus on impact. It drives them to take up strange bedfellows—to make common cause with would-be enemies or unlikely allies.

But this relentless drive comes at a cost. Every movement leader sacrificed and suffered, whether part of a successful movement or struggling one, or something in between. "If you want it to be a success, be prepared to give up your family," cautions Lightner. "And be prepared to work for nothing . . . we work seven days a week, twenty-four hours a day." Lightner recalls how she didn't earn a salary at MADD for some eighteen months, and she was ill-prepared for the role and the personal demands. "No one warns you—you're going to be competing as one of thousands of nonprofits, you're going to be competing with them, and be prepared for dissension—I dealt with that constantly with my board."

The emotional toll on movement leaders we met with was palpable. Two interviewees from the tobacco control movement teared up when we interviewed them. Feelings were so raw and frustrations still high from times when allies across the tobacco control spectrum turned against one another, first unwilling and later unable to find common ground with regard to negotiating with the tobacco industry. It was brutal.

What has kept movement leaders going is the never-ending quest for impact and a clear-headed belief that, whatever their side of the issue, they were on the "right" side of history. Matt Myers spent decades working on tobacco control issues, including at the Federal Trade Commission starting in 1980, then with the Coalition on Smoking OR Health, which he joined as legal director in 1982, then as executive vice president and legal counsel of the Campaign for Tobacco-Free Kids in 1996, where he now serves as president as the Campaign takes its fight globally. The same tenacity is true for Evan Wolfson, who worked for three decades on advancing marriage equality for same-sex couples before the 2015 Supreme Court ruling. Wayne LaPierre has battled fiercely for gun rights and expanded Second Amendment freedoms since he joined the NRA in 1977, rising to EVP in 1991, and continuing in the role today. When asked why he had such a passion for what he does, LaPierre replied: "It's people. . . . It's about helping them. It's about trying to do the right thing."

Of course, leaders possess deep passion and commitment on all sides of issues—whether the movement is winning, losing, or stuck somewhere in between. So this is not in itself a differentiating factor. But when combined with the other abilities explored in this chapter such as transcendent listening and ego-less leadership, it considerably tips the scale toward winning.

Leaderfull vs. Leaderless vs. Leader-Led Movements

Just as the successful movements of modern times appeared to us as "leaderfull," other movements seemed to embody traits that could be described as either "leaderless" or "leader-led." Perhaps the most visible modern "leaderless" movement is Occupy Wall Street (Occupy), which prides itself on having no central leadership. Occupy began in September 2011 as demonstrators camped out in Manhattan's Zuccotti Park to peacefully protest, under the "We are the 99 percent" rallying cry, against rising income inequality, criminality on Wall Street, and the corrupting influence of money in U.S. politics.

The Occupy movement has been structured on anarchist organizing principles, which means no formal leaders or hierarchy. "Occupy Wall Street is a people's movement. It is leaderless and party-less by design. It is not a business, a political party, an advertising campaign or a brand. It is not for sale."[38,39] Occupy does have some basic decision-making structure behind it, however; it has been organized by the New York City General Assembly (the General Assembly), a parliament-like group that describes itself as an "open, participatory, and horizontally organized process" which anyone can join.[40] The inclusive, flat, non-hierarchical structure helped rapidly fuel protests in "open spaces" like Wall Street. But it was so diffuse—with so many demands appearing on the protestors' list of grievances—that the wholly democratic decision-making process could not yield a consensus. In the Declaration of the Occupation of New York City—accepted by the General Assembly on September 29, 2011—the Occupy protestors' grievances amounted to more than twenty specific corporate injustices, including: "taking bailouts from taxpayers with impunity"; profiting from the torture, confinement, and cruel treatment of animals; stripping employees of the right to negotiate for better pay and safer working conditions; holding students hostage with exorbitant debt; promoting oil dependency; and creating weapons of mass destruction.* (The last item is affixed with an asterisk to denote, "*These grievances are not all-inclusive.")[41] With so many complaints and no apparent coordinated plan of action or unifying solution, it's not surprising that within a year of the Zuccotti Park demonstrations, Occupy was widely dismissed for disorganization and lack of a core message. Reports soon described Occupy as "fizzled" or "failed."[42]

However, being "leaderless" does not necessarily mean a movement lacks impact. Many credit Occupy with igniting a national conversation around income inequality. Signs of its impact were visible years later. In 2016 the Democratic presidential challenger Bernie Sanders's rallying cry was predicated on protesting Wall Street greed and breaking up big banks; Democratic nominee Hillary Clinton also struck a populist tone, declaring "the deck is still stacked in favor of those at the top."[43] Across the United States, campaigns for higher minimum wages built on the Occupy momentum, as grassroots coalitions crystallized from groups of fast-food workers and Walmart employees, convenience-store clerks, and adjunct teachers, who coalesced in the wake of the Zuccotti Park protests around the cause.[44] Other campaigns, such as environmentalists protesting the Dakota Pipeline, sprouted from seeds sown in the heat of Occupy.

At the same time, the Occupy movement at this writing was not a visible, identifiable movement driving a dominant cause or issue, in the same way MADD, Campaign for Tobacco-Free Kids, and Freedom to Marry were often synonymous with their causes. That was in part by design. But it illustrates a larger point: To be successful in the long run, it appears movements must strike a balance. Too little structure and totally democratic decision-making processes can lead to the lack of a unifying focus so a movement risks imploding or simply fading away. On the opposite end of the spectrum, movements risk also being "leader-led"—with chief executives amassing and asserting power and authority from above and controlling strategic decision-making processes—which often fail to maximize impact as well (see Figure 6.2).

At various times in the history of the gun control movement, torchbearers veered toward the "leader-led" end of the spectrum, particularly at a critical juncture in 2000 after the Million Mom March Across America for Sensible Gun Laws. In 2001, the Brady Campaign had an opportunity to transition and catalyze a more bottom-up grassroots-driven "leaderfull" movement when it absorbed

Anarchy		Central Control
Leaderless	**Leaderfull**	**Leader-led**
• Purely democratic decision making, each individual member has an equal voice • Flat/non-hierarchical structure • No recognized grass-tops leadership, only grassroots	• Multiple leaders drive collective decision making • Coalition or campaign structure • Simultaneous grass-tops and grassroots leadership • Multiple organizations share power, credit, and decision-making authority	• One dominant leader tries to control decision making • Competitive structure (groups compete vs. collaborate) • Grass-tops elites hoard power, authority, credit • Grassroots/individual members downplayed or non-existent

Figure 6.2   Leadership Spectrum of Social Movements

the 236 MMM chapters. But that opportunity dissipated when Brady was unable to fully embrace the state council structure created by the Million Mom March (based on the MADD model), which elevated state leaders with the help of the Bell Campaign.[45]

It would be another twelve years, when Shannon Watts launched Moms Demand Action with a Facebook page in the wake of the Sandy Hook School shooting and later merged with MAIG to form Everytown for Gun Safety, before a more leaderfull approach was adopted in the gun safety cause. It remains to be seen whether the four-year-old Everytown and its four million supporters will turn the tide against the nearly five million NRA members and the leaderfull gun rights movement LaPierre and his colleagues have been building for decades.

Toward More Leaderfull Movements

Leaderfull movements are phenomena of balance. They require strong leaders who possess clarity of vision and unbounded will to relentlessly pursue impact. But these same leaders must also be willing to let go of their egos, to deeply listen to and understand others who represent differing—often opposing—views. Successful movement leaders create a modicum of structure and organization by building effective coalitions and campaigns that enable multiple organizations and individuals to work together in common cause. But then they subsume their own organization's identity and needs and defer to what is best for the movement as a whole. Leaders who successfully achieve this balance embody traits that Senge, Hamilton, and Kania see in the "systems leader," which they describe in *Stanford Social Innovation Review* as "a person who catalyzes collective leadership."[46] Veer too far to the left side of the spectrum, and movements risk disintegrating into chaos. While they can make important points and reframe the way society sees or thinks about a problem, the decentralized approach doesn't appear to be the winning formula for long-term, sustained impact. Or swerve too far to the right side of the spectrum, and movements can be stifled by the grass-tops, where powerful influencers compete to control resources, make decisions, and focus less on empowering the grassroots than on shoring up their own organizations. They operate more like spiders, rather than starfish, and, as a result, are less powerful than they might otherwise be.

For movements that are struggling or are just emerging, the trick will be to navigate toward a more leaderfull equilibrium. In successful movements like marriage equality, gun rights, anti–drunk driving, and tobacco control, leaders have figured out how to strike a balance between being too leaderless or too leader-led. At the end of the day, winning movement leaders learn how to harness the energy around them and channel it toward a common cause—like catching lightning in a bottle. Hold on too tight, and risk snuffing out that energy. Or let it go too wild, and the fireworks might be spectacular—but only for a moment. The best movements keep the light burning bright for as long as it takes to *make change happen*.

Notes

1. Candace Lightner interview, August 8, 2016. See also Fell, James C., and Voas, Robert B. "Mothers Against Drunk Driving (MADD): The First 25 Years." *Traffic Injury Prevention*, 2006, 7(3), 197.
2. *Ibid.*
3. Weed, Frank J. "The MADD Queen: Charisma and the Founder of Mothers Against Drunk Driving." University of Texas at Arlington, *Leadership Quarterly*, 4(3/4), 341. JAI Press, Inc. 1993.
4. Candace Lightner, email exchanges on December 9 and 11, 2017.
5. Candace Lightner interview, August 8, 2016.
6. "Drunk Driving Deaths 1982–2016." Official Web site of MADD. https://www.madd.org/state-statistics/.
7. Payne, Charles. "Ella Baker and Social Change," *Journal of Women in Culture and Society*, 1989, 14(4). http://classes.maxwell.syr.edu/wmstory/EllaBaker.pdf. Accessed November 2017.
8. Weed, Frank J. "The MADD Queen," page 337.
9. *Ibid.*, page 338.
10. Christiane Amanpour, "How MADD Changed American Culture." Candy Lightner interview, December 20, 2012.
11. Candace Lightner interview, August 2016.
12. *Ibid.*
13. Fell, James C., and Voas, Robert B. "MADD: The First 25 Years," page 201.
14. *Ibid*, page 197.
15. *Ibid.*
16. *Ibid.*
17. Brafman, Ori, and Beckstrom, Rod A. *The Starfish and the Spider: The Unstoppable Power of Leaderless Organizations*. New York: Penguin Group, 2006.
18. Payne, Charles. "Ella Baker and Social Change," 1989.

19. "Misconceptions About the Black Lives Matter Movement." Black Lives Matter Web site, http://blacklivesmatter.com/11-major-misconceptions-about-the-black-lives-matter-movement/. Accessed September 10, 2017.

20. *Ibid.* Accessed September 10, 2017.

21. Stolberg, Sheryl Gay, and Kantor, Jodi. "Shy No More: NRA's Top Gun Sticks to Cause." *New York Times*, April 13, 2013. http://www.nytimes.com/2013/04/14/us/wayne-lapierre-the-gun-man-sticking-to-his-cause.html. Accessed August 18, 2017. See also Taddonio, P. "The Evolution of Wayne LaPierre." January 6, 2015. https://www.pbs.org/wgbh/frontline/article/the-evolution-of-wayne-lapierre/. From the documentary film, "Gunned Down: The Power of the NRA." *Frontline*, PBS. Aired January 6, 2015. https://www.pbs.org/wgbh/frontline/film/gunned-down/.

22. Zoroya, Gregg. "The Sunday Profile: On the Defensive." *Los Angeles Times*, June 25, 1995. http://articles.latimes.com/1995–06–25/news/ls-16843_1_wayne-lapierre. Accessed August 18, 2017.

23. Stolberg, Sheryl Gay, and Kantor, Jodi. "Shy No More."

24. Breslow, J. "NRA Insiders on the Politics of Guns." January 6, 2015. https://www.pbs.org/wgbh/frontline/article/nra-insiders-on-the-politics-of-guns/. Based on the film, "Gunned Down: The Power of the NRA." *Frontline*. PBS. https://www.pbs.org/wgbh/frontline/film/gunned-down/.

25. Taddonio, P. "The Evolution of Wayne LaPierre." January 6, 2015. https://www.pbs.org/wgbh/frontline/article/the-evolution-of-wayne-lapierre/. Based on the film, "Gunned Down: The Power of the NRA." *Frontline*. PBS. https://www.pbs.org/wgbh/frontline/film/gunned-down/.

26. Stolberg, Sheryl Gay, and Kantor, Jodi. "Shy No More."

27. *Ibid.*

28. *Ibid.*

29. *Ibid.*

30. *Ibid.*

31. *Ibid.*

32. *Ibid.*

33. Zoroya, Gregg. "The Sunday Profile: On the Defensive." *Los Angeles Times*, June 25, 1995. Accessed August 18, 2017.

34. Surowiecki, James. "Taking on the N.R.A." *The New Yorker*. October 19, 2015. https://www.newyorker.com/magazine/2015/10/19/taking-on-the-n-r-a. Accessed September 10, 2017.

35. Dunne, John S. *The City of the Gods: A Study in Myth and Mortality.* South Bend, IN: University of Notre Dame Press, 1978.

36. Solomon, Marc. *Winning Marriage: The Inside Story of How Same-Sex Couples Took on the Politicians and Pundits—and Won.* Lebanon, NH: ForeEdge, 2014, page 302.

37. Crutchfield, Leslie R., and McLeod Grant, Heather. *Forces for Good: The Six Practices of High-Impact Nonprofits*. San Francisco: Jossey-Bass, 2010.

38. Occupy Wall Street Web Site. http://occupywallstreet.net/learn. Accessed September 2, 2017.

39. NB: the Occupy Wall Street movement describes itself as ". . . full of people who lead by example. We are leader-full, and this makes us strong." This "leader-full" reference appears to be related to, but not the same as, the "leaderfull" approach we are describing in *How Change Happens*.

40. Ungerleider, Neal. "The Stealth Leaders of Occupy Wall Street," *Fast Company*, October 7, 2011. https://www.fastcompany.com/1785698/stealth-leaders-occupy-wall-street. Retrieved September 2, 2017.

41. Occupy Wall Street Web Site. http://occupywallstreet.net/learn. Accessed September 2, 2017.

42. Zara, Christopher. "Occupy Wall Street a Failure? OWS 2014 Marks Survival of Brand with Blurred Purpose." *International Business Times*, September 17, 2014. http://www.ibtimes.com/occupy-wall-street-failure-ows-2014-marks-survival-brand-blurred-purpose-1690198. Accessed September 2, 2017.

43. Levitin, Michael. "The Triumph of Occupy Wall Street," *The Atlantic*, Friday, June 19, 2015, Op-Ed. http://www.truth-out.org/opinion/item/31395-the-triumph-of-occupy-wall-street. Accessed September 2, 2017.

44. *Ibid.*

45. Former Brady Campaign grassroots division leader Brian Malte notes that a variety of factors prevented the Brady Campaign from fully embracing the state council structure and elevating the Brady/MMM chapters. These included difficulties locating and communicating with the chapters, and the fact that after the 9/11 terrorist attacks, Brady lost significant funding and had to lay off 20 percent of its staff; as a result there weren't sufficient resources at that point in time. Email exchange with Brian Malte, December 19, 2017.

46. Senge, Peter, Hamilton, Hal, and Kania, John. "The Dawn of System Leadership," *Stanford Social Innovation Review*, Winter 2015. Accessed September 3, 2017.

Conclusion:
Where We Go from Here
From Forces for Good to
How Change Happens

HOW CHANGE HAPPENS picks up where *Forces for Good: The Six Practices of High-Impact Nonprofits* leaves off. The driving question behind *Forces for Good* was: "What makes great nonprofits great?" The answer: High-impact nonprofits build *movements*, not just organizations. The best nonprofits work outside their four walls to advance causes that go beyond their singular missions or programs. The research findings in *Forces for Good* led to another question: What makes great *movements* great? The answer to that question is revealed in the chapters of this book.

Not surprisingly, many of the findings in *How Change Happens* echo or amplify ideas introduced in *Forces for Good*. However, there is a key difference: In this book, the unit of analysis was not just individual organizations, but entire *movements*—the constellations of nonprofits, government agencies, policy shops, businesses, faith-based organizations, associations, media, and millions of individual grassroots community members that make up any major change effort. The landscapes of movements are so broad, their histories so deep, and their intra-workings so complex that it has been supremely challenging to distill salient lessons readers can use. We realize we may not have captured *all* of the factors that explain why some movements succeed and others don't in *How Change Happens*, but we believe we found the important ones.

171

It's also worth noting that, when we set out to write *How Change Happens*, we didn't attempt to study *every* modern movement erupting in recent decades. We picked a handful that had achieved very clearly defined outcomes between the 1980s and 2010s. That way, we could easily distinguish successful movements from others and try to detect why some advanced, while others lost ground. There are many other important causes we might also have chosen to examine. But our focus on a select few movements that have definitely tipped the scales one way or the other still gave us plenty of material to consider. It allowed us to see patterns within mountains of data and to harvest insights that can help advocates fighting for almost every cause that concerns society in the 21st century.

So where do we go from here? What do the findings in *How Change Happens* mean for *your* movement?

Let's start with movements that are just now emerging. Progressive causes like Black Lives Matter, All Lives Matter, and the "Fight for 15" national minimum wage campaigns are surging, alongside conservative uprisings for immigration reform and other nativist campaigns. Every emerging movement can apply the lessons from this book [Author's note: We reject the thought that a hate group might use this knowledge to advance their goals.] As readers think about how to tackle issues like racism and other social justice concerns such as poverty and economic mobility, we encourage you to look at the lessons from the successful movements in this book and consider what you can do to incorporate them into your work. Where do you excel? Where do you fall short?

For instance, Black Lives Matter has strong momentum as its activists are capturing worldwide attention by "turning grassroots gold" through protests, marches, and demonstrations in response to new police shootings of unarmed black men. But what are the opportunities to win over hearts and minds *and* change public policies to advance their agenda of tolerance and equity? How can Black Lives Matter members and other civil rights groups leaders foster long-sought social norm shifts and overturn the stereotypes and misperceptions that cause such harm to communities of color in the United States? As activists consider the possibilities, they could think about how to sharpen a 10/10/10/20 = 50 vision so campaigns have a clear state-by-state policy focus and are designed to meet diverse communities where they are in cultural terms (for better or for worse). As Freedom to Marry National Campaign Director Marc Solomon noted, it's important to have a federal strategy *and* a national one. For most states, the LGBT movement's goal was to remove discriminatory laws from the books; in only a handful of states did they push for full marriage. But by nudging the country incrementally forward to greater tolerance—and putting the "love is love" message at the core—the collective weight of the LGBT movement bent the arc of history toward justice.

While some movements have been in progress for a century or more, others crop up as new problems in society arise. One startling trend since the 1980s has been the fast-growing rates of obesity in the United States. Nearly 75 percent of American men and more than 60 percent of women are now obese or overweight, along with one-third of young people.[1] With obesity comes increased rates of other diseases, such as diabetes and heart disease, and a range of other afflictions. How did Americans grow so big, so quickly? The answer isn't as simple as overeating. A combination of factors plays a role: ubiquitous marketing and almost limitless availability of corn syrup–laden soft drinks and fattening, hard-to-resist foods like salty snacks, sugary sweets, and quick-serve meals. Available now around the clock at rock-bottom prices, high-calorie, unhealthy foods today are the default sustenance for too many low-income families. While obesity afflicts both rich and poor communities, the paradox of low-income people being both overweight *and* food insecure is mind-boggling.

Further, bad-for-you food is not only everywhere, but there's *more* of it. Today the standard serving of ice cream is a half-cup; it used to be one modest scoop—as an occasional treat, not a daily milk substitute. While it's easy to blame profit-hungry food companies for the ballooning weight of the nation, food manufacturers and restaurants are not the sole source of the malady. Other factors come into play too: changing habits—screen time spent surfing mobile devices, playing video games, and binge-watching TV—combined with fewer safe outdoor places to exercise and play.[2]

What it will take to reduce an entire nation's weight is an extraordinarily complex challenge. Signs of progress in some communities are pointing the way. The collective impact approach deployed by Shape Up Somerville out of Tufts University offers hope, as cross-sector groups effectively reversed obesity trends among youth with a combination of grassroots activism, policy, and behavior change campaigns.[3] It will take time to replicate Shape Up Somerville's success in other communities, as ChildObesity180 is now attempting to do. What's needed on a national scale is the "full vaccine": coordinated changes in business policies and practices—especially with regard to portions and ingredient mixes; government policy changes at municipal, state, and federal levels; and societal norm and cultural attitude shifts.

As we know from our three years of research for this book, these changes will only happen when there is a grassroots-fueled movement led by people with the *lived experience* of the problem agitating from the bottom up, along with savvy *networked* coalitions of organizational leaders coordinating at the grass-tops who understand that their role is to coordinate and align the players around them in collective action. They do this by building "leaderfull" movements and by focusing on changing hearts as well as policies. These are the strategies that made the difference for the winning movements profiled in *How Change Happens*.

The six chapters at the core of this book form a framework for thinking about how to deliver the "full vaccine" for your movement. To win, movement leaders can strive to master all six of the elements described herein and work on them in tandem in order to achieve maximum impact. To stimulate your thinking, we've outlined some high-level questions in Table C.1 to ask as you think about the causes you lead or support.

The winning movements in this book advanced their causes by firing on all six of these cylinders. But it's important to note that even though certain movements had "won" by the time of this writing, none of their victories can be considered permanent. Nothing in today's socio-political landscape is fixed. As cigarette companies continue to enjoy a license to operate in the United States—albeit now a more restricted one—they focus on exporting their deadly products globally. For instance, Philip Morris recently launched a global marketing campaign for its best-selling Marlboro cigarettes: "Be Marlboro." The campaign rolled out in sixty countries featuring young people partying, falling in love, playing music, and engaging in risky behavior.[4] Domestically, smoking rates for adults hover just under one in five nationally, but that statistic hides a lumpier reality: In "tobacco nation," many states in the central and southern parts of the country have much higher rates of smoking than the national average.

Table C.1. Movement Best Practices

Practice	Questions to Consider
Turn Grassroots Gold	Does our movement . . . ■ Actively recruit, nurture, and grow a grassroots constituency, or do we collaborate closely with other groups that do? ■ Invest in building bonds between our members, creating and cementing trust *between* them, as well as connecting to our broader common purpose? ■ Offer modern and robust communications channels to keep the organizations in touch with grassroots and connect grassroots members with each other? ■ Put people with the *lived experience* of our problem at the front of the movement?
Sharpen Your 10/10/10/20 = 50 Vision	Does our movement . . . ■ Embrace a local *and* a national campaign strategy, working to influence all three branches of the federal government while also advocating in each of the fifty U.S. states? ■ If our cause is global, does our movement have a country-by-country change strategy and local boots on the ground to drive policy and social norm change? ■ Support coalitions at the local and regional level advancing policy and social change objectives within states? ■ Embrace a *networked* leadership structure that allows organizations to act within their own states or communities but also in centrally coordinated ways that advance the larger cause? ■ Engage in litigation, policy lobbying, and electoral influence strategies tailored to all fifty states (or if global, each targeted country)?
Change Hearts *and* Policy	Does our movement . . . ■ Have deliberate, resourced strategies to change individual attitudes, beliefs, and behaviors to shift broader social norms? ■ Convey messages and social marketing campaigns that penetrate people at their human cores, that is, have we found our core message of "love" (LGBT marriage), "truth" (teen smoking), or "freedom" (gun rights)?

Practice	Questions to Consider
	<ul><li>Conduct formative research to fully understand the minds of the people whose behaviors and attitudes we are trying to shift?</li><li>Segment our audience so we know exactly whose heartstrings need to be pulled in order to advance our cause? (Hint: It's usually the most powerful voting blocks and opinion leaders in society, not your core audience of already-converted supporters.)</li><li>Create social marketing strategies that take into account the full marketing mix across all four P's: product, price, place, and promotion?</li><li>Deploy differentiated but coordinated social media and traditional media strategies?</li></ul>
Reckon with Adversarial Allies	Does our movement . . . <ul><li>Realistically assess not only who our opponents are, but also who the allies are on *our* side of the issue who will likely reject or disagree with our approach?</li><li>Know our adversarial allies personally and try proactively to build relationships, or at least open communications with them? Or do we ignore them or dismiss them as extremists?</li><li>Knowing extreme views exist on all sides of every issue, have we built "enough" of a quorum behind our core cause that we can overcome the extremes?</li><li>Have we thought about what we will do to counteract or neutralize attacks from allies on our side of the issue?</li><li>Are we spending our time battling our true enemies, or do we actually spend our time mostly fighting among ourselves? If the answer is the latter, how can we refocus the movement on our foes, and away from attacking each other?</li></ul> As you answer these questions, keep in mind these four factors when it comes to dealing with adversarial allies: <ol><li>*Count on conflict:* The most common fights are waged over money, power, access, and credit. Some of these things can be sorted out in advance, because they are not central to the movement's cause. Work out an MOU or other working arrangements that settle what will happen with donor lists, leftover funds, and other assets *before* the campaign begins.</li></ol>

Practice	Questions to Consider
	2. *Plan for philosophical divisions:* There will be fault lines some sides simply cannot cross. You will not get beyond it. How can you deal with that fact head-on?
	3. *Let go of the ego:* Lose yourself in the coalition. Don't worry about your organization's identity or brand within the context of the coalition; you can advance it in other ways.
	4. *Don't dismiss your adversarial allies:* Even when the extremes are *very* extreme, you have to include them in the planning. Don't assume they are without power or supporters.
Break from Business as Usual	Does our movement . . .
	■ See corporations as "the enemy" or dismiss them as irrelevant to our cause?
	■ Have we assessed the four ways we might engage with business to advance our issue, including as . . .
	1. Policy first-movers
	2. Product innovators
	3. Advocates and educators
	4. Hyper-exposed targets of protest
	■ Have we fully considered how markets can be harnessed to advance our cause?
Be Leaderfull	Does our movement . . .
	■ Practice "leaderfull" leadership, versus a purely democratic "leader-less" approach or a top-down "leader-led" approach?
	■ Embrace the core tenants of being "leaderfull" by:
	1. Empowering leaders at the state and local levels to lead
	2. Creating "big-tent" coalitions of both likely and unlikely allies
	3. Embodying a "networked" leadership structure among grass-tops
	4. Putting people with the *lived experience* of the issue at the center and out front of the movement at all times
	■ Have leaders that share in common traits such as:
	1. Come from a mix of likely and unlikely backgrounds
	2. Listen to the point of transcendence
	3. Let go of the ego
	4. Relentlessly pursue *impact* (rather than credit, power, fame, or fortune)

"Progress is never permanent, will always be threatened, must be redoubled, restated, and reimagined if it is to survive," writes author Zadie Smith, as quoted in a recent Ford Foundation e-newsletter sent by CEO Darren Walker. To protect progress—or to overturn it if you're advocating from the other side—readers can use the ideas in this book to their advantage. Which ideas, and how you engage with them, depends on where you sit within the larger ecosystem that makes up each of these movements.

Who You Are Matters

Whether you lead a nonprofit, chair a coalition, head a foundation, hold an elected or appointed public office, run a business, volunteer, or are simply an individual who cares about a cause, you can use the knowledge in this book to advance it. How you deploy the best practices depends on where you sit. If you work for or represent . . .

Foundations or High-Net-Worth Individuals

Your role in movements is critical—whether you help advance them or unwittingly hamper them. We've seen funders do plenty of both. We looked closely at how each of the movements in this book raised resources and saw a great deal of variation—both among the winning causes and across the also-rans.

Certainly the $700 million the Robert Wood Johnson Foundation committed to tobacco control over a decade played a critical role in the success of the anti-smoking cause. It wasn't just the *amount* of money (although significant and unprecedented); it was the *way* RWJF's then-CEO Steve Schroeder and vice president Nancy Kaufman and their colleagues invested it. The biggest chunk went to *SmokeLess States*, fueling coalitions and alliances of grassroots groups to agitate, educate, and persuade at local and state levels. The next biggest amount went to Campaign for Tobacco-Free Kids, which was set up to play the central networked leadership role, or "backbone," for the cause, pulling into its coalition leaders from the American Cancer Society, American Heart Association, American Medical Association, and others to collaborate for collective wins. RWJF seeded the campaign, then stepped back. The Campaign for Tobacco-Free Kids went on to engage in national and federal policy advocacy pushes, and it provided technical assistance to the state-based coalitions.

Most importantly, RWJF leaders understood that they needed to support advocacy, not just individual smoking cessation programs. And they recognized that money toward marketing and communications wasn't extraneous but well spent. Conversely, more traditional foundations have made mistakes and shied away from funding in ways that enable grassroots advocates to flourish and have ignored the need for social marketing—to their causes' peril.

In the less effective movements we studied, we saw funders often playing more harmful than helpful roles. In one scathing report commissioned in 2002 by a gun control funders collaborative, a consultant unsparingly assessed the state of the movement after the Million Mom March merged with the Brady Campaign.[5] Stories of policy conflicts, territorial scraps, and other destructive behaviors among the nonprofits involved in the gun control movement were documented. But equally disturbing was the behavior of the *funders* in the movement. Granted, only a handful of foundations at that time, including George Soros's Open Society Institute, Joyce Foundation, and others, had an appetite for funding gun control. But most of the funders in the game could not seem to agree on which policy positions and campaign strategies to back, so philanthropists scattered their support to myriad pet projects, backing opposing organizations in ways that reinforced the competitive dynamics in the field rather than soothing them.

In one case, multi-millionaire Monster.com founder Andy McKelvey had offered $2 million to the fledgling Million Mom March (MMM) grassroots group. But after MMM merged with The Bell Campaign (and then Bell re-named itself Million Mom March and soon merged with the Brady Campaign), McKelvey chose not to fund it after all. Writes Donna Dees-Thomases, ". . . instead he put his $2 million into a new Washington, D.C.–based group called Americans for Gun Safety."[6] This resulted in further distortion and splintering of an already disjointed gun safety field—at the exact time the NRA was aggregating power by building up its dues-paying membership rolls and *doubling down* on its grassroots campaigns.

Gun violence preventions funders would be well-served to take a page from the marriage equality campaign playbook. An instrumental behind-the-scenes player in that movement was mega-donor Tim Gill.

Gill poured $422 million into the cause of equal rights for the LGBT community over three decades—more than any one person in America.[7] In 1994 he launched the Gill Foundation to underwrite research, polling, litigation, data analytics, and field organizing to advance LGBT causes. A decade later he launched Gill Action, a political group that has helped elect hundreds of pro-equality lawmakers at the local, state, and federal levels. As *Rolling Stone* reports, "Gill's fingerprints are on nearly every major victory in the march to marriage."[8]

Like RWJF, Gill poured big money into the movement in exactly the right ways: He funded grassroots organizations and state and local electioneering, and he tailored his support to the 10/10/10/20 = 50 strategy that ultimately tipped the Supreme Court in favor of LGBT marriage. He also leveraged his power as a mega-donor/convener rather than a dictator; he helped convene the transcendent Jersey City meeting described at the start of Chapter Two. At that point in history, the marriage movement was at a crossroads, and he helped coax major LGBT group leaders to gather behind closed doors to reflect on why they were losing so badly, and he helped them coalesce around a different path forward. Gill didn't come up with the plan. He helped set the table so the field could come to it, together.

Donors have the power to dramatically propel a cause forward, and they can also smother it, undermine it, or destroy it in myriad other ways.

Government—Policy Officials and Agency Heads

Whether elected, appointed, or career hires, government actors play vital roles in movements. They can steer research to help advance causes, like CDC-funded studies that helped unearth the dangers of smoking, or the National Highway Traffic and Safety Administration's backing of MADD and other group efforts to advance road safety. Conversely, movements can tie up government support to block their opponents: The NRA has shrewdly influenced government policies so that federal agencies could not engage in gun safety and violence prevention research.[9] Without a government patron, it's very difficult for public campaigns to gain traction—unless there is ample private support.[10]

Another role officials who hold high office can play is to throw their political clout behind a cause. This non-financial support can be priceless. When New York Governor-Elect Andrew Cuomo promised to make LGBT marriage a priority of his administration, this was a mighty lever. To make use of it, sparring LGBT groups needed to align behind a common strategy and collaborate rather than compete. Cuomo's offer proved potent—his pledge of support was the carrot activists needed to "get their shit together and work together," as Solomon recalls.[11]

Business

Whether you run or work for a corporation, think about the myriad ways business can help advance causes you care about. Although conservative thinkers like Milton Friedman argued that corporations should stay out of funding or engaging in charitable or advocacy causes, many companies today from global *Fortune* 500 companies to mom-and-pop Main Street businesses are getting in the game. Some do it by creating shared value, blending financial, social, and environmental goals. Others do it through strategies outlined in Chapter Five, "Break from Business as Usual." They can act as first policy movers, as the airline industry did in enacting the first smoking bans; as allies in advocacy and education; or as engineers of innovative products and services. But businesses must also beware: Now more than ever, they risk being hyper-exposed targets of protests and extreme "actions" mounted by NGOs. To avoid being put under the global glare of activists, companies can at the very least stop engaging operations and activities that harm workers, community members, or the environment.

Nonprofits and Citizen Activists

If you lead, work for, volunteer with, or in other ways support nonprofits, this book is made for you. Every chapter contains ideas and advice you can employ to advance the causes you care about. You can use it whether you serve at the helm, on staff, on the board, or as a volunteer, member, or donor.

And as for readers who aren't currently part of any nonprofits, we urge you to join some. Your impact is more limited when you act alone than if you join up with others. You can also take heart in the fact that many of the leaders profiled in this book had no or limited experience with nonprofits—or social activism, for that matter—before they became involved with their movements. While some were experienced lawyers or seasoned lobbyists, the majority were not.

Whether your role is as a leader on the front lines of national change or as a supporter inching a cause forward locally one petition signature, phone call, or town hall meeting at a time, you can make a difference—just as the diverse people profiled in this book have done. You multiply your impact when you join networks and collaborate with others, because then you are part of a system that can achieve something greater together than any one element could do alone. That's what makes systems work.

As Robert F. Kennedy said, "Few will have the greatness to bend history itself, but each of us can work to change a small portion of events. It is from numberless diverse acts of courage and belief that human history is shaped. Each time a man stands up for an ideal, or acts to improve the lot of others, or strikes out against injustice, he sends forth a tiny ripple of hope, and crossing each other from a million different centers of energy and daring those ripples build a current which can sweep down the mightiest walls of oppression and resistance."

That is *how change happens*.

Notes

1. The Institute for Health Metrics and Evaluation (IHME), a population health research center at UW Medicine, part of the University of Washington. http://www.healthdata.org/news-release/vast-majority-ameri can-adults-are-overweight-or-obese-and-weight-growing-problem-among. Accessed November 9, 2017.
2. Full disclosure: Global Social Enterprise Initiative is working on a project funded by Nestlé to explore seeding a portion-focused anti-obesity campaign.
3. Kania, John, and Kramer, Mark. "Collective Impact." *Stanford Social Information Review*, 2011.
4. Campaign for Tobacco-Free Kids Web site: https://www.tobaccofreekids.org/ press-releases/2017_09_13_pmi. Accessed November 9, 2017.
5. Report archived at Alliance for Justice, 11 DuPont Circle NW, Suite 200, Washington, DC, 2006. Accessed July 29, 2016.
6. Dees-Thomases, Donna, and Hendrie, Alison. *Looking for a Few Good Moms*. Harlan, IA: Rodale Press, 2004, page 201.
7. Kroll, A. "Meet the Megadonor Behind the LGBTQ Rights Movement: How Tim Gill Turned a $500 Million Fortune into the Nation's Most Powerful

Force for LGBTQ Rights." *Rolling Stone*, June 23, 2017. http://www.rolling-stone.com/politics/features/meet-tim-gill-megadonor-behind-lgbtq-rights-movement-wins-w489213. Accessed November 9, 2017.

8. *Ibid.*
9. Couric, K. narrator, *Under the Gun* documentary film, directed by Stephanie Soechtig. 2016.
10. Goss, Kristin A. *Disarmed: The Missing Movement for Gun Control in America*. Princeton, NJ: Princeton University Press, 2006.
11. Marc Solomon interview.

Appendix A: Research Parameters

THE DRIVING QUESTION behind the research for *How Change Happens* was: Why do some movements succeed while others don't? We wanted to understand why successful movements triumphed and others did not, with the specific purpose of extracting insights that could be applied by today's changemakers to advance causes.

Research for this book was led by author Leslie Crutchfield, who was joined by twenty-one colleagues and graduate student assistants who made up the *How Change Happens* research team. This team was housed at the Global Social Enterprise Initiative (GSEI) at Georgetown University's McDonough School of Business. Founded by Professor of the Practice Bill Novelli in 2011, GSEI delivers research, education, and actionable solutions that drive shared social, environmental, and financial impact. The GSEI team is currently comprised of sixteen Georgetown staff and affiliated project leaders, and thirty-nine GSEI student leaders participate in the academic year 2018. For the *How Change Happens* research project, seven graduate student researchers contributed to the project on a work-study basis. All team members are recognized in the Acknowledgments.

Research for *How Change Happens* began in earnest in 2015, when Leslie Crutchfield joined the GSEI team as a senior research fellow. Working closely with Bill Novelli and former GSEI Executive Director Ladan Manteghi, supported by the team of seven graduate student researchers, Crutchfield has spent nearly three years studying some of the most significant social changes of the last few decades, specifically, changes that had occurred between 1980 and 2016.

As a research team, we made deliberate choices based on a few parameters to help us narrow the list of movements for study. One choice was around timing: We focused specifically on societal shifts that had occurred *since the 1980s*. We wanted to understand how change happens in the *modern era*—within current political, social, and economic contexts. This meant we did not study movements that had peaked prior to the 1980s (such as the civil rights, suffrage, and earlier waves of the environmental movement—although writings about these movements significantly informed our thinking). And while we took into consideration the fact that many modern movements have long tails, we tried to focus primarily on events and actions occurring since the 1980s. For instance, emerging movements like Black Lives Matter; "We are the 99 percent" campaigns for economic equality and a livable minimum wage; and the LGBT marriage equality campaign are all modern extensions of long-waged civil and labor rights struggles.

Another choice was to exclusively study changes that resulted in some form of specific social or environmental impact. We were interested in what led to demonstrable societal *outcomes*—lives saved through smoking cessation or drunk-driving reduction; liberties expanded through gun rights expansion or LGBT marriage rights. Therefore, we did not specifically look at political movements *per se*, such as the Tea Party, or other libertarian or populist movements. Nor did we study closely the progressive resistance erupting against the 2016 presidential election of Donald Trump, or the Green Party that supported presidential runs of Ralph Nader and Jill Stein. While political movements like these have unarguably influenced the major social and environmental outcomes of our time—as well as impacted the political elections on which they were focused—we looked at political movements mostly on the periphery, rather than as central foci of the research.

Geography and scale of impact also came into play as we chose the movements in our book. Each of the changes we examined occurred either at the national level within the United States or bi-nationally (across the United States and Canada), or they were led largely by U.S. actors on a global scale (the worldwide push for polio eradication led largely by Rotary International). Most of the changes we studied were manifest within the United States; all of them involved predominately U.S. organizations and individuals playing lead or prominent roles. Of course, globally significant, paradigm-shifting changes have happened in all corners of the earth since the 1980s. But what it takes to make fundamental societal change in socialist democracies of Western Europe or in the BRIC countries of Brazil, Russia, India, and China that are rapidly rising up or in emerging economies across Eastern Europe, Southeast Asia, Africa, or the Middle East, is largely determined by the unique social, political, economic, and cultural contexts of each of these very different places.

We hope the lessons from our study of changes occurring in the United States, or led largely by U.S. actors, will be helpful in influencing social change thinking and practice in other parts of the world. But we know these lessons are not uniformly transferrable—any more than "technology transfers" from the West have helped solve many developing-world problems (some have regretfully done more harm than good). We sincerely hope that scholars and change makers interested in how change happens in other parts of the world will conduct analyses of movements in countries outside of the United States, and share openly what they learn.

On the topic of comparative analysis: We purposely chose movements that had clear winners. We wanted to understand whether there was anything different about the way triumphant change campaigns were waged versus the opposing sides, as we've seen great insights emerge from comparing and contrasting divergent phenomena. Jim Collins popularized this approach in his business books *Built to Last* and *Good to Great*, which demonstrated why certain companies out-performed their industry peers under similar conditions. We found the compare-and-contrast model to be very revealing when writing *Forces for Good: The Six Practices of High-Impact Nonprofits*, which served as an important precursor to *How Change Happens*. So for this book, we picked a handful of causes with clear winners—such as tobacco control, gun rights, LGBT marriage equality, acid rain, and polio elimination.

Conversely, we chose not to delve into causes for which contenders seemed more evenly matched, such as the life versus choice battles over abortion. We also didn't closely examine issues that were "in progress" or whose outcomes had not yet been definitely determined as of this writing (such as immigration reform). Finally, it's worth noting: The purpose of this book is not to provide an all-encompassing assessment of every modern movement. We instead set out to study a select portfolio of movements and attempted to generate insights by comparing their approaches designed to help change makers advance causes, regardless of what side of the issue they stand on.

Which raises another research parameter: In selecting the causes for this book, we aimed for political and social neutrality. We tried to be objective and withhold normative judgment on whether a particular change was "good" or "bad." Some issues were crystal clear in their "rightness" or "wrongness": Eliminating a scourge like polio can only be seen as a positive change. But issues like expanding gun rights or curtailing smokers' liberties through tobacco control can be seen as more complicated. Finally, we chose to study changes that had happened on very wide scales—national or global population-wide changes.

In sum, the key elements of the extremely diverse causes we chose to study are twofold: (1) they represent large-scale, population-wide social or environmental impacts and (2) they unarguably *happened*. What we wanted to know is how, and why.

Appendix B:
List of Interviews

Anti–Drunk Driving

Barnes, Michael. Former president of Brady Campaign, board member of MADD, and Congressional Representative from Maryland, July 11, 2016

Lightner, Candace (Candy). Founder, Mothers Against Drunk Driving and president of We Save Lives, August 8, 2016, Arlington, Virginia, and December 18, 2017, via telephone; email exchanges on December 9 and 11, 2017

McGuire, Andrew. Executive director, Trauma Foundation; former board member, Bell Campaign/Million Mom March, and former board member, MADD, June 20 and 22, 2016

Weir, Debbie. CEO of MADD, July 12, 2016

Environment: Acid Rain and Climate Action

Boeve, May. Executive director, 350.org, July 28, 2016

Drayton, William. Founder, Ashoka, and former assistant administrator, Environmental Protection Agency, November 15, 2017

Dudek, Dan. Vice president of Environmental Defense Fund (excerpts from interviews for *Forces for Good*)

Goldmark, Peter. Former head of Climate Programs, Environmental Defense Fund, February 1, 2016

Hawkins, David. Director of NRDC Climate Programs and lecturer, Yale Forestry School, March 7, 2016

Krupp, Fred. President of Environmental Defense Fund, January 7, 2015

Shelby, Michael. Chief economist, Office of Transportation and Air Quality, Environmental Protection Agency, July 29, 2016

Wirth, Tim. Former senator from Colorado and vice chair of the United Nations Foundation and the Better World Fund, February 1, 2016

Guns

Aaron, Stephen. SVP, Mercury; former federal liaison, NRA, January 5, 2017

Aborn, Richard. Former president, Brady Campaign, and current president of the Citizens Crime Commission of New York City, August 1, 2017

Aron, Nan. Founder and president of Alliance for Justice, July 20, 2016

Barnes, Michael. Former president, Brady Campaign, board member of MADD and Congressional Representative from Maryland, July 11, 2016

Blek, Mary Leigh. President emeritus of Million Mom March, September 29, 2016

Caroline, Glen. Director, NRA-ILA Grassroots Division. Interview conducted at NRA Headquarters, Fairfax, Virginia, November 16, 2016, and email exchange on December 15, 2017

Feinblatt, John. President of Everytown for Gun Safety, August 1, 2017, and email exchange on December 18, 2017

Feulner, Ed. Former president, The Heritage Foundation, August 2, 2016

Horwitz, Joshua. Executive director of the Coalition to Stop Gun Violence, July 18, 2016

Makris, Anthony (Tim). Founder and managing director, Sandy Hook Promise, October 4, 2017, and email exchange on December 18, 2017

Malte, Brian. Former senior national policy director, Brady Campaign, June 9, 2016, Washington, DC, and email exchanges on December 17, 2017

McGuire, Andrew. Executive director, Trauma Foundation; former board member, Bell Campaign/Million Mom March, and former board member, MADD, June 20 and 22, 2016

Miller, Brian. Heeding God's Call/CeaseFire NJ, August 1, 2016

Morrison, Alan. Associate dean for public interest and public service law, George Washington University Law School, January 20, 2015

Rodgers, Samantha. Former chief organizing officer, Everytown for Gun Safety, June 7, 2016

Thomases, Donna Dees. Founder, Million Mom March, June 3 and June 7, 2016

Watts, Shannon. Founder, Moms Demand Action for Common Sense Gun Laws, August 1, 2017

LGBT Marriage Equality

Barrios, Jarret. Former member of both the Massachusetts House of Representatives and the Massachusetts Senate and first Latino and first openly gay man elected to the Massachusetts Senate, March 9, 2016

Coles, Matt. ACLU deputy legal director and director of the Center for Equality, April 19, 2016

Rose, Carol. Executive director, ACLU of Massachusetts, March 17, 2016

Rouse, Marty. Human Rights Campaign (HRC) national field director and former director, MassEquality, April 20, 2016

Shapiro, Norma. Legislative director, ACLU Massachusetts, May 2, 2016

Solomon, Marc. Author of *Winning Marriage* and former national campaign director, Freedom to Marry, November 16, 2015

Swislow, Lee. Director of Facing Cancer Together, Inc., former executive director, Gay & Lesbian Advocates & Defenders (GLAD) and former member of the MassEquality coalition, April 8, 2016

Wolfson, Evan. Founder, Freedom to Marry, August 2, 2017, and September 2, 2017

Mass Incarceration and Criminal Justice Reform

Busansky, Alex. President, Impact Justice, October 28, 2016

Knight, Ali. Chief development officer, Fly, October 7, 2016

Morial, Marc, CEO, National Urban League, October 13, 2017

Norris, Zachary. Executive director of the Ella Baker Center for Human Rights and former director of Books Not Bars, January 19, 2017

Polio

Aylward, Bruce. Former executive director, GPEI; executive director ad interim of the Outbreaks and Health Emergencies Cluster, World Health Organization (WHO), July 26, 2016

Bates, Nicole Bates. Deputy director, Polio Advocacy, Bill & Melinda Gates Foundation, July 12, 2015

Calvin, Kathy. CEO, The UN Foundation, February 1, 2016

Frieden, Thomas. Director of the Centers for Disease Control and Prevention (CDC) and administrator of the Agency for Toxic Substances and Disease Registry (ATSDR), August 8, 2016

Guirguis, Sherine. Senior communications manager, Polio Eradication, UNICEF, July 28, 2016

Lange, John Lange. Former ambassador and senior fellow, Global Health Diplomacy, UN Foundation, July 30, 2016

McGovern, Michael McGovern, member of the Board of Trustees, Rotary International, July 6, 2016

Pandak, Carol. Director, PolioPlus, Rotary International, July 15, 2016

Teen Pregnancy

Brown, Sarah. Former CEO, The National Campaign to Prevent Teen Pregnancy and Unplanned Pregnancy, June 29, 2016

Panjabi, Chitra. President and CEO, Sexuality Information and Education Council of the United States (SIECUS), July 12, 2016

Tobacco

Glantz, Stanton A. Professor of Medicine, University of California, San Francisco, and director, UCSF Center for Tobacco Control Research and Education, March 7, 2016

Hallett, Cynthia. CEO of American for Nonsmokers Rights, September 21, 2016

Kaufman, Nancy, RN, MS. President, Strategic Vision Group LLC, and former vice president, Robert Wood Johnson Foundation, March 9, 2015

Myers, Matthew. President and CEO, Campaign for Tobacco-Free Kids, January 5, 2015, email exchange on December 26, 2017.

Novelli, William. Professor of the practice, Georgetown University McDonough School of Business, co-chair of the Coalition to Transform Advanced Care, and founding president, Campaign for Tobacco-Free Kids, November 24, 2015

Parrish, Steve. Former general counsel at Philip Morris, current principal, Steve Parrish Consulting Group, LLC, December 30, 2015

Spegman, Jerry. Former RWJF program officer, *SmokeLess States*, March 21, 2016

Appendix C: Additional Resources on Movements and Systems

THIS APPENDIX CONTAINS select recommended readings, films, and organizational information for readers who want to delve more deeply into the specific histories of some of the movements featured in this book. These listings are organized by movement (or cause) in alphabetical order. The listings are not exhaustive, and not every modern movement peaking since the 1980–2016 period is mentioned. Included at the end are also recommended readings on social movements and marketing, systems, networks, and complexity.

Guns

Select Books on Gun Violence Prevention and Gun Rights

Cook, Philp J., and Goss, Kristin A. *The Gun Debate: What Everybody Needs to Know*. New York: Oxford University Press, 2014.

Dees-Thomases, Donna, and Hendrie, Alison. *Looking for a Few Good Moms: How One Mother Rallied a Million Others Against the Gun Lobby*. Harlan, IA: Rodale Books, 2004.

Goss, Kristin A. *Disarmed: The Missing Movement for Gun Control in America*. Princeton, NJ: Princeton University Press, 2006.

LaPierre, Wayne. *Guns, Crime, and Freedom*. New York: HarperPerennial: 1994.
Meltzer, Scott. *Gun Crusaders: The NRA's Culture War*. New York: New York University Press, 2009.
Winkler, Adam. *Gunfight: The Battle Over the Right to Bear Arms in America*. New York: W.W. Norton & Company, 2011, 2013.

Select Films and Videos for Gun Violence Prevention

"Gunned Down: The Power of the NRA." *Frontline*, PBS, aired January 6, 2015. https://www.pbs.org/wgbh/frontline/film/gunned-down/.
"Tomorrow's News" video posted on Sandy Hook Promise official Web site https://www.sandyhookpromise.org/tomorrowsnews.
Under the Gun, directed by Stephanie Soechtig. New York: Epix, 2016, online documentary.

Select Organizations and Coalitions for Gun Rights

American Conservative Union

www.conservative.org/

Founded in 1964 by author William F. Buckley Jr., the American Conservative Union Foundation is a 501(c)3 organization best known for putting on the Conservative Political Action Conference, which is also co-sponsored by the NRA. The American Conservative Union Political Action Committee formally endorses and funds conservative candidates for federal office.

Gun Owners of America

www.gunowners.org/

Founded in 1975 by H.L. Richardson when legislation to ban all handguns was introduced in California, GOA is a 501(c)4 nonprofit. Gun Owners Foundation (GOF) is a nonprofit, tax-deductible educational foundation that acts as the research arm for GOA. Its main objective is to hold seminars around the country to inform the public, media outlets, and various government officials on Second Amendment issues.

National Association for Gun Rights

www.nationalgunrights.org/

Founded in 2000 by Dudley Brown, NAGR is a 501(c)4 nonprofit that supports no-permit constitutional carry; their political action committee is NAGR-PAC.

National Rifle Association (NRA)

www.home.nra.org/

The NRA is dedicated to defending the Second Amendment and to prevent and remove restrictions on gun ownership and use. Founded in 1871 in New York City as a charitable 501(c)3 nonprofit, this sportsmen's membership group was originally dedicated mainly to advancing rifle marksmanship and teaching firearm competency and safety. In the 1970s, the NRA became politically active under new libertarian leaders, who aimed to link gun ownership with American notions of freedom and limited government. The NRA launched in 1975 the Institute for Legislative Action (ILI), a 501(c)4 functioning as the NRA's main lobbying and campaign operation, and a PAC, the NRA Political Victory Fund in 1976 to support pro-gun political candidates and challenge gun control candidates. Since then, the NRA's membership has grown from a couple hundred thousand members to nearly five million by 2016.

Second Amendment Foundation

www.saf.org/

Founded in 1974, SAF is a 501(c)3 nonprofit, and publishes gun rights magazines and public education materials, funds conferences, provides media contacts, and has assumed a central role in sponsoring lawsuits. In addition, the Citizens Committee for the Right to Keep and Bear Arms (CCRKBA) is the lobbying affiliate of the SAF. As of January 2015, both groups reported having over 650,000 members.

Select Organizations and Coalitions for Gun Violence Prevention

Americans for Responsible Solutions

www.giffords.org

Founded by Gabrielle Giffords and Mark Kelly after the Sandy Hook Elementary shooting in 2012, Americans for Responsible Solutions is a 501(c)4 super PAC. Giffords, a former member of Congress (D-AZ), was a victim of an assassination attempt at a Safeway supermarket near Tucson, Arizona, where she was meeting publicly with constituents.

Brady Campaign to Prevent Gun Violence

www.bradycampaign.org/about-brady

The mission of the Brady Campaign is to create a safer America that will lead to a dramatic reduction in gun deaths and injuries. Brady's approaches to accomplish this includes a policy focus to "Finish the Job" so life-saving Brady background checks are applied to all gun sales; to "Stop 'Bad Apple'

Gun Dealers"—the 5 percent of gun dealers who supply 90 percent of all crime guns; and to lead a new national conversation and change social norms around the real dangers of guns in the home, to prevent the homicides, suicides, and unintentional shootings that happen every day as a result.

CeaseFire New Jersey

www.nj.gov/oag/ceasefire/

CeaseFire New Jersey is a gun violence prevention group, a project of New Jersey–based Coalition for Peace Action. Founded in 1988, the group advocates for common-sense gun laws, policy, and education, in an effort to end senseless gun violence.

Coalition to Stop Gun Violence and Educational Fund to Stop Gun Violence

www.csgv.org/ and http://efsgv.org/

In 1974, the United Methodist General Board of Church and Society formed the *National Coalition to Ban Handguns*, with the goal of addressing "the high rates of gun-related crime and death in American society" by licensing gun owners, registering firearms, and banning private ownership of handguns with "reasonable limited exceptions" for police, military, etc. In 1989, the group changed to its current name. The coalition is a 501(c)4 comprised of forty-eight member organizations.

Everytown for Gun Safety

www.everytown.org/

Founded in 2014 by philanthropist and former New York Mayor Michael Bloomberg, Everytown merged with Mayors Against Illegal Guns (MAIG) and Moms Demand Action for Gun Sense in America. Everytown operates as both a 501(c)3 and 501(c)4, and has four million supporters.

Faiths United to Prevent Gun Violence

www.faithsunited.org

An inter-denominational group formed in 2011 to mobilize members of the faith community to advocate for common sense gun laws.

Heeding God's Call

www.heedinggodscall.org/

A faith-based movement to prevent gun violence, primarily located in Washington, D.C., and Pennsylvania.

Lawyers for a Safer America

www.bradycampaign.org/our-impact/campaigns/lawyers-for-a-safer-america

A national alliance of lawyers and law firms that actively partner with the Legal Action Project to reduce gun violence in America through the courts.

Mayors Against Illegal Guns

https://everytown.org/mayors/

Founded in 2006 by former New York City Mayor Michael Bloomberg and former Boston Mayor Thomas Menino as a coalition of 15 mayors.

Million Mom March

www.bradycampaign.org/million-mom-timeline-15-year-anniversary

Million Mom March (MMM) is a grassroots movement started by Donna Dees-Thomases after a tragic shooting at the Los Angeles Jewish Community Center in Granada Hills, California, on August 10, 1999. More than 750,000 people marched in Washington, D.C., on Mother's Day, May 14, 2000. Initially, the group was part of the Trauma Foundation at San Francisco General Hospital. When Million Mom March merged with The Bell Campaign, the organization was re-named Million Mom March. In 2001, Andrew McGuire separated the MMM from The Bell Campaign and formed its own 501(c)3 and 501(c)4 organization. In 2001, MMM united with Handgun Control, Inc., and the Center to Prevent Handgun Violence to form the Brady Campaign to Prevent Gun Violence and the Brady Center.

Moms Demand Action for Gun Sense in America

https://momsdemandaction.org/

Founded by Shannon Watts in Indianapolis in 2012, after the Sandy Hook Elementary shooting in Newtown, Connecticut. By the end of 2013, the group had grown into an advocacy group with chapters in all fifty states; it merged with Everytown for Gun Safety in 2014.

National Gun Victims Action Council

www.gunvictimsaction.org/

The council was founded by Elliot Fineman after his only son, Michael, was fatally shot in 2006 by a mentally ill man with a legally purchased gun. The group is known for originating the 2010 "Brew Not Bullets" boycott against Starbucks, to change their policy on allowing open carry in their stores.

Sandy Hook Promise

www.sandyhookpromise.org/

Formed in the wake of the shooting at Sandy Hook Elementary School in 2012, the group is a national movement of parents, schools, and community organizations promoting the prevention of gun violence, along with passing sensible state and national gun laws.

States United to Prevent Gun Violence

ceasefireusa.org/

A grassroots network of thirty-two state affiliates who encourage existing gun violence prevention groups at the state level and work to bring new partners on board. The groups' efforts also focus on the importance of educating communities and reaching out through grassroots initiatives.

Violence Policy Center

www.vpc.org

Founded by Josh Sugarmann in 1988, VPC works to stop gun death and injury through research, education, advocacy, and collaboration.

Washington Alliance for Gun Responsibility

www.gunresponsibility.org/

The Alliance works to end gun violence and promote safe gun ownership.

Women Against Gun Violence

www.wagv.org/about-wagv/

Founded by Ann Reiss Lane and Betty Friedan in 1993, the group focuses their approach at a community level.

Drunk Driving

Select Books, Studies, and Films

Dorius, Cassandra R., and McCarthy, John D. "Understanding Activist Leadership Effort in the Movement Opposing Drinking and Driving." *Social Forces*, 1 December 2011, 90(2), 453–473. https://doi.org/10.1093/sf/sor035. Published 22 December 2011. Available at https://academic.oup.com/sf/article/90/2/453/2235904.

Fell, James C., and Voas, Robert B. "Mothers Against Drunk Driving (MADD): The First 25 Years." *Traffic Injury Prevention*, 2006, 7(3), 197.

Lerner, Barron H. *One for the Road: Drunk Driving Since 1900*. Baltimore: The Johns Hopkins University Press, 2011.

Mothers Against Drunk Drivers: The Candy Lightner Story, aired on the NBC Television Network, March 14, 1983.

Robin, Gerald D. *Waging the Battle Against Drunk Driving*. New York: Praeger, 1991.

Select Organizations and Coalitions

D.A.R.E. America

www.dare.org/

D.A.R.E was launched in 1983 to address drug-related issues pertaining to K–12 students and to provide education programs in schools around the country. The group's curricula has now grown to address violence, bullying, Internet safety, and other concerns.

DrinkingAndDriving.Org (DADO)

www.drinkinganddriving.org/

A national nonprofit 501(c)3, DADO aims to prevent drunk driving and encourage public safety through educating and inspiring individuals to prevent driving under the influence.

International Drunk Driving Prevention Association (IDDPA)

www.iddpa.org/

The goal of IDDPA is to prevent drunk driving, aid those who are victims of drunk driving, and focus on legislative efforts to end drunk driving.

Mothers Against Drunk Driving (MADD)

www.madd.org

Mothers Against Drunk Driving (MADD) was formed in 1980 by Candy Lightner, after her thirteen-year-old daughter was killed by a drunk driver. MADD works to end drunk driving, while also acting as a support network for those affected by drunk driving. MADD works to combat underage drinking and create stricter laws for those who drive under the influence. With offices in every state in the United States and every providence in Canada, MADD is the largest and most influential player in the battle against drunk driving.

National Highway Transportation Safety Association (NHTSA)

https://www.nhtsa.gov/

NHTSA is part of the U.S. Department of Transportation and focuses on drunk driving issues as just one part of its highway safety efforts. NHTSA has created several media campaigns to bring awareness to the issue of drunk driving, including "Drive Sober or Get Pulled Over," "Buzzed Driving Is Drunk Driving," and "The Ultimate Party Foul." Through these campaigns, as well as through research and working with state governments, NHTSA works to reduce alcohol-related crash fatalities.

National Transportation and Safety Board (NTSB)

www.ntsb.gov/Pages/default.aspx

NTSB is an independent federal agency that investigates transportation accidents and promotes transportation safety. In addition, NTSB issues recommendations to avoid future accidents and safety violations, and helped bring about increasing the legal drinking age to twenty-one.

RID USA, Inc.

www.rid-usa.org/rid-usa-inc/

Founded by Doris Aiken, Remove Intoxicated Drivers (RID) is the original anti–drunk driving organization in the United States. The group focuses on legislative efforts in regard to ending drunk driving.

Students Against Destructive Decisions (SADD)

www.sadd.org/

SADD has a national network of chapters that engage in peer educational training and awareness events in an effort to empower students to confront daily pressures that face them.

Environment—Acid Rain and Carbon Emissions

Select Books and Publications

Dunlap, Rileu E., and Angela G. Mertig, eds. *American Environmentalism: The US Environmental Movement, 1970–1990*. Washington, DC: Taylor & Francis, 1992.

Gore, Al. *An Inconvenient Truth: The Planetary Emergence of Global Warming and What We Can Do About It*. Harlan, IA: Rodale Books, 2006.

Gore, Al. *Earth in the Balance: Ecology and the Human Spirit*. Harlan, IA: Rodale Books, 2006.

Hansen, Paul Walden. *Green in Gridlock: Common Goals, Common Ground, and Compromise*. College Station, TX: Texas A&M University, 2013.

Jones, Van. *The Green Collar Economy: How One Solution Can Fix Our Two Biggest Problems*. New York: HarperOne, 2008.

McKibben, Bill. *The End of Nature*. New York: Random House, 2006.

Pooley, Eric. *The Climate War: True Believers, Power Brokers, and the Fight to Save the Earth*. New York: Hatchette Books, 2010.

Reinhardt, Forest L. *Environmental Defense*. Harvard Business School Case 9–703–029. Boston: Harvard Business School Publishing, 2003.

Shabecoff, Philip. *A Fierce Green Fire: The American Environmental Movement* (rev. ed.). Washington, DC: Island Press, 2003.

Skocpol, Theda. *Naming the Problem: What It Will Take to Counter Extremism and Engage Americans in the Fight Against Global Warming*. Harvard University, January 2013. Prepared for the Symposium on The Politics of America's Fight Against Global Warming, co-sponsored by the Columbia School of Journalism and the Scholars Strategy Network, February 14, 2013, Tsai Auditorium, Harvard University.

Snow, Donald. *Inside the Environmental Movement: Meeting the Leadership Challenge*. Washington, DC: Island Press, 1991.

Stavins, Bob. Project 88: Harnessing Market Forces to Protect the Environment. https://scholar.harvard.edu/files/stavins/files/project_88–1.pdf.

Welzer, Harald. *Climate Wars: What People Will Be Killed for in the 21st Century*. Cambridge, UK: Polity Press, 2012.

Select Organizations and Coalitions

Alliance for Climate Protection (the Climate Reality Project)

www.climaterealityproject.org/

An international initiative to end fossil fuel consumption and move toward more environmentally friendly energy sources; the group also pushes for all countries to adhere to the Paris Climate Agreement.

Center for Energy and Economic Development (CEED)

CEED represents the interests of the coal community in environmental issues.

Climate and Clean Air Coalition

www.ccacoalition.org/en

The Coalition works in both the public and private sectors to effect environmental change policy worldwide.

Climate Institute

climate.org/

Founded in 1986, this was the first worldwide organization focused only on climate change. The group looks to spearhead non-partisan collaboration with regard to climate initiatives.

Climate Project

www.theclimateproject.org/

Climate Project includes staff and volunteers from the United States, Australia, Canada, India, Spain, and the UK, all personally trained by Al Gore to inform the public about climate change.

Earth First!

earthfirst.org/

A group of environmental activists who use grassroots organization, legal proceedings, and civil disobedience to further the causes related to the environment.

Environmental Defense Fund

www.edf.org/

An environmental advocacy group founded in 1967, EDF uses scientific study, economic incentives, corporate partnerships, and government policy initiatives to further environmental issues. To achieve its program goals in areas such as climate and air, health, land, water and wildlife, and oceans, Environmental Defense brings together experts in science, law, and economics to tackle complex environmental issues. With more than two million members and a staff of 675 scientists, economists, policy experts, and other professionals around the world, EDF acts on the belief that financial prosperity and environmental stewardship go hand in hand.

Friends of the Earth

www.foe.org/

The group works with policymakers on national and statewide levels to defend the environment.

Greenpeace

www.greenpeace.org/usa

A global, independent organization, Greenpeace uses social media, media, and peaceful protests to bring about a peaceful and green world.

League of Conservation Voters

lcv.org/

LCV is strongly involved in policymaking and advocating for sound environmental laws at all levels of government.

Izaak Walton League

www.iwla.org/

A national conservation organization focused on sustainability and the importance of preserving natural resources in the United States.

Natural Resources Defense Council

www.nrdc.org/

The Natural Resources Defense Council (NRDC) was founded in 1970 by a team of law students and lawyers to ensure the rights of people to clean air and water and healthy communities. NRDC combines more than three million members and online activists with the expertise of some five hundred scientists, lawyers, and policy advocates across the globe to ensure the rights of all people to the air, the water, and the wild.

Sierra Club

www.sierraclub.org/

Formed in 1892 by conservationist John Muir, Sierra Club is recognized as the largest and most influential grassroots environmental organization.

Union of Concerned Scientists

www.ucsusa.org/

An independent organization focused on scientific answers to environmental issues such as global warming, sustainability, and reducing the threat of nuclear war.

USCAP (Climate Action Partnership)

merid.org/en/Content/Projects/United_States_Climate_Action_Partnership .aspx

A partnership organization that includes businesses and environmental groups working toward the goal of reducing greenhouse gas emissions through governmental regulation.

World Resources Institute (WRI)

www.wri.org/

As advocates for scientific analysis of environmental and development challenges in the United States, WRI focuses on forests, water, food, climate change, energy, and cities/transport.

LGBT Marriage Equality

Select Publications

Armstrong, Elizabeth A. *Forging Gay Identities: Organizing Sexuality in San Francisco, 1950–1994*. Chicago: University of Chicago Press, 2002.
Boswell, John. *Christianity, Social Tolerance and Homosexuality*. Chicago, IL: University of Chicago Press, 1981.
Coles, Matt. "The Plan to Win Marriage." In *Love Unites Us: Winning the Freedom to Marry in America*, edited by Kevin M. Cathcart and Leslie J. Gabel-Brett. New York: The New Press, 2016.
Freedom to Marry official Web site. "Winning the Freedom to Marry Nationwide: The Inside Story of a Transformative Campaign" Available at http://www .freedomtomarry.org/pages/how-it-happened#section-2. Accessed February 29, 2017.
Solomon, Marc. *Winning Marriage*. Lebanon, NH: ForeEdge, an imprint of University Press of New England, 2014.

Select Organizations and Coalitions

American Civil Liberties Union (ACLU)

www.aclu.org/

ACLU is a nonpartisan, nonprofit organization with a mission "to defend and preserve the individual rights and liberties guaranteed to every person in this country by the Constitution and laws of the United States." ACLU has worked for the freedom to marry for members of the LGBT community and also for the recognition of domestic partnerships.

Empire State Pride Agenda

The Empire State Pride Agenda (ESPA) was a statewide political advocacy organization in New York that advocated for lesbian, gay, bisexual, and transgender (LGBT) rights, including same-sex marriage. ESPA has since disbanded.

Freedom to Marry

www.freedomtomarry.org/

Founded by Evan Wolfson, Freedom to Marry led the campaign to win marriage equality rights in the United States and also helped spark a global movement. Their "Roadmap to Victory" strategy set the stage for a national victory at the Supreme Court by winning a critical mass of states, building strong public support, and ending federal marriage discrimination.

Gill Foundation

https://gillfoundation.org/

Founded in 1994 by software entrepreneur and philanthropist Tim Gill, the foundation supports efforts to achieve equality for LGBT individuals, as well as those with HIV/AIDS. Gill was a major proponent and funder of the freedom to marry movement.

GLBTQ Legal Advocates & Defenders (GLAD)

www.glad.org/

GLAD is a nonprofit legal rights organization in the United States that works to end discrimination based on sexual orientation, HIV status, and/or gender identity and expression through litigation, advocacy, and education work in all areas of LGBT (lesbian, gay, bisexual, transgender) rights and the rights of people living with HIV. GLAD played the lead role in the 2003 victory in *Goodridge v. Department of Public Health*, making Massachusetts the first U.S. state to grant same-sex couples full marriage equality. GLAD also played key roles in winning marriage equality in Vermont, New Hampshire, Maine, and Rhode Island.

Human Rights Campaign

www.hrc.org/

The Human Rights Campaign represents more than 1.5 million members and supporters in the United States. As the largest national lesbian, gay, bisexual, and transgender civil rights organization, HRC envisions an America in which LGBT people are ensured of their basic equal rights and can be open, honest, and safe at home, at work, and in the community. HRC led the effort to enact marriage equality in the District of Columbia, among others.

Lambda Legal

www.lambdalegal.org/

Founded in 1973, Lambda Legal is the oldest and largest national legal organization. Its mission is to achieve full recognition of the civil rights of lesbians, gay men, bisexuals, transgender people, and those with HIV through impact litigation, education, and public policy work. They were part of the legal arm (along with ACLU and others) of the marriage equality movement.

MassEquality

www.massequality.org/

MassEquality is the leading statewide grassroots advocacy organization in Massachusetts, working to ensure everyone in that state thrives, without discrimination and oppression based on sexual orientation, gender identity, or gender expression. The coalition was formed in the late 1990s in response to the first attempts in the Massachusetts state legislature to prohibit recognition of same-sex marriage. MassEquality was formally incorporated in late 2001 as a 501(c)4 advocacy organization, although it operated previously without staff.

National LGBTQ Task Force (formerly the National Gay Task Force)

www.thetaskforce.org/

This task force was founded in 1973 in the wake of the Stonewall Riots, the first major protest in favor of equal rights for gay people. At the time of its founding, homosexuality was still considered a mental illness, and many states had anti-sodomy laws.

Polio Eradication

Select Book

Seytre, Bernard, and Shaffer, Mary. *The Death of a Disease: A History of the Eradication of Poliomyelitis*. New Brunswick, NJ: Rutgers University Press, 2005.

Select Organizations and Coalitions

Bill & Melinda Gates Foundation

https://www.gatesfoundation.org/

This foundation focuses on healthcare issues for children and young people around the world. They have been instrumental in the battle to eradicate polio, pledging millions of dollars and thousands of hours of manpower.

Centers for Disease Control and Prevention

https://www.cdc.gov/

The CDC focuses on health security, disease prevention and control, public health, and improving medical care.

Global Polio Eradication Initiative (GPEI)

http://polioeradication.org/

The initiative was launched in 1998 following a World Health Assembly resolution to eradicate polio. To date, polio rates around the world have decreased by 99.9 percent.

Rotary International—PolioPlus Program

https://my.rotary.org/en/take-action/end-polio

Rotary and its worldwide partners have advocated, raised money, and built awareness regarding polio and the importance of inoculating children around the world.

UN Foundation

http://www.unfoundation.org/

The healthcare arm of the United Nations, the UN Foundation works with businesses, governments, and NGOs on issues such as healthcare, climate change, peace, security, and more.

UNICEF

https://www.unicef.org/

Focused on health issues related to children, UNICEF works on policy advocacy and partnerships with other organizations to ensure access to the polio vaccine.

USAID "CORE Group Polio Eradication Initiative"

https://coregroup.org/our-work/programs/core-group-polio-project/

The group is now in a second phase of funding lasting from 2008 through 2012 and known as the CORE Group Polio Project or CGPP.

World Health Assembly

http://www.who.int/mediacentre/events/governance/wha/en/

The Assembly is the decision-making body of the World Health Organization (WHO), focused on specific health-related topics set forth by the Executive Board.

World Health Organization (WHO)

http://www.who.int/en/

Health organization that works alongside governments and NGOs from around the world to ensure high-quality healthcare. The group also created World Polio Day, October 24.

Tobacco Control

Select Books and Publications

Kessler, David. *A Question of Intent: A Great American Battle with a Deadly Industry*. New York: Public Affairs, 2001.

Kluger, Richard. *Ashes to Ashes: America's Hundred-Year Cigarette War, the Public Health, and the Unabashed Triumph of Philip Morris*. New York: Vintage Books (Random House), 1997.

Pertschuk, Michael. *Smoke in Their Eyes: Lessons in Movement Leadership from the Tobacco Wars*. Nashville, TN: Vanderbilt University Press, 2001.

"Smoking and Health: A Report of the Surgeon General." Report by the Office on Smoking and Health, available at the official Web site of National Institutes of Health (NIH) U.S. National Library of Medicine. Appendix A: Cigarette Smoking in the United States, 1950–1978. https://profiles.nlm.nih.gov/ps/access/nnbcph.pdf.

"Tobacco Campaigns of the Robert Wood Johnson Foundation and Collaborators, 1991–2010." A report commissioned and published by Robert Wood Johnson Foundation as part of the Robert Wood Johnson Foundation Retrospective Series and authored by the Center for Public Program Evaluation. Published April 2011 and available at https://www.rwjf.org/en/library/research/2011/04/the-tobacco-campaigns-.html.

Select Organizations and Coalitions

American Academy of Pediatrics

https://www.aap.org/en-us/Pages/Default.aspx

A professional society of pediatricians in the United States, AAP offers professional resources and education, as well as policy and advocacy for infant, children, adolescents, and young adults, with a major focus on smoking prevention.

American Cancer Society

https://www.cancer.org/

ACS funds and conducts cancer research, provides patient support, and informs the public about preventing cancer. ACS was a founding partner of the Campaign for Tobacco-Free Kids.

American Heart Association

http://www.heart.org/HEARTORG/

AHA provides public health education in regard to lifestyle choices, treatment guidelines for healthcare professionals, and education for policymakers in regard to health issues. ACS was a founding partner of the Campaign for Tobacco-Free Kids.

American Lung Association

www.lung.org

ALA is dedicated to improving lung health and preventing lung disease through research, education, and advocacy.

American Medical Association

www.ama-assn.org

The American Medical Association is focused on patient health, well-being, and satisfaction, as well as doctor training and education. It was an early partner of the Campaign for Tobacco-Free Kids.

Americans for Nonsmokers' Rights (ANR)

https://nonsmokersrights.org/

Americans for Nonsmokers' Rights is a national 501(c)4 lobbying organization formed in California in 1976 dedicated to non-smokers' rights, taking on the tobacco industry at all levels of government, protecting non-smokers from exposure to secondhand smoke, and preventing tobacco addiction among youth. ANR has promoted clean indoor air ordinances in the United States and works globally to help enact smoke-free regulations. ANR's sister organization, Americans for Nonsmokers Foundation (ANF), is an educational nonprofit, focused on preventing secondhand smoke, and educating smokers and the public about the dangers of secondhand smoke.

APPEAL (Asian Pacific Partners for Empowerment, Advocacy, and Leadership)

http://www.appealforcommunities.org/

A national organization working toward social justice for Asian-Americans, Native Hawaiians, and Pacific Islanders. The group focuses on policy, advocacy, and critical public health issues for these groups, including tobacco use.

Bloomberg Philanthropies

Bloomberg.org

Headed by former NYC mayor Mike Bloomberg, the foundation focuses on arts, education, the environment, government innovation, and public health. The Bloomberg Initiative to Reduce Tobacco Use is working to limit the harmful effects of tobacco around the world through policy change.

Campaign for Tobacco-Free Kids

https://www.tobaccofreekids.org/

The Campaign for Tobacco-Free Kids (the Campaign) was launched in 1996 by Matt Myers and Bill Novelli with support from RWJF as the leading national voice for tobacco control. The Campaign focuses on protecting children from tobacco use—the number one cause of preventable death among young people. Working in the United States and around the world, the Campaign uses strategic communications and policy advocacy to promote the most effective anti-smoking programs. The Campaign's work has contributed since 1996 to a 70 percent decrease in youth smoking, driving youth smoking rates to under 6 percent by 2017 and a 39 percent decrease in adult smoking—down to under one in five; and helped protect 185 million Americans from secondhand smoke. The Campaign has also helped save millions of lives by reducing cancer, heart disease, and other tobacco-related conditions. The Campaign involves youth in its efforts, including in its "Kick Butts Day," "Taking Down Tobacco" initiative, Youth Engagement Alliance, and National Youth Ambassadors programs.

Centers for Disease Control and Prevention Office of Smoking and Health

https://www.cdc.gov/tobacco/about/osh/index.htm

The CDC and its partners work to reduce the number of deaths and incidences of chronic disease related to smoking and tobacco use. Programs include interventions, promoting smoke-free environments, cessation programs, and more.

Food and Drug Administration Center for Tobacco Products (CTP)

https://www.fda.gov/TobaccoProducts/default.htm

CTP regulates the manufacturing, marketing, and distribution of tobacco products, in an effort to reduce the number of tobacco-related deaths and diseases. The group focuses on public education, enforcement, policy making, and research.

National African American Tobacco Prevention Network

http://www.naatpn.org/about

NAATPN works to promote public health efforts for the African American community. Created in 1998, the organization has created and put in place numerous tobacco control activities and programs geared to minorities, who are disparately affected by tobacco consumption.

Robert Wood Johnson Foundation

https://www.rwjf.org/

The United States' largest philanthropy focused solely on health, today RWJF focuses on issues primarily related to the healthcare system, health leadership, healthy communities and healthy kids, and healthy weight. RWJF contributed more than $700 million over a decade to prevent and reduce tobacco use in the United States, including providing seed funding to the Campaign for Tobacco-Free Kids (listed previously) and to underwrite the RWJF *SmokelessStates Initiative*, a statewide tobacco initiative that ran from 1993 to 2004 focused reducing tobacco use, especially among children and youth. https://www.rwjf .org/en/library/research/2009/07/smokeless-states-national-tobacco-policy-initiative.html.

Tobacco Control Legal Consortium

http://www.publichealthlawcenter.org/category/programs/tobacco-control-legal-consortium

A legal organization program focused on tobacco control policy. The group includes lawyers and policy specialists who work with government and community leaders and public health organizations on tobacco-related issues.

Truth Initiative

https://truthinitiative.org/

The nation's largest public health nonprofit focused solely on tobacco, Truth engages in education, reduction in tobacco use, policy studies, and community activism.

Additional Resources on Causes, Movements, and Social Change

Articles

Grantmakers for Effective Organizations, Monitor Institute. "Catalyzing Networks for Social Change: A Funders Guide." November 1, 2011.

Katcher, Robin. "Unstill Waters: The Fluid Role of Networks in Social Movements," *Nonprofit Quarterly*, Summer 2010.

Wei-Skillern, Jane, and Marciano, Sonia. "The Networked Nonprofit," *Stanford Social Innovation Review*, Spring 2008.

Networks, Complexity, Systems

Aaker, Jennifer, and Smith, Andy. *The Dragonfly Effect: Quick, Effective, and Powerful Ways to Use Social Media to Drive Social Change*. San Francisco: Jossey-Bass, 2010.

Barabasi, Albert-Laszlo, and Frangos, Jennifer. *Linked: The New Science of Networks*. New York: Perseus Books, 2002.

Brafman, Ori, and Beckstrom, Rod A. *The Starfish and the Spider: The Unstoppable Power of Leaderless Organizations*. New York: Penguin Group, 2006.

Crosby, Barbara C., and Bryson, John M. *Leadership for the Common Good: Tackling Public Problems in a Shared-Power World*. San Francisco: Jossey-Bass, 1992.

Eggers, William D., and Goldsmith, Stephen. *Governing by Network: The New Shape of the Public Sector*. Washington, DC: Brookings Institution, 2004.

Gladwell, Malcolm. *The Tipping Point: How Little Things Make a Big Difference*. Boston: Little, Brown and Company, 2006.

Gladwell, Malcolm. *David and Goliath: Underdogs, Misfits, and the Art of Battling Giants*. New York: Back Bay Books/Little, Brown and Company, 2015.

Godin, Seth. "The Tribes We Lead." https://www.youtube.com/watch?v=uQGYr9bnktw.

Goldsmith, Stephen, Georges, Gigi, and Burke, Tim Glynn. *The Power of Social Innovation: How Civic Entrepreneurs Ignite Community Networks for Good*. San Francisco: Jossey-Bass, 2010.

Grant, Heather McLeod, Bower, Amanda, and Johnston, Jenny. *Pioneers in Justice: Building Networks and Movements for Social Change*. San Francisco: Levi Strauss Foundation, 2014.

Heifetz, Ronald A. *Leadership Without Easy Answers*. Boston: Harvard University Press, 1998.

Holley, June. *Network Weaver Handbook: A Guide to Transformational Networks*. Athens, OH: Network Weaver Publishing, 2012.

Howe, Jeff. *Crowdsourcing: Why the Power of the Crowd Is Driving the Future of Business*. New York: Three Rivers Press, 2009.

Johnson, Steven. *Emergence: The Connected Lives of Ants, Brains, Cities, and Software*. New York: Scribner, 2001.

Johnson, Steven. *How We Got to Now: Six Innovations That Made the Modern World*. New York: Riverhead Books, 2014.

Lipnack, Jessica, and Stamps, Jeffrey. *The Age of the Network: Organizing Principles for the 21st Century*. New London, NH: Oliver Wright Ltd., 1994.

Meadows, Donella. *Thinking in Systems: A Primer*. Diana Wright, ed., Sustainability Institute. White River Junction, VT: Chelsea Green Publishing, 2008.

Mitchell, Melanie. *Complexity: A Guided Tour*. New York: Oxford University Press, 2009.

Plastrik, Peter, Taylor, Madeleine, and Cleveland, John. *Connecting to Change the World: Harnessing the Power of Networks for Social Impact*. Washington DC: Island Press, 2014.

Senge, Peter M. *The Fifth Discipline: The Art & Practice of The Learning Organization.* New York: Doubleday, 2006.

Shirky, Clay. *Here Comes Everybody: The Power of Organizing Without Organization.* New York: Penguin Books, 2008.

Skidmore, Paul. "Leading Between: Six Characteristics of Network Leaders." In *Network Logic: Who Governs in an Interconnected World?* Helen McCarthy, Paul Miller, and Paul Skidmore, eds. London: Demos, 2004.

Stroh, David Peter. *Systems Thinking for Social Change.* White River Junction, VT: Chelsea Green Publishing, 2015.

Surowiecki, James. *The Wisdom of Crowds: Why the Many Are Smarter than the Few and How Collective Wisdom Shapes Business, Economies, Societies, and Nations.* New York: Doubleday, 2004.

Watts, Duncan J. *Six Degrees: The Science of a Connected Age.* New York: W.W. Norton & Company, 2004.

Westley, Frances R., Zimmerman, Brenda, and Patton, Michael. *Getting to Maybe: How the World Is Changed.* Toronto: Vintage Canada, 2009.

Wheatley, Margaret J. *Leadership and the New Science: Discovering Order in a Chaotic World.* San Francisco: Berrett-Koehler, 2006.

Occupy Wall Street

Roberts, Alasdair. "Why the Occupy Movement Failed," *Public Administration Review,* 72, 754–762. DOI:10.1111/j.1540–6210.2012.02614.x. http://onlinelibrary.wiley.com/doi/10.1111/j.1540–6210.2012.02614.x/abstract.

Van Gelder, Sarah. *This Changes Everything: Occupy Wall Street and the 99% Movement.* San Francisco: Berrett-Koehler, 2011.

Writers for the Ninety-Nine Percent. *Occupying Wall Street: The Inside Story of an Action That Changed America.* New York: OR Books, 2012.

Political, Racial, and Cultural Movements

Alexander, Michelle. *The New Jim Crow: Mass Incarceration in the Age of Colorblindness* (rev. ed.), 2010, 2012. New York: The New Press, 2011.

Alinsky, Saul. *Rules for Radicals.* New York: Vintage Books, 1989.

Cole, David. *Engines of Liberty: The Power of Citizen Activists to Make Constitutional Law.* New York: Basic Books, 2016.

Mayer, Jane. *Dark Money: The Hidden History of the Billionaires Behind the Rise of the Radical Right.* New York: Anchor Books, 2017.

Skocpol, Theda, and Williamson, Vanessa. *The Tea Party and the Remaking of Republican Conservatism.* New York: Oxford University Press, 2013, 2016.

Taylor, Keeanga-Yamahtta. *From #BlackLivesMatter to Black Liberation.* Chicago: Haymarket Books, 2016.

Vance, J.D. *Hillbilly Elegy.* New York: Harper, 2016.

Social Change and Social Marketing

Andreasen, Alan R. *Marketing Social Change: Changing Behavior to Promote Health, Social Development, and the Environment.* San Francisco, CA: Jossey-Bass, 1995.

Chetkovich, Carol A., and Kunreuther, Frances. *From the Ground Up: Grassroots Organizations Making Social Change.* Ithaca, NY: Cornell University Press, 2006.

Davis, Gerlad F., McAdam, Doug, Scott, W. Richard, and Zald, Mayer N. *Social Movements and Organizational Theory.* New York: Cambridge University Press, 2005.

Ganz, Marshall. *Why David Sometimes Wins: Leadership, Organization, and Strategy in the California Farm Worker Movement.* New York: Oxford University Press, 2009.

Kotler, Philip, and Lee, Nancy R. *Social Marketing: Influencing Behaviors for Good.* Thousand Oaks, CA: Sage, 2008.

Kotler, Philip, and Zaltman, Gerald. "Social Marketing: An Approach to Planned Social Change," *Journal of Marketing,* July 1971. 35, 3–12.

Novelli, Bill, and Workman, Boe. *50: Igniting a Revolution to Reinvent America.* New York: St. Martin's Press, 2007.

Pertschuk, Michael. *Giant Killers.* New York: Norton, 1986.

Pertschuk, Michael, and Schaetzel, Wendy. *The People Rising: The Campaign Against the Bork Nomination.* New York: Thunder's Mouth Press, 1989.

Plastrik, Peter, Taylor, Madeleine, and Cleveland, John. *Connecting to Change the World: Harnessing the Power of Networks for Social Impact.* Washington DC: Island Press, 2014.

Schmitz, Paul. *Everyone Leads: Building Leadership from the Community Up.* San Francisco: Jossey-Bass, 2012.

Tilly, Charles. *Power in Movement.* New York: Cambridge University Press, 1994.

Acknowledgments

I FEEL PRIVILEGED TO have collaborated on this book with one of the true legends of social change, Bill Novelli. Many people know Bill from his leadership roles at AARP and CARE or his co-founding of Porter-Novelli, the pioneering social marketing firm, or his current work as a professor of the practice at Georgetown University. But his contributions as co-founding president of Campaign for Tobacco-Free Kids have most inspired me. I've had the privilege of learning at the feet of an advocacy and social marketing master, both through working with Bill on this book and as executive director of the Global Social Enterprise Initiative, which he launched with a group of students at Georgetown's McDonough School of Business in 2011. Bill, your generosity of thought, time, ideas, and spirit inspire me every day.

I also am deeply grateful to Ladan Manteghi, GSEI's founding executive director. Ladan brought me in the GSEI fold and believed so strongly this book needed to happen that she created a research fellowship to enable me to come to Georgetown and work on it full-time. She even graciously opened her office so I'd have a quiet place to write. (Luckily, we found an extra office elsewhere at the business school so we could maintain both our friendship and colleagueship.)

This book has benefitted from the camaraderie of the incredible team Ladan and Bill have built here at Georgetown. My deep respect and gratitude go to our special project leaders, including AgingWell Hub directors Liddy Manson and Diane Ty; Rural Opportunity Initiative founder and GSEI Executive in Residence Matt McKenna and former ROI director Sam Rikkers; EARN project director Judi Kennedy

215

and analyst Lauren Gilbert; Sustainable Oceans Alliance founder Daniela Fernandez; and our fabulous New Strategies Forum team, including founder Curt Weeden, director Chico Rosemond, and lecturer Chris Gates. You all inspire me with your masterful leadership and entrepreneurship. To Chris, I owe a special note of thanks for your thoughtful critique of early drafts of the manuscript and for applying your expert lenses of policy and philanthropy to make this book stronger.

Here on campus at Georgetown, I am indebted to GSEI's core group of incredibly capable operations team members: GSEI Associate Director Natalia Rankine-Galloway brings good humor, thoughtful insight, and a sympathetic co-working mom's take on everything we do. GSEI Program Manager Bich Le brings the exquisite combination of surgical precision and inspired beauty to every project she touches. And Kevin Iraheta, our intrepid administrative assistant, brings boundless enthusiasm and infectious curiosity to work every day. Our remote Executive Assistant Dana Frazeur supports all of us in every conceivable way, especially on this book: Her editing prowess and writing abilities have buoyed the book from beginning to end. I owe a special word of thanks to Dana as well for proofreading multiple drafts and helping prepare the manuscript for publication; your work on the endnotes alone puts me squarely in your debt.

To our Georgetown student researchers: You've inspired me with your dedication to learning and passion for the causes in this book. Each of you went beyond the call of duty in your own unique ways— some extending for multiple modules and putting off other projects to keep the research moving forward. Special thanks are in order to Ben Brown, Ja Eon (Jane) Cho, Magdelena Filippone, Annabelle Haynes, Minjeong Hong, Erica Shi, and Luis Trenard. I know each of you will make change happen in your own unique ways beyond Georgetown.

Faculty at Georgetown also deserve their own note of thanks: To Paul Almeida, the dean of the McDonough School of Business, your vision for making Georgetown both best in the world and best *for* the world inspires us. Former Dean David Thomas also championed the book from the moment Ladan introduced the idea. Associate Dean Pietra Rivoli, Undergraduate Program Dean Patricia Grant, and faculty members Ricardo Ernst and Ed Soule have been inspiring colleagues, along with other GSEI faculty advisors, including Vishal Agrawal,

Doug McCabe, Rachelle Sampson, Jose Luis Guerrero, Daniela Brancaforte, Ron Anton, and Kasra Ferdows. I also want to recognize Visiting Professor and Researcher Consuelo Bonito—although you've returned to Spain, you will always be with GSEI.

A core group of friends and thought partners encouraged and inspired me to take on writing this book. To my life-long friend, non-profit co-founder, and *Forces for Good* co-author, Heather McLeod Grant, I owe the deepest expressions of gratitude. If you hadn't shown me what it takes to be a great writer when we collaborated on *Forces for Good*, then *How Change Happens* could never have happened! Thank you for taking the time to read chapter drafts and sharpen my thinking for this book—especially around networks and systems. Your pioneering work in the field has been inspirational, and my only regret is that we didn't get to work on this one together; creative endeavors are always more fun when done with you.

To John Kania and Mark Kramer at FSG, I also extend notes of deep appreciation. You brought me in to FSG to collaborate on *Do More Than Give* as co-authors, and I was inspired by your insights and writing prowess. It is amazing to look back and see the kernels of the ideas that blossomed into your articles on Collective Impact and Shared Value after our book was released; the contributions these works have made to advancing social innovation thinking and practice have been immeasurable—and have significantly shaped this book. I also appreciate your reviewing of early chapter drafts, serving as thought partners in the research and writing process, and keeping me in the FSG fold as a senior advisor and kindred spirit. Likewise, the camaraderie and colleagueship of FSGers Val Bockstette, Dane Smith, Laura Herman, Fay Hanley Brown, and FSG alumni Kyle Peterson and Jeff Kutash have each fortified me at various stages along the journey.

To the foundation supporters who made working on this book a financially viable endeavor: I would like to thank Kerry Sullivan at Bank of America Foundation, Anne Marie Burgoyne at Emerson Collective, Kathy Calvin at UN Foundation, Mary Snapp and Sue Gluek at Microsoft Philanthropies, and Steve Glikbarg of the Glikbarg Foundation. Your intellectual, moral, and financial support made the difference between this book being a sideline project that might never have happened, and a hard-copy reality. There is no way I could have researched and written this book without your help.

To my agent, Rafe Sagalyn, I owe a special note of thanks. You championed the idea from the start and pushed me to break out of the academic ether to turn this into a book that anyone who cares about causes can use. To my editor at Wiley, Brian Neill, thank you for seeing the possibilities here and shepherding this book through the publishing process. I am particularly grateful to Pete Gaughan, who read multiple chapter drafts, grappled with structure, and pushed my thinking and prose with each iteration.

I also thank each of the leaders and activists who spoke with me for this book. Conversations with icons like Matt Myers, Bill Novelli, Robin Koval, Stan Glantz, Cynthia Hallet, Nancy Kaufman; Evan Wolfson, Marc Solomon, Marty Rouse, Lee Swislow, and Carol Rose; Donna Dees-Thomases, Mary Leigh Blek, Shannon Watts, John Fineblatt, Brian Malte, Richard Aborn, Michael Barnes, Tim Makris, and Glen Caroline; Candy Lightner and Deb Weir; Fred Krupp, David Hawkins, Tim Wirth, and May Boeve; Bruce Aylward, John Lange, and Nicole Bates; Nan Aron, Ed Feulner, Mark Fraley, and many, many more—all of whom are listed in the Appendices—you were generous with your time and thoughts. I particularly want to recognize some of the phenomenal change-making women featured in this book whom I had the pleasure to speak with at length. Donna, Shannon, Mary, Candy, Nancy, and Deb: As entrepreneurial founders and courageous activists, you did it on high heels, backwards, and with kids in tow. You are my personal heroines.

Additional friends have also helped shape this book. Early nuggets of the idea for it bubbled up during a hot tub session with Peter Mellen & co. at Esalen one brisk winter weekend. Bike rides with Victoria Vrana fortified me with ideas and inspiration. Betsy Fader provided a New York office crash pad, and a sounding board throughout this process through her Surdna colleagues; Anne Marie Burgoyne and Robbie Kellman Baxter offered the same kind of support out on the West Coast. Hometown friends provided much-needed moral and logistical aid when this book pulled me away from family. My Westbrook posse kept Finn, Quinn, and Caleigh in good company and efficiently transported, rested, and fed; you had my back when deadlines loomed. Many thanks to Li, Jen, Mike, Ami Susan, Michael, Elizabeth, Joanne, Lara, Shaun, Judy, Peter, Amanda, Leslie, and Kristi, Liz, Zoe, Kristin, Sarah, Rachel, and all of Troop 1357.

Finally, my most intimate and heartfelt thanks goes to Anthony. Without you, none of this would have happened—or have been worth it. With loving support from you—and assistance from Nicole, Didi, Iris, and Melina—you've kept the kids and selflessly made sure I had time to finish this book, while also helping hurricane victims and caring for patients, too. You are my inspiration and my rock.

Caleigh, since I started working on this book, you've grown from being a young girl into a brilliant and beautiful young woman, and your unconditional love and moral support—especially when things got really tough with the writing—is appreciated beyond what you will know. I am so proud of you, and I hope that one day I will become half as good a writer as you are!

To Quinn, I want to thank you for your creative ideas and awesome sense of humor. You helped by introducing me to things on social media I had no clue about. You were understanding when I was working late and long hours on this book, and you have become such a mature guy since I started this book. I am so proud of you, too.

And to Finn, I dedicate this book. Your older sister and brother already have books dedicated to them, and even though you're just learning how to read, now you have a book dedicated to you, too. It's a miracle you came into our lives, and we believe you will make miracles happen with yours.

To all three of our kids, I hope this book inspires you to make change happen.

About the Author and GSEI

Leslie R. Crutchfield is an author, the executive director of the Global Social Enterprise Initiative at Georgetown University's McDonough School of Business, and a senior advisor at FSG Social Impact Consultants. Crutchfield is an author of two previous books, including *Forces for Good: The Six Practices of High-Impact Nonprofits* with Heather McLeod Grant. *Forces for Good* was recognized by *The Economist* on its Best Books of the Year list and is published in three languages globally. Crutchfield also co-authored with John Kania and Mark Kramer *Do More Than Give: The Six Practices of Donors Who Change the World*, a game-changer for philanthropy in the 21st century. Crutchfield served as managing director at Ashoka, the global venture fund for social entrepreneurs, and she co-founded a national nonprofit social enterprise in her twenties. She has contributed to *Fortune, Forbes, The Chronicle of Philanthropy,* and *Stanford Social Innovation Review* and has appeared on programs such as NPR and ABC News.

Crutchfield frequently lectures at domestic and international events on topics including social movements, entrepreneurship, leadership, management, corporate social responsibility, and shared value, among others. She also conducts workshops and facilitates training for cross-sector leaders and teaches a *Lynda.com* course on nonprofit leadership. She has served as a trustee of several nonprofit boards and volunteered with Crossroads Africa. Crutchfield holds an MBA and a bachelor of arts degree from Harvard, and resides in the Washington, D.C., region with her family.

www.forcesforgood.net

www.domorethangivebook.com

The Global Social Enterprise Initiative (GSEI) at Georgetown University's McDonough School of Business delivers world-class education, research, and actionable solutions that drive lasting social, economic, and environmental impact. Founded by Georgetown University Professor of the Practice Bill Novelli, GSEI's work is grounded in the belief that business can be a powerful force for good. Complex societal problems will only be solved by leaders working systemically across sectors—private, public, and nonprofit. GSEI works with companies to do well by doing good, helping them improve business performance while creating social and environmental value. GSEI also helps nonprofits to grow stronger, become more sustainable, and achieve greater impact though its New Strategies Forum, which has educated more than 450 nonprofit leaders through its revenue diversification programs. GSEI partners with government agencies, guiding them to adopt innovative approaches to advance the public good. And GSEI empowers students to be high-impact leaders in their careers, communities, and the world. GSEI is comprised of sixteen team members, including project leaders in the areas of Rural Opportunity, Aging Well, and Disability Employment, among others who bring deep expertise in creating strategies designed to solve complex social and environmental issues.

The Global Social Enterprise Initiative
Hariri Building
37th & O Streets, NW
Georgetown University
Washington, D.C. 20057
email: GSEI@georgetown.edu
http://socialenterprise.georgetown.edu/about/leadership

Index

Note: Page references in *italics* refer to figures and tables.